SAY THEIR NAMES

SAY THEIR NAMES

HOW
BLACK LIVES
CAME TO MATTER
IN AMERICA

CURTIS BUNN, MICHAEL H. COTTMAN, PATRICE
GAINES, NICK CHARLES, AND KEITH HARRISTON

GRAND CENTRAL
PUBLISHING

NEW YORK   BOSTON

Grand Central Publishing
Hachette Book Group
1290 Avenue of the Americas, New York, NY 10104
grandcentralpublishing.com
twitter.com/grandcentralpub

First Edition: October 2021

Grand Central Publishing is a division of Hachette Book Group, Inc. The Grand Central Publishing name and logo is a trademark of Hachette Book Group, Inc.

The publisher is not responsible for websites (or their content) that are not owned by the publisher.

The Hachette Speakers Bureau provides a wide range of authors for speaking events. To find out more, go to www.hachettespeakersbureau.com or call (866) 376-6591.

Library of Congress Cataloging-in-Publication Data
Names: Bunn, Curtis, author. | Cottman, Michael H., author. | Gaines,
    Patrice, author. | Charles, Nick (Journalist), author. | Harriston,
    Keith, author.
Title: Say their names : how Black lives came to matter in America / Curtis
    Bunn, Michael H. Cottman, Patrice Gaines, Nick Charles, and Keith
    Harriston.
Description: First edition. | New York : Grand Central Publishing, 2021.
Identifiers: LCCN 2021023045 | ISBN 9781538737828 (hardcover) | ISBN
    9781538737842 (ebook)
Subjects: LCSH: African Americans--Social conditions--1975- | Black lives
    matter movement. | African Americans--Politics and government. | United
    States--Race relations.
Classification: LCC E185.615 .B84 2021 | DDC 323.1196/073--dc23
LC record available at https://lccn.loc.gov/2021023045

ISBNs: 978-1-5387-3782-8 (hardcover), 978-1-5387-3784-2 (ebook)

Printed in the United States of America

LSC-C

Printing 1, 2021

For the courageous Brothers and Sisters who have marched, spoken, rallied, stood up, fought, and died for Black people to matter.

CONTENTS

Foreword   *ix*

Why Black Lives Matter Matters   1

The Black Carnage of the Coronavirus   63

Dealing with Policing in America   111

Locking Up Black Lives   155

Church in the Age of the BLM Movement   214

Black Political Lineage: From Adam Clayton Powell to Barack Obama   252

Black Women Stand Tall   269

The Rise of Georgia Black Voters   287

The Need for Fair Legislation   292

The Matter of the Wealth Gap   300

Moving On   312

Hope for the Future   316

Bibliography   *325*

Acknowledgments   *331*

About the Authors   *335*

FOREWORD

BY MARC H. MORIAL, PRESIDENT AND CEO, NATIONAL URBAN LEAGUE

I WAS ALREADY MAYOR of New Orleans, and Michael Cottman was a seasoned journalist with a Pulitzer Prize under his belt when first we met. But we share a deeper connection as children of the Civil Rights Movement. Born into the waning days of Jim Crow, we are a generation whose childhood was shaped by desegregation and Black Power, who came of age during the cultural backlash of the Reagan Revolution.

In the years since I moved on from mayor to president and CEO of the National Urban League, we have spoken frequently about the issues and developments impacting Black Americans, from the devastation of Hurricane Katrina, through Barack Obama's historic election as the nation's first Black president, to the alarming rise of white supremacist ideology under Donald Trump.

There are perhaps no journalists working in the United States better positioned to put the Black Lives Matter movement and the cultural uprising of 2020 into historical perspective than Michael Cottman, Curtis Bunn, Patrice Gaines, Nick Charles, and Keith Harriston. Through moving personal accounts and a detailed grasp of history, they trace the spiritual legacy of anti-lynching crusader Ida B. Wells to the fearless women who created #BlackLivesMatter and laid the groundwork for "a moment when the world is cracked wide open."

I call myself a "child of the movement" in the most literal of senses: My mother, Sybil Haydel, was home in New Orleans on summer break from her graduate studies at Boston University when she attended a Great Books discussion of W. E. B. Du Bois's *Souls of Black Folk*. After the book discussion, she became immersed in a conversation with a self-confident young civil rights attorney about *Brown v Board of Education of Topeka*, which had been decided just weeks earlier. She returned to Massachusetts that August wearing Ernest "Dutch" Morial's fraternity pin.

The struggle for civil rights and social justice and its violent backlash have been an ever-present force in my life from my earliest childhood. I remember my father honking his car horn each evening when he arrived home from work and waiting for my mother to flash the car port lights on and off; this was the system they devised in response to the constant death threats he received as president of the New Orleans chapter of the NAACP. Racially motivated police brutality was among the greatest challenges both during my father's term as Mayor of New Orleans and during mine. When I took office, New Orleans led the nation in the number of civil rights complaints against its police department.

But 2020 was a year like no other. Even as the COVID-19 pandemic was just beginning to tighten its grip on the nation, the National Urban League identified it as a crisis of racial equity. The limited access to quality health care, lower rates of health insurance, higher rates of chronic illness, and implicit bias in health care delivery that saturated Black America before 2020 were the accelerant that spread the flame of COVID-19 racing through our communities. African Americans and Latinos were more than three times as likely to contract the coronavirus as whites, and African Americans nearly twice as likely to die.

Black workers were overrepresented among low-income jobs that could not be done from home as the economy cratered, and Black unemployment soared by nearly 250% from February to April.

As the nation's economic first responders, the National Urban League and our network of ninety affiliates around the nation faced our greatest challenge in a generation. As our affiliates leaped into service as COVID testing facilities, distribution points for food and medical supplies, and emergency employment clearinghouses, we waged a fierce and unrelenting advocacy campaign to target economic relief to communities' Black-owned businesses.

Into this simmering cauldron of grief and economic desperation—already overheated by the staggering rollback of civil rights protections under the Trump administration—fell the brutal killing of George Floyd.

For Black Americans battling a disease that left its victims gasping for air, George Floyd's final words, "I can't breathe," became a heartbreaking emblem of systemic racism. The aloof expression on Officer Derek Chauvin's face, as he calmly crushed the life from Floyd's body, became an emblem of white indifference to Black suffering.

It was a time to respond—not with despair, but with determination. The National Urban League joined with other civil rights organizations to demand the reforms that became the George Floyd Justice in Policing Act. As a community, we demanded justice for the victims of racially motivated police violence across the country.

This book, like 2020 itself, ends with what *Washington Post* journalist Dorothy Butler Gilliam calls "an explosion of Black hope." But our hope must be tempered with caution. We cannot emerge from this year of crisis only to fall back into the same patterns and practices that created the crisis in the first place. We need to see the span of history encapsulated in these pages and let it inform the future. We must be vigilant, we must be forceful, and we must continue to "Say Their Names" if we are to sustain the momentum of this movement.

SAY THEIR NAMES

WHY BLACK LIVES MATTER MATTERS

BY CURTIS BUNN

OF ALL THE ACTION Black Lives Matter has taken, all the change it has effected, all the controversy it has engendered, its most significant feat is this: It has awakened anew the power that resides within Black people.

From every part of the United States, African Americans charged to the forefront of the BLM movement. They brought all of their emotions—their anger, their fears, their boundless optimism, and, mostly, their courage. BLM was born in the shadows of the 2013 acquittal of George Zimmerman, who had gunned down seventeen-year-old Trayvon Martin. It rose to a world-shaking phenomenon in 2020, after George Floyd was murdered under the knee of Minneapolis police officer Derek Chauvin.

That heinous act illuminated why Alicia Garza, Patrisse Khan-Cullors, and Opal Tometi—three Black women—created what they describe as a "Black-centered political will and movement."

It was Garza, who is from Los Angeles and lives in Oakland, who coined the phrase "Black Lives Matter." Trayvon Martin was shot and killed on February 26, 2012, when confronted by an armed Zimmerman as Trayvon returned to his father's fiancée's home from a convenience store in Sanford, Florida. Garza posted the phrase as an emotional proclamation on Facebook in response to the anguish she felt, a suffering magnified by knowing there were so many others like it.

It became the most used phrase in the lexicon around the world. It was a rallying cry, a call for justice, an exaltation of human worth, an expression of desperation.

Garza's mother is Black, her father Jewish. She calls herself a "queer social justice activist" and is married to Malachi Garza, a transgender male activist.

Khan-Cullors, whose mother is a Jehovah's Witness, is gay and an activist from Los Angeles. She served in the trenches of criminal justice reform and led Reform LA Jails' "Yes on R" campaign, a ballot initiative that passed by a 73 percent landslide victory in March 2020. Her Twitter use of the hashtag #BlackLivesMatter sparked an explosion on that social media platform.

Tometi is the daughter of Nigerian immigrants. She lives in New York, has been involved in social movements for two decades, and is the executive director of Black Alliance for Just Immigration. Tometi is married with children. She built the BLM website.

These are the three women who have changed the world.

These are the three women who, in changing the world, thrust its vicious underbelly into everyone's consciousness.

They are not the first to do so, however. They are, indeed, following a legacy of female leaders who fought tirelessly for justice since the 1800s. There was Ida B. Wells, a former slave who became a journalist and activist who spearheaded an anti-lynching campaign in the United States in the 1890s.

Long before Rosa Parks and others refused to give up their seats and move to the back of the bus, Wells, in May 1884, would not relinquish the first-class train seat she purchased to retreat to the "Colored Car," as ordered. She was forcibly removed from the train, but not before she bit one of the men on the hand. Wells won a $500 settlement in a circuit court case. But the Tennessee Supreme Court later overturned the decision. That's when she began writing about social injustices and became an activist.

"One had better die fighting against injustice than to die like a dog or a rat in a trap," she said.

There was Charlotta Bass, the first Black woman to run for vice president, in 1952. She was on the ballot with presidential candidate Vincent Hallinan of the left-wing Progressive Party. A former journalist, Bass was the co-president of the Universal Negro Improvement Association in the 1920s and created the Home Protective Association, which fought against laws that prevented Black people from becoming homeowners. So aggressive were her stances that the FBI put her under surveillance.

After becoming the vice presidential nominee, Bass said: "For the first time in the history of this nation a political party has chosen a Negro woman for the second highest office in the land. It is a great honor to be chosen as a pioneer. And a great responsibility. But I am strengthened by thousands on thousands of pioneers who stand by my side and look over my shoulder—those who have led the fight for freedom, those who led the fight for women's rights, those who have been in the front line fighting for peace and justice and equality everywhere. How they must rejoice in this great understanding which here joins the cause of peace and freedom."

There was Shirley Chisholm, who went from voicing her strong views on racial and gender discrimination as a member of the NAACP and the League of Women Voters to becoming the first Black woman elected to Congress. The former New York state legislator, who had worked as a nursery school teacher and later as a director of schools for early childhood education, served seven terms in the House of Representatives and introduced more than fifty pieces of legislation.

There was Patricia Harris, who worked with many presidents of the United States and became the first African American woman to serve in a presidential cabinet, under Jimmy Carter in 1977. She also was named co-chair of the National Women's Committee for Civil Rights by President John F. Kennedy in 1963 and was made an American envoy by President Lyndon Johnson in 1965.

"I feel deeply proud and grateful to knock down this barrier, but also a little sad about being the 'first Negro woman' because it implies we were not considered before," Harris said.

There were countless other Black women who felt, like the Black Lives Matters founders, the call to address systemic racism—enduring police killings of mostly Black people and social injustice—and acted.

With BLM, its ultimate strength rests with its revealing force and its galvanizing influence. Things about America, shameful things that had been pushed aside but mostly ignored, were illuminated as if by the sun. And leaders have emerged, many young, eager, and courageous, who will extend this fight into the future.

And they did so without the Black church as the anchor of its organization, as it was during the civil rights movement of the 1950s and '60s. That religious entity took its concerns from the pulpit to the pavement, led by the indomitable Dr. Martin Luther King Jr. and a band of faith leaders who were relentless and courageous.

The marches and boycotts inspired change and iconic milestones in history, including the Supreme Court declaring bus segregation unconstitutional in 1956 and the Civil Rights Act of 1964, among many other society-changing policies.

Dr. King and the army of civil rights troops showed the way. Black Lives Matter adopted those principles and kicked it up several notches, eschewing the church and relying instead on a not-taking-no-for-an-answer, unrelenting, in-your-face methodology, led by young people, that did not slow down, even during the coronavirus pandemic that disproportionately devastated Black communities across America.

So how did we get here? Structural and systemic racism have been at the heart of Black people's suffering since the first ships with enslaved

Africans arrived on the shore of Jamestown, Virginia, on August 20, 1619. The killings of Trayvon Martin and George Floyd, Michael Brown and Breonna Taylor, Sandra Bland and John Crawford...and on and on, are a part of the white supremacy ideology that has made the United States go. The three founders of Black Lives Matter had had enough and moved to reenergize the civil rights movement.

BLM, as it would turn out, is the biggest movement in American history, according to analysts, with up to 26 million people participating in the nationwide demonstrations. On the world stage, there were protests in sixty countries and all continents except Antarctica. Its global reach was the result of savvy leveraging of social media platforms, where messaging and rally locations were shared widely.

Much more than that, it was its way of enhancing the citizenry's understanding of structural racism, using racist incidents that were different in nature but connected in spirit. And there were many.

Its mantra: "There's a Mike Brown in every town."

And yet, the idiom Black Lives Matter was an "umbrella" term, Tometi said. As Black people are not monolithic, the term captured all lifestyles and heritages of Black people. Indeed, it was the organization's most viable attribute: It stood for everyone, endowing every Black person's vested interest.

At the same time, the founders were intentional in not being the focal point of the cause. There were at least forty chapters in American cities, the idea being that vast leadership will allow the movement to sustain itself through numbers.

The co-founders travel with security. Their lives have been threatened by white supremacists. They are followed by law enforcement. The FBI raided the home of an extremist and found two of the founders' names on a watch list. The risk of death is real.

In an interview with the *Guardian*, Tometi explained why having a single confirmed leader out front would be a disadvantage. "I see what has happened in the past, where there has been one or two figure-heads and those people have been assassinated," she said. "It really destabilized their organizations. So, what we're trying to do now is be stronger than we ever were before. Leaders are everywhere. Yes, one might go, but there will be ten more that pop up."

Translation: They were prepared to die for the cause.

THE MATTER OF PROTESTS

BLM was ignited by the tragic killings of Black men by white men, either law enforcement, wanna-be law enforcement, or so-called vigilantes. The uprisings were heightened by the death of Black women, Sandra Bland in police custody in Texas, and later by the shooting death of Breonna Taylor in Kentucky, with many others in between. But the vast issues that plague Black life spread about like tributaries flowing from a river.

The movement had multiple layers—police reform at the top to eliminate the blatant disregard for Black life, but also with job equity, the wealth gap, public health, fairness in housing and education—just about every element of life where being Black was a disadvantage, which was every walk of life.

"We primed the ground for a moment when the world is cracked wide open," said Melina Abdullah, co-founder of the Los Angeles BLM chapter. "We set things up to get folks to reimagine public safety and think beyond policing. I think we've ushered in transformative change in many different regards."

In her best-selling book *When They Call You a Terrorist*, Khan-Cullors wrote: "In Los Angeles, working primarily with women, many of them students from Cal State, I begin planning what will become the largest march I've ever planned up until that point. I put a call out on Facebook for people to come to Saint Elmo's Village to meet...and Thandisizwe Chimurenga, one of our most beloved local journalists and radio hosts, helps get people to come. She brings Melina Abdullah, who teaches black studies at Cal State, and Melina brings her students, and together we formed the core of what will become the organizing committee for our March, indeed for who we are in LA. It is the beginning of the build-out of our Black Lives Matter, Los Angeles DNA."

Similar efforts rose across the country. The movement had legs—and critics. The name Black Lives Matter scared and put off some white people, who called the organizers "terrorists," the participants "radicals," and the emphasis on Black lives exclusionary.

There were critics of the sexual orientation of the three founders, as if their views on and commitment to protecting all Black lives had anything to do with sexuality.

"I'm not going to entertain it or engage it," Abdullah said. "That's not how Black people get free. You know, fifty-seven years ago, they made the same accusations and allegations around Bayard Rustin (who fought for civil and gay rights in the 1960s and was the primary organizer of the 1963 March on Washington) and it's fifty-seven years ago, a bunch of Black male pastors said, 'You know what? Bayard Rustin is too important to the movement. Barbara Jordan is too important to the movement.' All of these queens and trans folk who helped to conceptualize, conceive of and usher forward the movement need to be given priority. And we're not going to entertain it, certainly. Fifty-seven years later, we should be taking at least that strong of a position."

She added: "There's always been homophobic and transphobic people, and those are the people we want to engage. So, you know, it's our proclamation that all Black lives matter. And anybody who thinks that someone's Black life doesn't matter because of sexual orientation or gender identity or class, then [that's] their problem."

That dogged perspective permeated the BLM movement. *You have a problem with how we do things? Get over yourself.*

The confidence in how the leadership went about its work was decisive and unyielding, which created a unified approach, whether the march was in New York or Denver, Detroit or Memphis.

"I am clear, we are clear," Khan-Cullors wrote, "that the only plan for us, for Black people living in the United States—en masse, if not individually—is all tied up to the architecture of punishment and containment. We are resolute in our call to dismantle it."

Tacuma Peters, an assistant professor at Michigan State University in the James Madison College, which focuses on politics and social politics and society, said the 1960s efforts led mostly by clergy and the 2020 BLM efforts led mostly by Black women are the same, but different.

"So, there are things that we can point to that have historical precedents," Peters said. "And then there's things that are wholly new. So I think that the things that we have seen before is the care that Black communities have for their children and have for their mothers and fathers and sisters and brothers and their neighbors, and rallying around particular people or particular events as a way to both honor those who have been taken away, but also as a way to really push politically and socially for change that is affecting the supermajority, if not all Black people.

"So, I think there's a way just to think about how this is different. I think people have pointed out repeatedly how the protests, the initial Black Lives Matter protests, are actually important for understanding our contemporary moment: that something happened five or six years ago that allowed for a particular groundswell of particular individuals."

Peters said the formulation of BLM in response to Zimmerman's acquittal for killing Martin set up the power of the 2020 movement. It was a strong, established organization and prepared to mobilize. And for their work, Black Lives Matter was nominated for a 2021 Nobel Peace Prize. In Norwegian MP Petter Eide's official nomination papers, obtained by CNN, he wrote that he nominated the movement "for their struggle against racism and racially motivated violence." Eide added, "BLM's call for systemic change [has] spread around the world, forcing other countries to grapple with racism within their own societies."

Peters said: "If you were to ask me two years ago about the effectiveness of the first iteration of Black Lives Matter, part of it, would it be talking about maybe [laws passed that required police to wear] body cams. But [in 2020], if we want to talk about the impact of Black Lives Matter, it is the fact that that first iteration made the second iteration possible. I always want to think about how the consciousness of people, Black people, but not exclusively Black people, was raised. People were making policy decisions. They came to the center at least for a little bit for a certain discussion. And [in 2020] we [saw] an extension of that with new players, but also some of the same people in a further raising in Black communities, in Latino communities, in larger white America of a certain type of consciousness of death at the hands of the police.

"Part of the newness from the perspective of larger white, but not only white America, is a visceral reaction to particular deaths...visceral reaction that we didn't see three, five, six years ago. That is part of the newness. Another part of this is the way in which calls for defunding police and the calls for abolition, calls for really dismantling...the police state are gaining more traction in places within the Black community and outside of the Black community where they were never given any credence. That is very important because there has been a shift [in] understanding that what needs to happen is a radical dismantling of a whole system that captures many Americans in its maws, and that there needs to be some radical change on the local level that is not going to be just 'reform.' And I think that's a pretty big change."

Black Lives Matter, Peters said, "confounded people" because it energized a base that had been tired of being marginalized, especially in the aftermath of the killing of Black people in suspect circumstances.

Law enforcement, on the other hand, was hardly energized by BLM. Rather, there was a tangible contempt for the organization and what it represented, evident by its aggressive posture and its persistent counter-message of "Blue Lives Matter."

Often in riot gear and contentious, police and, in some cases, the National Guard aggressively confronted BLM protesters and used physical tactics, including clubs, shields, pepper spray, and rubber bullets to assert their authority.

Additionally, the intimidation factor was omnipresent. There were countless images of officers pointing weapons at unarmed protesters, including women and children, marchers knocked to the ground, choking on tear gas, getting pushed back, run over and arrested. Army tanks traveled up Pennsylvania Avenue in D.C. during the BLM march following George Floyd's killing.

"As we were fighting police brutality, we're also experiencing police brutality," Melina Abdullah said.

"I didn't feel safe with the police wearing riot gear, holding automatic weapons and tasers just feet away from me," said Samantha Myers, who participated in the BLM protests in Washington, D.C., where there was a significant show of force. "I felt uncomfortable in the presence of the police, in fear that I or a loved one would be injured while demanding justice for Black lives and the end of systemic oppression."

Jordan Sims, a high school student in Atlanta, was pepper-sprayed in the face at a protest in Georgia's capital city. "I was on the front line," Sims recounted. "We were chanting. Everything was fine. Then the police officers got agitated and started pushing us back. And it turned into chaos, and someone pulled out the pepper spray and got me—for no reason."

A Black woman, Leslie Furcron of San Diego, was shot in the eye with a rubber bullet during a Black Lives Matter demonstration on May 30, 2020, after she tossed an empty Red Bull can several feet away from the line of police officers dressed in riot gear, with weapons aimed at protesters. The officer who permanently blinded Furcron in one eye was never brought up on charges.

In Minneapolis, 650 people, mostly Black, were arrested during a march on a highway that had been peaceful—until state troopers surrounded the demonstrators and ordered everyone to sit on the ground. A nineteen-year-old was charged with felony riot. Her offense? She shone a laser pointer in the eyes of a police officer.

Officers in riot gear disrupted a solemn violin vigil on a lawn for a Black man who had died during a police arrest in the Denver suburb of Aurora. They gushed pepper spray at families with kids, sending them scurrying.

Those are only a handful of the countless uses of force around the country against BLM marchers, unprovoked acts against Black people that were magnified by the contrast of law enforcement's reaction on January 6, 2021, to the mob of largely white Donald Trump supporters who marched to and commandeered the U.S. Capitol. Many believed that Trump had incited the crowd at a rally, exhorting his followers, many of whom were connected to white supremacist and conspiracy theorists' groups, to march to the Capitol and to be "strong" in their actions.

With little resistance from Capitol Police, the gang—wearing Trump paraphernalia, carrying Confederate flags and weapons, and spewing nonsensical gibberish about America being "their" country—stormed a building that was supposed to be one of the most secure in the world. Capitol Police, overrun and understaffed, essentially played matador, stepping aside to let them bull-rush the hallowed building constructed by enslaved Black people beginning in 1793. The National Guard was called in much too late to stop the mob.

The magnitude of the invasion was monumental. People knocked over barricades, scaled the walls like wild squirrels, and broke windows, a breach of the Capitol unmatched since the British burned the building during the War of 1812. It was not enough to illegally enter the structure. The terrorists deposited feces in the hallways, ransacked offices, smoked marijuana, and stole lawmakers' property. Their thwarted intent was to abduct and harm lawmakers.

Members of the mob mounted statues and posed for photos, took seats at politicians' desks, and set up a makeshift hanging post with a noose at the entrance—an egregious but telling act.

A Capitol Police officer died, and many others were beaten and injured in the insurrection that forced many Trump sycophants to distance themselves from the disgraced president. Four others died as well, including a woman shot by a Capitol Police officer, and three others with medical emergencies.

Remarkably, when done with their carnage, the invaders/terrorists strolled out of the building, after more than three hours of occupying and plundering offices, as if they were enjoying a fine afternoon in the park.

There was no distress on their faces or concern in their gait that there would be repercussions for their treasonous crimes.

All this occurred at the U.S. Capitol, where in 2013, a Black woman, Miriam Carey, with her thirteen-month-old daughter in the backseat, was shot multiple times and killed by the same Capitol Police that did little or not enough to stop—and, in fact, in some cases invited in—a white mob with bad intentions. Carey had made a U-turn at the White House and initiated a police chase for a quarter mile up Pennsylvania Avenue. The lethal forced used against the young Black mother, who was suffering from postpartum depression and other mental health issues, her sister said, was symptomatic of the concerns of Black Lives Matter protesters who peacefully demonstrated.

What happened at the Capitol on January 6, 2021, displays the tale of dueling Americas: one in which Black peaceful demonstrators are intimidated and physically handled by an abundance of law enforcement, and the other America in which a violent, angry white mob can seize the U.S. Capitol against understaffed police, abuse and cause the death of officers, wreck a government building, and walk out without concern of suffering consequences.

Responses to the blatant differences were swift and carried the same theme: hypocrisy.

Black Lives Matter posted on Twitter: "When Black people protest for our lives, we are met by National Guard troops or police equipped with assault rifles, tear gas and battle helmets. When white people attempt a coup, they are met by an underwhelming number of law enforcement personnel who act powerless to intervene.

"Make no mistake, if the protesters were Black, we would have been tear gassed, battered, and perhaps shot."

Americans from all walks of life, all races and political affiliations, made the obvious comparison. It was undeniable.

"The events [at the Capitol showed us] that there have always been multiple Americas," Garza, the BLM co-founder, said. "There's been an America that we read about in history books—a romantic America that is made of fairy tales. And then there's America that some of us live in—an America where the rules have been rigged against us for a very long time.

"It's an America where the rules around race and gender and class are fundamental, and they shape and impact people's everyday lives. It's also an America where we function under a particular sense of amnesia."

When it comes to law enforcement, Black people were not looking for equal violence toward whites. Rather, as a cogent meme on Instagram expressed: "We're not asking you to shoot them like you shoot us. We're asking you to *not* shoot us like you *don't* shoot them."

"THE TALK" INTENSIFIES

The trust of law enforcement, which had been precarious at best, vaporized in 2020 with the seemingly endless stream of Black deaths at the hands of white officers or vigilantes keen on taking the law into their own hands. It reached an explosive tipping point when Floyd's horrifying death played out on televisions, computers, and cell phones. The world rebelled. For Black parents, it was a clarion call to rally their kids.

Floyd's death, amplified by twenty-five-year-old Ahmaud Arbery's senseless slaying in Georgia a few months earlier on February 23 by a shotgun-toting civilian son and his father, put into alarming context the struggle and fear Black parents have for their children.

"It's an insidious form of racial profiling," Rodney Coates, a sociologist and professor of critical race and ethnic studies at the University of Miami of Ohio, said.

"I'm terrified that my son might go to prison or get killed just by being Black," said Jeri Byrom, a teacher in Nairobi, Kenya, who said she was excited about her son, Adam, starting college at Howard University a few years ago. That excitement, though, was laced with concern he would fall victim to a targeted attack.

"I live in this constant fear," she said. "Young freshmen do stupid things, and young Black men cannot afford to make one mistake. I happened to call him on Halloween during his freshman year. Good thing I did, because he and his friend were about to go trick-or-treating in an affluent area of D.C.

"I freaked out and started yelling: 'Are you out of your mind?' I could imagine what could happen to a group of Black boys, with or without costumes, going to a white neighborhood. Again, we had 'The Talk': 'You can't do things like that. You are a target. You don't have to do anything at all, and you can still be shot or arrested or attacked. Please don't go.' Thankfully, they didn't."

New York native Carlton Riddick, an information technology specialist, recalled the talk he had with his mother before he left to attend Johnson C. Smith University in 1988 in Charlotte, North Carolina.

"She told me to avoid being considered a criminal by watching whom I would associate with, so I would not be arrested," he said.

Before his oldest son departed for college, Riddick had a different talk. "I said, 'Son, the police are not your friends.' I wanted him to fully understand what it means to walk out of the safety of his home into a world that would see him as a suspect just because he was walking down the street. This admonishment also included being cautious and suspicious of those of other cultures, many of whom now seem emboldened to take matters into their own hands."

A miffed Riddick added: "What kind of world do we live in when a parent has to have these types of conversations with their children? What pained me the most is here I am a father basically instilling a level of trepidation in my sons. All they hear normally from me is that they can be anything they want to be if they work for it. I had to add a caveat: even in a world that only sees you as a suspect."

Hauntingly, Samar Moseley, thirty-seven, of Minneapolis, said he lives in fear that an officer will kill him. He said he leaves social events early to avoid the potential for confrontations that often come at the end of the night. The area has been the scene of so much Black pain, including the deaths of Floyd, Jamar Clark in 2015, and Philando Castile in 2016, across the bridge in St. Paul.

"I feel like I could be next," he said. "It's that bad. Black men in this city feel like targets," said Moseley, who was so disturbed by killings of Black men by cops that in 2019 he wrote and released a music video on YouTube called "When They Gonna Stop?"

Family therapist Porsha Jones advises that parents take a stronger position on instilling pride in their young Black men when they have "The Talk."

Too many Black children believe, "I could be next," Jones said, a burden non-Black youths do not have to bear.

"That's such a powerful force, believing what you have seen on television could happen to you also, that the police or a random person could take your life just because you're Black."

It becomes a mental game.

"Black parents have to implement a talk around new protective factors," Jones said. "But we have to balance the message so that he does not believe he is less than. You must communicate a sense of all love for your child and let him know that he is not broken, that he is equal. Reinforce his attributes and make sure he understands his heritage. This is necessary to reinforce because this is certainly not about him."

Coates, the sociologist, equated the trauma Black males feel to Reconstruction, when gangs of whites would hunt down and kill African Americans for sport and with no consequences.

Arbery's death in Georgia was also hunting. He was on a jog when he was essentially run down by a father-son vigilante duo, eventually got into a struggle with a man who pulled a shotgun on him and killed him. Arbery had done nothing wrong. The men were not police officers, though the father had once been an officer and had also worked as an investigator for a district attorney's office.

"When these [vigilante] cases occur, [Black young men] must try to defuse," Coates said. He said his son had an incident where he tried to run and was fortunate he was not shot in the back. Coates hugged his son "with tears in my eyes, knowing it could have worked out tragically.

"[Defusing a situation] goes against their brain and instincts," Coates said. "But it's not about being a coward. It's not about backing down. It's being strategic. It's about living.

"It's the time we are living in, it's infuriating that we have to take these measures. But we do. Black people have to be strategic about protecting their lives because there are clear forces that are against us...And it's the ultimate form of racism in America."

THE MATTER OF YOUNG LEADERS

Out of the agony of 2020, which sparked national insurrection about an American system that has disproportionately kept its knee on Black people's necks, came a collection of young leaders who, simply, are not having it.

They are younger than the founders of Black Lives Matter. In some cases, they are too young to vote. But as teenagers, they possess an innate sense of responsibility in a moment in history that calls for responsible stalwarts.

They are leaders, the next wave of rabble-rousers, that promise to be needed, as the changes required will not occur at warp speed. Indeed, the process will be painstakingly slow, so deliberate, in fact, that it will require more energy and passion and strong voices to keep the movement moving over the years. And, again, these emerging leaders are young women.

In 2020, four high school students were among the many young people who, inspired by BLM and devastated by the George Floyd killing, emerged as prominent voices—and plan to stay there.

At eighteen, Brianna Chandler concluded what many Black adults have not: "We don't need politicians," the St. Louis native said.

"We are all we have as people and all we need as citizens. We don't have to rely on politicians." That position is one of the reasons she has taken on a role as "a student of a revolutionary movement," she said.

To that end, Chandler organized a "teach-in" in her city for local students to learn about racial injustice. The idea was that the more they knew, the more they'd be inspired as she has been, and the more young people would join the fight.

"We have to bring sheer radical hope," she said. "We've lived under capitalism for so long that it's taken a mental toll."

That mental toll is played out in passivity, which is the polar opposite of Chandler's posture. "One of the pitfalls of activism is that people get tired. You post ten messages on Instagram and you're done. No. Real activism comes from conversations and commitment.

"Social media plays a large role, yes. The educational system is not filled to the brim with Black history or the liberation movement. Social media is good for sharing what we can from home and reaching a lot of people around the world. It's good for getting donations. We have a mutual need."

And when fatigue sets in? "It's comforting knowing that I am not alone," Chandler said. "There is no hierarchy in this. We all carry this weight equally."

Her sentiments were shared by Tiana Day, a seventeen-year-old in the San Francisco area. Much of her life she said she had a "burning desire to protest injustices." But she "didn't know what to do. I felt hopeless. But I wanted to do something. I never had that talk with my dad. We made it to the suburbs and never thought we'd have to face racism, police brutality."

Inevitably, she learned that racism was everywhere. She also learned that her father marched while at San Jose State in protest after the beating of Rodney King by police officers in 1991 and that her grandfather was a part of the Black Panthers movement in the 1960s.

"I was shocked that my father hadn't told me about his activism. But it made sense. I had that burning desire. It's literally in my blood."

Her father and family were proud when Tiana led thousands in the first-ever Black Lives Matter march across the Golden Gate Bridge in a demonstration after George Floyd was killed. At the apex of the bridge, she spoke to the mass of people. Doing so was liberating.

"I want to share my voice," she said. "We need representation. We need a future to fight for. These are the most influential times for us. There is so much to fight for: against police brutality, for climate change and women's rights.

"My family has had the strength and persistence to keep going. We have to take a stance now if we want to see change when we are adults."

She founded the organization Youth Advocates for Change. "One of the things that keeps me going is thinking what if, as an adult, I get a call saying my son was shot, my friend was shot," she said.

The burden of balancing school and activism and the state of America drains her, she said. "Sometimes depression sets in and I cry for twenty-four hours. I feel so helpless. But I always find a reason to get back out there. We have work to get done."

Politics, however, is also not in her future. She said Joe Biden would receive her first-ever vote for president over Donald Trump, "because I relate to him the most…Politics are messy. You have to step on people to get up there…I have enough anxiety. My name is out there. My address is out there. It's very dangerous to stand on that pedestal. There are people who absolutely don't agree with what I'm saying…But it's in my blood."

Zee Thomas asked permission from her mother to become an activist. Given the go-ahead, the sixteen-year-old went full bore and ended up leading a march of 10,000 protesters in Nashville, Tennessee, against police brutality.

"The oppression we've felt has lasted hundreds of years and it won't stop," Thomas said. "People think that teenagers don't care about what's going on around the world. We care. Tennessee is a red state, but we still care."

She said it is imperative that Black girls take the mantle. "Because if we don't, it won't get better. We have to continue the generational strength and pass it on."

Soft-spoken and withdrawn when not speaking in public, Zee said taking on a leadership role has been a challenge, but worth the effort.

"I have severe anxiety [about public speaking]," she said. "It's very frustrating. Sometimes I want to do more, but physically I can't." But she said she will not stop. "It's empowering."

Asked what it takes to do what she's doing? "Bravery."

Shayla Turner found her bravery when she saw a peer speaking to students about racism. It was a Friday during her sophomore year. She skipped class and was moved. "I said, 'I can do that.' And I did."

At eighteen, she connected with community and grassroots organizations and grew more impassioned by the day. She spent some of her week of graduation campaigning in her hometown of Chicago to improve the city's schools.

"My anger and passion covers up my introverted nature," she said. "I have a passion and rage and desire to make change."

She said she cried when she voted. "But it was not a good thing. I was counting on voting for Bernie [Sanders]. Kamala [Harris]'s policies…there were a lot of Black and brown people in jail because of her. So, I literally cried.

"All this is happening [in America] because of racism, and the people at the bottom are suffering. It's so corrupted because it's rooted in corruption and based on racism and white supremacy."

She is so emotional about her work that she said she "overexerts" herself. "My mom has to remind me to take a mental health day. So, I cut off social media and relax. I don't think I'm obligated to fix all that is wrong. But I would feel guilty if I did nothing."

Peters, the professor who studies civil rights movements, said young activists represent a wave of revolutionaries who have and will continue to immerse themselves in the movement to make Black lives matter.

"The fact that there are generations who are younger who now know that protest is possible," he said, "that coming together is possible, that there could be significant cohesion and a way of attacking and demanding is powerful. This is important."

THE MATTER OF MINNEAPOLIS

A city was deconstructed in the wake of George Floyd's killing. Minneapolis had a reputation as a progressive place that championed inclusivity and mobility, with a downtown replete with high-end shopping and fine culinary options.

Outside of the Chamber of Commerce's depiction, Minneapolis also had a reputation for tension between its police force and its Black male population—and for sound reasons. Black men and women were appalled when, in 2015, Jamar Clark, twenty-four, was shot during a scuffle with two white Minneapolis police officers. In July 2016, cops shot Philando Castile in his car while his girlfriend recorded the tragedy in St. Paul, the state capital and neighboring Twin City. Police also shot to death Mario Philip Benjamin, thirty-two, when responding to a domestic incident in 2019.

In each case, the shooters were either not arrested or found not guilty.

In between those occasions, in 2017, a Black police officer named Mohamed Noor, born in Somalia, shot and killed a white woman in a dark alley, something Noor called "a mistake." He was the only Minnesota officer to be convicted in an on-duty shooting in recent history.

And then George Floyd happened, and the powder keg the city had become exploded.

Andrea Jenkins, the Minneapolis city council vice president who represents the neighborhood where Floyd was killed, lives a five-minute walk from Cup Foods at 38th and Chicago, the site of the tragedy.

Jenkins said she shopped at Cup Foods for decades.

"I've been there hundreds of times."

The Memorial Day 2020 when Floyd was killed, Jenkins said she was at home, watching Netflix, a show called *The Politician*. She did not learn of the tragedy until she received a call late that evening from a colleague and then the mayor of Minneapolis, asking if she had seen the video.

She hadn't. It took her forty-five minutes to find it on Facebook. It was 1 a.m.

"It was sickening," Jenkins said of the video that shows Chauvin resting his knee and the force of his weight on Floyd's neck for nine minutes, twenty-nine seconds as Floyd begged for relief. "Absolutely sickening."

And then she thought: "Here we go. Here we go again. The overall disregard for human life, disregard for Black life. I didn't really start thinking about the social unrest that would eventually ensue or any of that. It was just a real emotional response [and] feeling."

That same feeling permeated the Watts section of Los Angeles in August 1965, when a white California Highway Patrol officer stopped a Black man named Marquette Frye in his vehicle on suspicion of driving while intoxicated. A roadside argument broke out, which then escalated into a fight with police. In the commotion, witnesses said the police injured a pregnant woman.

Frye's encounter was the accelerant on the fire—the culmination of consistent mistreatment by white officers—that sent Black residents into a fervor. Six days of civil unrest followed, with Watts set ablaze in the most destructive uprising: thirty-four deaths and $40 million in property damage.

Fifty-five years later, it happened in Minneapolis. Jenkins was aware of the Watts riots, also called the Watts Uprising and Watts Rebellion, and was fearful the same could happen in her city. After all, the parallel was striking: Both cities had a history of violence against Black people by law enforcement. Both cities had citizens who were fed up with the disregard. Both cities were one incident from an explosion. And America itself was rife with police brutality cases.

The difference that made all the difference: In Minneapolis, Floyd's death was captured on video—all nine minutes, twenty-nine seconds. There was no hiding behind the shield, no tainted, one-sided reports from enabling police officers. The world saw George Floyd murdered.

The world heard him beg for his life. It saw a cop, Chauvin, show no concern that the man could not breathe. It saw three other officers hold him down—and none of them come to the aid of a man who had been accused of passing a counterfeit $20 bill.

And so, the next day in Minneapolis, there was a rally as the nation and eventually the world shrieked in horror while viewing the video. The anger was palpable, the pain intense. But because so many Black men had died at the hands of law enforcement, few Black people were surprised. They had been desensitized to the violence. But that did not lessen the anguish or rage.

The gathering in Floyd's memory was peaceful, Jenkins said. "It was very peaceful. I mean, there was deep anger and frustration," she said. "But it was being expressed, you would say, in traditional ways. You know, there were speakers.

"There were people from all over the city, people just kind of gathering, and supporting each other, calling for justice. Then that scene moved to begin marching down eastward on 38th Street towards the third precinct, which was about two and a half miles from 38th and Chicago.

"Things started around five in the evening. We cried and all of those kinds of things. I spoke. Many ministers and community activists and [the] community took off towards the precinct, maybe about seven-thirtyish, to march that two and a half miles to the police station.

"I did not go that far; I have multiple sclerosis, so walking that distance in a large crowd was not healthy for me.

"When I learned that it became this confrontation, I was surprised. There have been many reports about it, that the police maybe overreacted...I did not anticipate it."

"Actually, there was nothing to be surprised about," said Greg

Agnew, a Minneapolis native who has had encounters with white officers. "You have a situation where a man gets killed as George Floyd did in a city with a terrible history of police not only killing Black men, but constantly harassing us. Yes, there would be confrontations during the protests because the cops still act like cops and the Black people are tired of it."

Jenkins said she called the police chief and "begged" him to not use tear gas on the demonstrators. The fact that she knew that type of aggressive tactic would be employed speaks to the history of the city and America.

But the inspector on duty, who had the authority, called for tear gas, rubber bullets, and riot gear, elements that sent a clear and alarming message: They were prepared for war with the protesters, even if the protesters were only there to make a statement.

Those actions set the scene for the next night of protests, nights and actions that would define Minneapolis in this moment. Chaos erupted. Fires. Looting. Destruction. Leaders of the protests, who implored peaceful protests, decried the disruptions and were often recorded stopping white marchers from painting "BLM" on buildings and inciting mayhem.

Jenkins said she stayed at her partner's home and watched it all play out on television for four days.

"Minneapolis was spared the damage that could have come because the BLM movement isn't about violence and destruction," said Ray Richardson, a radio host who has lived in Minneapolis for more than twenty-five years. "We had a right to be fed up and pissed off—and not just because of George Floyd. There's a history in this town that pushed us to the edge. But the organizers pushed an agenda that was not like the 1960s nonviolent marches, but still not to turn things into chaos. It takes away from the message."

"It was very spontaneous," Jenkins said. "I mean, there were clearly reports of white supremacists in the area definitely involved...like cutting a fire hose and destroying property and burning down banks and post offices.

"We were getting reports from neighbors that people were driving around in trucks with no license plates, starting fires behind people's houses. Garages were on fire. Those are the kinds of reports that people were seeing.

"And they were suggesting that these were not typical protesters. Many white neighbors [were] reporting that they [saw] white supremacists. Some had Confederate flags, lots of guys with tattoos. These were actually being confirmed by the law enforcement agencies that I was communicating with. Even though they were stating that these guys weren't there to harm anything.

"[But] they were reporting some of the same things that . . . happened in Kenosha [Wisconsin] later in the summer, that white supremacist militias were just in town to protect their stores and protect things. But it was downplayed quite a bit by state authorities. I guess they thought they weren't a threat.

"That's the only thing I can assume . . . even though we do know that since then many people who have been affiliated with those groups [were] arrested."

The harsh reality is that there will be another Minneapolis—many of them, if history continues to repeat itself. In 1967, two years after the Watts riots, a Black cabdriver in Newark, New Jersey, was stopped for a minor traffic violation and beaten badly by two white police officers.

The news of the Newark incident spread quickly, and a crowd formed at the police headquarters where the injured driver was held. Protesters, exhausted from police misconduct and more, expressed their discontent by hurling rocks at police station windows.

The next two days were turbulent. New Jersey governor Richard Hughes called in the National Guard. The violence escalated, with twenty-six people dead and many Black people injured in the streets.

Then, two weeks after the Newark unrest of 1967, police raided an after-hours club in Detroit, where a welcome-home party was being held for two Black Vietnam War veterans. Police busted up the celebration and arrested eighty-two African Americans who were in the club.

The arrests lit the bomb within the Black community that had been waiting to go off. After five days of the disorder, thirty-three Black people were dead, 7,000 people were arrested, and more than 1,000 buildings were burned. This incident is considered to be one of the inspirations for the creation of the Black Panther movement.

Police brutality was the spark in these moments, but the true causes were the boiling resentment behind racism in general and in particular unemployment, poverty, segregation, inferior education, and other systemic issues of oppression.

Three months before the Detroit and Newark uprisings of 1967, Dr. Martin Luther King Jr. foreshadowed what was to come in a speech he delivered at Stanford University called "The Other America."

In it, Dr. King said: "All of our cities are potentially powder kegs…But in the final analysis, a riot is the language of the unheard. And what is it that America has failed to hear? It has failed to hear that the plight of the Negro poor has worsened over the last few years. It has failed to hear that the promises of freedom and justice have not been met. And it has failed to hear that large segments of white society are more concerned about tranquility and the status quo than about justice, equality, and humanity…And as long as America postpones justice, we stand in the position of having these recurrences of violence and riots over and over again."

More than five decades later, Dr. King's words continue to ring true in America.

A week after the protests in Minneapolis began in 2020, Jenkins returned to her home in the neighborhood where she had lived since 1999, uncertain of what to expect after daily demonstrations mixed with nightly unrest that were pervasive in New York, Atlanta, Chicago, Los Angeles, Buffalo, and countless other cities across the country, as law enforcement maintained an aggressive posture against the protesters' determination to be heard.

"During the day it seemed like just regular old, beautiful, bucolic Minneapolis," she said. "Summer was coming. The grass was turning green. People were walking their dogs. It's your regular old neighborhood. But during those first few weeks, still people were on edge, and at night mostly people were on edge because there were these huge firecrackers. It kind of started slowing down after the Fourth of July. But for Juneteenth, the fireworks were mixed with gunshots.

"It was unnerving. The fireworks were more rapid. They had a certain cadence. And then the gunshots were louder and had their own particular sort of rhythm."

In addition, the demonstrations occurred during the coronavirus pandemic, which sent the message that the cause was worth defying the stay-at-home orders that were in place.

The perpetual concern during the marches centered on following— or not following—Centers for Disease Control guidelines on wearing masks and maintaining six feet of social distancing. Many demonstrators wore masks; some did not. Maintaining social distance was difficult as the gatherings grew in size. But it was the same for law enforcement, although it was not noted nearly as much. They lined up in riot gear, presenting a show of force—but masks were absent, and social distancing did not exist.

Dr. Enid Neptune, a Black pulmonologist at Johns Hopkins University School of Medicine, said she watched the protests with equal parts pride and uneasiness. "As a physician I had a heightened degree of concern. The demonstrations were overly populated with African Americans. But that concern is balanced against the need to protest…The Black body is being devalued, so the protesters are protesting on merit, despite a pandemic.

"This is about people having to make these decisions in this [racially divided] climate and what they hope to gain from the protests being more important than the need to employ every possible strategy to block the risk of COVID transmission. That's a very personal choice [to march] and it's not a choice that anyone can make for anyone else."

Dr. Pierre Vigilance, founder and principal at HealthUp Strategic Advisors and associate dean of public health practice at George Washington University, noted that the purpose of the movement was so powerful that any critique of following COVID-19 protocols rang hollow.

"I often heard of these comparisons of the protests versus the mass [social] gatherings, how they are all the same," Vigilance said. "Those are inappropriate. The point of the protests was to speak out on wrongdoings. That was valid. And many of the images showed people wearing masks.

"The point of these other [social] gatherings, like in the Ozarks, was to socialize. So, if we're going to talk about the protests and their impact on this pandemic, they also need to be talking about the mass gatherings of [white] people who are socializing not wearing masks or social distancing."

There was another, deeper reason, Neptune said, that Black people often did not wear masks as they demonstrated.

"One aspect of police-involved events that target African American men is the subtext that these persons are not seen, not recognized as people of value," she said. "The ability to show one's face is a way of saying, 'This is what I look like, and I matter.' So, a mask can attenuate that assertion of individuality and importance and 'This is who I am.' That part of the protests has been underexamined."

Interestingly to Jenkins, as the summer moved on, she could look out of her window and see normalcy. "Fall came. The leaves were turning red," she said. "I live right across the street from the park. Kids played soccer. They've got their dogs running loose, getting exercise. There was a church service. It was like the regular neighborhood.

"That area became known as George Floyd Square. It's barricaded off. But for all of the burning and looting and then fires and all of these things, the intersection at 38th and Chicago? No destruction.

"You would have suspected that maybe Cup Foods may have been burned out. That's what happened in many other cities, like Atlanta." (The Wendy's was set ablaze where unarmed Black man Rayshard Brooks was shot twice, once in the back and once in the buttocks, by an Atlanta police officer. He died in the hospital. A white woman was arrested for arson in that case.)

"In Ferguson, when Michael Brown got killed, they burned down the [store] that he went to [where the worker had called the police]. But Cup Foods remained completely untouched by the destruction and the looting, which is very, very interesting because 38th and Chicago has historically been kind of gang territory. For decades, the Bloods."

Jenkins also found the racial makeup of the demonstrators interesting. Black people led the rallies. The communities participating were comprised of multiple ethnic groups, including Latino and Somalian. But "the protesters were overwhelmingly white," Jenkins said. "Young white males were very visible early on. It was remarkable in the sense of people were talking about it—the news media and the elected officials."

The predominant number of white demonstrators in Minnesota was unique compared to most BLM protests around the country, especially in the cities where a Black life was taken. But that show of support spoke to the horrific nature of Floyd's death, and the outrage crossed racial differences. The civil disobedience in the 1960s had some participation from non-Blacks, but the demographic was predominately brothers and sisters exalting their pain and anguish on a social order that limited their growth. So they pushed back with little consideration for property—or consequences.

In the case of Minneapolis, Jenkins said the site of the tragedy became a "sacred place" and a rally point.

"George Floyd Square was like ground zero," Jenkins said. "So, either people would start their march somewhere else and end up at 38th and Chicago. Or they would gather at 38th and Chicago and march to the capital or march to the precinct or march to City Hall."

There was not much discussion on television about the priority placed on the location where Floyd was killed.

"There's sort of an eight-block [area], for lack of a better term—protesters or advocates get mad when I use this language—an autonomous zone. The general public [was] monitored and controlled on who and when people can enter by these self-proclaimed George Floyd Square protector residents. They're completely disassociated from any governmental or law enforcement agencies, and their distrust and their disgust to those very agencies [was strong]. People have come to 'Hold down this space until they get justice.'"

The barricade stopped the traffic flow on one of the state's busiest thoroughfares, Route 5, which runs through six different communities: Bloomington, Richfield, Minneapolis, Golden Valley, and Brooklyn Center, and extends to the Mall of America and the nearby airport.

Emergency vehicles could not get through George Floyd Square. And law enforcement exploited this as an opportunity to "take a break from enforcing the law, meaning citizens who needed protection often did not get any," Jenkins said. She added that law enforcement's lack of policing was in retaliation to the call to defund the police.

"Right," Agnew said. "The people paid to protect the citizens didn't want to do their jobs because they were mad. That about sums it up. And it's disgusting."

Indeed, the feel of law enforcement—in riot gear and with weapons drawn—treating protesters as terrorists reigned. The National Guard was called in, presenting another intimidating presence.

"It wasn't a comfortable feeling being there, exercising our right to protest and have the cops looking like they were ready to attack," Samar Moseley said. "And because they've shot us before, I definitely had the feeling that it could happen again. Why did they have guns out? Why dressed like something's about to go down? We came in peace. We got treated like the bad guys."

There was no official Black Lives Matter chapter in Minneapolis, which was the epicenter of the national unrest. There were BLM protesters there in its name and BLM representatives there, but the movements were not Black Lives Matter–organized.

Rather, BLM spawned other organizations in Minnesota with similar ambitions that were key players in the 2020 demonstrations. There was Black Visions Collective, an organization that describes itself as "dedicated to Black liberation and to collective liberation, we need a radical and ongoing investment in our own healing. By claiming love for our own bodies, our own psyches, our own experiences, and by building the resources we need to integrate healing justice into all that we do, we are insisting on conditions that can carry us towards the next generation of work, and towards a deeper place of freedom for all of us."

Based in the Twin Cities, BVC says it "has been putting into practice the lessons learned from organizations before us in order to shape a political home for Black people across Minnesota." BVC took the lead in most of the marches after Floyd's death.

There was also Reclaim the Block, a grassroots organization founded in 2018. It "organizes Minneapolis community and city council members to move money from the police department into other areas of the city's budget that truly promote health and safety."

The Reverend Al Sharpton visited Minneapolis in the early

days of the protests. His appeals to turn down the volume of the demonstrations were unwelcome. People needed to voice their anger and pain.

"Ultimately, I think many people around the country who are 'abolitionists' and Black Lives Matter members…see it as the start of a process, not the end," Jenkins said.

In Watts, Detroit, and Newark, while they rebuilt, the remnants of the civil unrest persist in a number of ways: police violence against Black people continues there; quality jobs are not plentiful; food deserts exist; public education is subpar. And on and on.

"What I would hope that we could trace back to these protests is that we have rebuilt our city on a foundation of sustainability and equal opportunities for everybody," Jenkins said. "And I hope that for the entire country, I hope that through these protests we can see universal health care in our society, that we can see universal basic income in our society. We have a real huge problem of income inequality. And I believe that that is the main reason why you have millions of people in the street marching and protesting, George Floyd, Breonna Taylor, Ahmaud Arbery are just the sparks that lit this flame.

"But people are angry about the blatant runaway capitalism that has created a caste system in this country. People are tired of it. So, I hope we see a more equitable society in terms of income, in terms of access to home ownership, education, and to safe health care. And that is what I think these protests are getting at. And I hope that in the end, we will see those things as a response."

THE SHIFT IN PUBLIC CONSCIOUSNESS

Long-distance freight driver Ed Hughes remembers—said he will not forget, in fact—the day a white woman approached him and his wife, Leigh, at a restaurant in northern Virginia. She served them dinner and had grown comfortable enough over their experience to share what Ed Hughes considered deep feelings of guilt.

"She said, 'I understand the battle and I just want to know what I can do differently and what I can say.' I was touched by that," Hughes said. "She could have kept that to herself. The fact that she didn't made me believe she was sincere. She was in her twenties from Louisiana. That was an outstanding moment, considering the climate of the country."

Hughes answered her simply, "Treat everyone like you treated us."

He said: "That's all that was needed to be said. She was wonderful to us, very nice and personable. My point was we need more of that."

The server's comments to the Hugheses represented a shift in public consciousness that was palpable in 2020. The turmoil Black people lived with daily—and had been living with all along—came to the forefront in the aftermath of the callous nature of George Floyd's killing in Minneapolis. Emotions of anyone with a tinge of empathy spilled over from seeing a man killed as he begged for his life.

Ten days after Floyd's murder, Marcy Sampson drove to Atlanta from Bessemer, Alabama, with two friends, a trio of young white women who said they felt compelled to be counted among those who agreed that the racial tide needed to be turned.

"We all are people, all should be treated like humans," Sampson said.

She admitted that the devastating image of Floyd dying under a police officer's knee was so heart-wrenching that she, for the first time in her life, gave serious consideration to the disparities she had heard African Americans share.

"I don't know. I mean, I thought I understood where Black Lives Matter was coming from. I thought I understood that there were biases in America," she said. "But that... the way George Floyd died, as if his life didn't matter... and worse, the officer seemed to know nothing would happen to him. It broke my heart.

"And as a person living in the world, white, Black, or otherwise, we can't just sit back; I couldn't just sit back. When I saw that, I got it that something is really wrong. All this time, I...I guess I didn't understand."

Sampson held a sign that read: "Black Lives Matter." Her friends' signs read: "No Justice, No Peace" and "Stop the Killing of Innocent PEOPLE."

They were a microcosm of the paradigm shift of public sentiment that emerged from Floyd's death.

"You can't do that to people. Period," J. Lee Young, a white man from Cummings, Georgia, north of Atlanta, said. Like Sampson, he said that before this year he did not believe racism was a prominent force in America.

"I know there is racism in the world," he said. "But that was what you call a watershed moment for me, seeing that man die like that for no reason. White people have to take a stand, too. I feel a sense of guilt for not understanding before now. If we don't take a stand, we are wrong. And we shouldn't be wrong on this issue."

The guilt manifested itself in other ways beyond protest participation. On social media, thousands of posts surfaced by non-Black people determined to share that they'd had a revelation about race in the United States. Books on anti-racism became bestsellers. "Black Lives Matter" signs appeared in front lawns of white homes and businesses.

"And I had a white co-worker come to me and apologize," Diana Wright, a pharmaceutical sales representative in suburban Chicago, said. "I said, 'For what?' She said, 'For what's happened to your people—the past and now. I'm ashamed.' I was shocked. But when I told my friends about it, more than one of them said they had a similar situation happen to them."

Gentrifying the demonstrations ran its course, though, with some Black protesters, who believed many whites participated on the condition that they lead the marches. They respected and appreciated their support, but they insisted on leading.

"It's our turn to lead our own fight, to frame our own conversations," Benjamin O'Keefe, a Black political organizer in Brooklyn, said. "We exist in a white supremacy culture in which even people who want to do good do not necessarily want to be led by a Black person."

Black leaders were more interested in how white Americans—inspired by brutality of white officers on Black people—would integrate anti-racism into their lifestyles, and not just when the country was mired in unrest.

The word and concept of "allyship" took on prominent roles in white people's quest to help with change. Allyship is defined as the continuous process in which someone with privilege and power seeks to first learn about the experiences of a marginalized group of people, and then ultimately empathize with their challenges and build relationships with that group of people.

Another way of putting it is allies acknowledge their lofty status—and recognize their favor should not override the virtue of helping.

"Allyship is language, and being a co-conspirator is about doing the work," said O'Keefe, a Black activist who was a former senior aide to Massachusetts senator Elizabeth Warren. "It's taking on the issue of racism and oppression as your own issue, even though you'll never truly understand the damage that it does."

He added: "There are a few important things to think about as we're having that conversation. Don't put your burden of your sadness or your fear onto your Black friends or onto Black leaders that you follow, because the truth is it's not the job of Black people to educate you or to make you comfortable. Anti-racism isn't comfortable, just like racism isn't comfortable for Black people and people of color.

"Listen more than you speak. Do your research. Ignorance by very definition is a lack of knowledge, so the only way to break down ignorance and your ignorance and the ignorance of others is through education. It's really important to learn the history of the struggle you're putting yourself into, to learn about the systems of oppression that exist and how you're complicit in them, and then, again, remember that it's not our job to educate you. It's not hard to educate yourself. You can literally Google it."

And one more thing, O'Keefe pointed out: Black people were grateful for whites' support, but urged them to know their place.

"When white people show up to protests for the Movement for Black Lives, they are our guests," he said. "This might be exciting to them now, but this has been something that we have been living for generations and fighting for generations. So, you are showing up, and we're happy to have you, you are our guests.

"A white person's job at a protest isn't to spray paint 'Black Lives Matter' on a building. It's not to destroy stuff. It's not to loot stores. Their job is not to mess with the cops and throw stuff. Their job at that protest, what they are there to do, is to do everything they can in their power to put their bodies between the bodies of Black people and police. They should know if they're there that they have the privilege of at least knowing that there will be more action taken if they die than if a Black person does. Because not only is it disrespectful to disrupt our protests, but it actually is also doing direct harm to the Black lives that these folks are supposed to be there to try to protect.

"Countless times it's white people who are doing this provocation (burning buildings, throwing things at law enforcement), who are escalating this, and it's not them who are suffering the consequences, both physically there in person and with tear gas and pepper spray thrown in our faces, but also they're not doing service to the narrative that we're trying to build. They're continuing to give fodder that will be used and is currently being used against Black people.

"If you show up to a protest, you're there to be an ally, you can say.

You are there to listen and to learn and to follow the leadership of the Black folks, to follow the leadership of the marginalized."

Forensic psychologist Dr. Christopher Bass in Atlanta said he could not rule out white guilt as part of white people's participation in the demonstrations.

"The idea that a revolution cannot be diverse has been proven incorrect throughout our time here in this country," Bass said. "This time was somehow different, though. As the media looked for answers to help them understand this diverse participation, some asked about the concept of 'white guilt.' In summation, we conclude that the term refers to the feelings of shame and remorse some white people experience when they recognize the legacy of racism and racial injustice, and perceive the ways they have benefited from it."

It was not just the media that questioned white people's participation. Those in the movement had questions and doubts, too.

"If history teaches us nothing else, it teaches us that history in many cases can repeat itself," Bass said. "Similar to protests in the 1960s for civil rights, a theme began to emerge as old lessons took center stage. The lessons that were taught earlier on included the fictitious narrative that African Americans, when emotionally charged, resort to aggressive tendencies and lack the intellectualism and socialization to remain peaceful during difficult or uncertain times.

"The tendency by the white media is to create the narrative that African Americans must be controlled with more aggression to quell the instinct, which is stereotypically innate. As we have seen in the media countless times, even those who were killed by police and others quickly have their previous encounters with the legal system (if a history exists) prominently displayed and circulated to consciously justify the actions of the authority figure. Victimize the victim. Yet, when the African American community cries out, the lenses of support and change only become clearer when there is white community support."

Bass said there were signs of potential for systemic changes following the protests, because many looked at the demonstrations as multiracial instead of just Black. It was bothersome that "white community support and participation changed the temperature of the visual. It is much more difficult to categorize and demean a diverse group of emotionally charged protesters," he said. "For, when you see those who resemble you, or your family, common descriptions used by the media to describe African American youth, like 'wild animals' (which was used consistently since Reconstruction) cease."

White people's participation did not assuage Black people's feelings or correct injustices. Significantly, Bass pointed out, there was a difference between the awareness that guilt brings and the caring that comes with being awakened by the atrocities.

"Being awake alludes to a complex connection to an ideal, whereas, being aware does not necessarily mean that," Bass said. "An individual's external state of awareness of their social surroundings, thoughts, and feelings can be procured from cues in the environment. Thus, behavior based on just awareness of perceived themes can be ill-timed, ill-themed, or worse—ill-intentioned.

"This should not suggest that being awake automatically makes one aware. The immediate reaction of Mr. Floyd's death was a display of raw pain. In context, it must be understood that this was not an isolated incident. In fact, within the first five months of 2020, over one hundred eight African Americans had been identified as being killed by police in America. The numbers reflected an *epidemic* within the pandemic."

The stress of seeing Floyd killed combined with the history of police shootings and Black people's demise at law enforcements hands—all occurring during a pandemic that devastated the African American community—created an almost unstoppable wave of emotions, Bass said.

"It all set the stage for this kettle pot of raw reaction and emotional expression to spill out. While the nation watched the events play out at home, the stress of being confined to their homes, the loss of family members, without the opportunity to utilize traditional methods of grieving and process, and the sheer uncertainty of a future life (as we knew it previously) also played significant roles in the groundswell of emotion and reaction."

And it goes deeper, Bass said. The protesters were guided by an urgent need to be heard and to effect change, even in the face of a pandemic, and even with law enforcement that viewed them as a foe rather than someone to be protected.

"The idea of being aware is present," he added. "It can guide our behavior. It has the ability to show up. Social consciousness, when viewed through the lens of philosophical and psychological glasses, is a multifaceted paradigm. It must be emphasized that our motivation for behavior lies much deeper than the surface of being aware of an issue. The perception involved in deciphering the multitude of sensational data is overwhelming. If the Freudians taught us anything about what sparks our thinking and subsequent behavior, it is that sometimes being awake, aware, and conscious really can be confusing, ill-directed, and self-preserving."

THE MATTER OF BLACK ATHLETES

Naomi Osaka, the women's tennis phenomenon born to a Haitian father and a Japanese mother, wore seven different masks to her matches at the 2020 U.S. Open, each bearing the name of an unarmed Black person killed by law enforcement. It was a strong display of support of Black Lives Matter—and an indication that the movement spilled into the sports world.

It was an audacious move by Osaka. She took BLM's concerns to the predominantly white, affluent, pretentious tennis world—where

Black players are scarce—and its vast international television audience. She won the major tournament and won a legion of fans that may not have known her as a star, but identified her as courageous after her two-week stand.

Asked after she took the title what she wanted to get out of displaying the names of unnecessarily fallen Black people, Osaka was unflappable: "Well, what was the message that you got was more the question. I feel like the point is to make people start talking."

Lewis Hamilton, the most dominant Formula One racecar driver in the world, was equally committed to BLM in Europe. The Black man of British heritage had "Black Lives Matter" painted on the Mercedes he drove in competition. He took a knee on the track and wore anti-racism slogans supporting BLM all of the 2020 season. And he dominated, winning seven races. Hamilton said the urgency of the Black Lives Matter movement made him a better driver.

"It was a different drive than what I've had in me in the past—to get to the end of those races first so that I could utilize that platform [for Black Lives Matter] and shine the light as bright as possible," he said. "There is no way that I could stay silent. And once I said that to myself, I didn't hold any fear."

That lack of fear existed throughout the athletic world. The NBA, 80 percent of whose players are Black, stood with the BLM movement by using its vast national platform to share the organization's concerns to its community, international audience, corporate sponsors.

"Black Lives Matter" was painted on the court at NBA games during the truncated 2020 season to send a consistent expression of support. Players wore calls for justice or expressions of hope on the back of their jerseys instead of their names.

LeBron James, perhaps the most popular athlete in the world, expanded his standing in the community by racing to the forefront of BLM support, taking on Donald Trump, Fox News host Laura

Ingraham, and anyone who did not share the ideals of change to make life equitable for Black lives.

In a very real way, they all followed in the courage of Colin Kaepernick, the former NFL quarterback who essentially sacrificed his career during his prime. When Kaepernick knelt during the national anthem to protest police brutality before an NFL game on September 12, 2016, he made a statement about the power of the Black Lives Matter movement.

He was their contemporary, a Super Bowl quarterback athletes could relate to, and they drew courage from his audacity. Considered a radical and a potential distraction—at least that was the public position of NFL executives—no team would sign him in what can only be described as "blackballing."

"He's a modern-day Rosa Parks and Muhammad Ali all in one," said Stephen A. Green, president of the People's Consortium, a civil rights group with nonviolent ideals. "When you think about what he has put on the line for himself personally, with what he could lose...that's not [an exaggeration]. He risked a lot to elevate the issues that affect Black and brown bodies in America. For our community, we can't afford to let him be silenced."

Over the years, Kaepernick had been strategic in his activism, doing more and saying less. Hardly did he grant interviews, but his voice had been heard nonetheless.

"Kaep was very deliberate about staying in the public eye," said Sarah J. Jackson, author of *Black Celebrity, Racial Politics, and the Press: Framing Dissent*. "It's also relevant, of course, that Kaepernick's activism came in the middle of the mainstream visibility of the Black Lives Matter movement and several high-profile police killings, as well as alongside the rise in a newly emboldened far-right that focuses a lot of energy on publicly attacking those that critique police or make outspoken stances against anti-Black racism."

NFL owners, some following the demands of Trump and their own biased ideals, forced their players not to follow Kaepernick's peaceful protest of kneeling during the pregame national anthem, conflating the issue of kneeling to protest police brutality with disrespecting the military.

In the NBA, while the league actively joined forces with the players, many of its owners—all white except Michael Jordan—were circumventing those actions.

A study by the sports and pop culture website The Ringer revealed that many of the same NBA owners who publicly professed their unity with the players and the BLM movement were making donations to causes designed specifically to undermine the demonstrations.

After a year spent analyzing five years of records from the Federal Election Commission, John Gonzalez, who wrote the report, found that league owners paid $28 million in political donations to Republican causes and candidates whose ideology clashed with those of the Black protesters and the NBA players.

"We found political contributions by twenty-seven different owners (as well as 20 significant others) over a period of more than five years. Of that $28 million total, more than $14.9 million (53.4 percent) went to Republican politicians and PACs, while over $12 million (43.1 percent) was directed to Democrats," the report said. "That leaves roughly $1 million to nonpartisan issues, such as the University Public Issues Committee, the National Cable and Telecommunications Association, or PACs that give to candidates from both parties."

Orlando Magic owner Dan DeVos is the son of Amway co-founder Richard DeVos and brother-in-law to Betsy DeVos, the much-maligned former secretary of education appointed by Donald Trump. Dan DeVos donated $50,000 to the Congressional Leadership Fund, "a super PAC that funnels money to the same Republican representatives who accounted for all but one of the nay votes against HR 7120," which was crafted to address police reform after George Floyd's killing.

Dan DeVos and his wife, Pamella, gave more than $220,000 to two Senate super PACs directly tied to Republican committees responsible for keeping the vote on HR 7120 from happening. The report also reveals that DeVos donated $200,000 to America First Action, one of Trump's super PACs, just two weeks after Floyd's death on May 25.

DeVos said he strongly condemned "bigotry, racial injustice, and the unwarranted use of violence by police against people of color" in public statements of unity with the players and said their mostly one-sided political donations didn't necessarily reflect their personal leanings, according to the report.

Billionaires typically donate equally to both political parties, according to a study by Americans for Tax Fairness and the Institute for Policy Studies. But in the NBA, 80.9 percent of the owners' donations have gone to Republicans and Republican causes, with 18.4 percent going to Democrats, and another 0.7 percent to nonpartisan issues, according to the report.

In fact, as the league professed its support of Black Lives Matter, NBA team owners collectively donated more money to Trump-related super PACs than all Democratic donations combined in 2020, according to the report. The DeVoses donated about half of that amount—more than $2 million—to Republicans, records show.

Michele Roberts, the first Black woman to be the executive director of the National Basketball Players Association, said in the report: "There are some people who purport to despise Trump but believe as long as he keeps those taxes low, he's their guy. Now, I think that's a disgraceful excuse for why you would support someone with his politics. But I know people who look me in the eye and say that to me: 'Look, I think [Trump is the] scum of the earth. And I would never have him in my home. And I tell my children all the time don't listen to him, he's a jackass. But you know how much money I saved in taxes the last four years?' And that's important to them. It drives me mad that there are ways for people to justify supporting Trump while taking a very progressive position on other issues."

As the NBA players balked at playing during the coronavirus pandemic, the league and Players Association negotiated to establish a social justice coalition that included players, coaches, and owners. Believing the league and owners supported their concerns for social justice, the players agreed to play.

The NBA paid for social justice advertising during playoff games that promoted "greater civic awareness in national and local elections and raising awareness around voter access and opportunity."

Franchise owners pledged $300 million collectively over ten years toward economic empowerment in the Black community and agreed to convert their massive arenas into polling facilities for the November 2020 election—a sound victory of BLM.

The league and owners also, at least publicly, supported the Milwaukee Bucks, who boycotted a playoff game in the aftermath of yet another shooting of a Black man by a white person. In Kenosha, Wisconsin, Jacob Blake was shot seven times in August 2020. He survived, but was paralyzed. A few days later, the Bucks refused to play their playoff game against Orlando, sparking a three-day NBA protest.

The pain of the shooting registered with the Bucks. It happened close to their training facility, and one of their players, Sterling Brown, had been Tasered and arrested by Milwaukee police, but he was never charged with a crime. He sued and was awarded $750,000 after the city admitted wrongdoing.

"You're supposed to look at the police to protect and serve. Now, it's looked as harass or shoot," Bucks player George Hill said. "To almost take a guy's life...I know the cops are probably upset he's still alive because I know they surely tried to kill him. But to almost take a man's life, especially in front of one's kids, that wasn't resisting, in his back at point-blank range, is a heartless and gutless situation. We need some justice for that."

All teams in the playoffs backed the Milwaukee 2020 boycott. It was an escalation of past acts of consciousness by athletes, including wearing "I Can't Breathe" T-shirts after Eric Garner's death by police in New York in 2014.

The Bucks' stand raised memories of the 1961 Boston Celtics protest of an exhibition game in Lexington, Kentucky. The Black players, led by Hall of Famer Bill Russell, sat out because they were refused service in a restaurant. Their white teammates did not support them and played in the game.

To bring attention in the hope for change in America in 1968, U.S. sprinters Tommie Smith and John Carlos raised their black-gloved fists and bowed their heads on the Olympic podium in Mexico City during "The Star-Spangled Banner" after winning gold and bronze medals, respectively, in the 200 meters. Their Black Power salute is among the most iconic images in sports history.

"It was a cry for freedom and for human rights," Smith said in 2008. "We had to be seen because we couldn't be heard."

There were countless acts of activism by athletes—including Muhammad Ali's well-documented moral stand and refusal to fight in the Vietnam War. NBA champion Craig Hodges had his career blackballed after Rodney King was beaten by officers in Los Angeles. Hodges, a member of the Chicago Bulls, attempted to organize a protest of Game 1 of the 1991 NBA Finals on June 2. But he failed to get support from other players, including teammate Michael Jordan. When the Bulls visited the White House after winning the title, he handed President George H. W. Bush a letter expressing concerns about racism and U.S. military involvement. Hodges, one of the best shooters in the NBA, could not get a team to sign him to a contract after the 1991–92 season.

Donald Trump wanted Black athletes to keep quiet. He inflamed tensions when he called NFL players such as Kaepernick "sons of bitches" for kneeling and attacked NBA players for the boycott in general and superstar LeBron James in particular. In his zest to reopen the country that had been shut down by the coronavirus and his affection for anti-Black sentiments, Trump lashed out.

"I think people are a little tired of the NBA," he said. "Frankly, they've become like a political organization, and that's not a good thing…It's terrible. I think what they're doing to the NBA in particular is going to destroy basketball. I can't—I don't even watch it…You know when you watch sports, you want to sort of relax, but this is a whole different world…You don't want to stay in politics. You want to relax."

James was unfazed by Trump, saying, "I really don't think the basketball community [is] sad about losing his viewership."

The all-time great, who led the Los Angeles Lakers to the NBA championship in October 2020, ascended to become a prominent social justice figure. He used his platform to advance the Black Lives Matter messaging, speaking out on political and social issues and helping form the program More Than a Vote, which advocated for African Americans exercising their right to participate in the electorate.

This adds to James's legacy of service. He has contributed millions to his hometown of Akron, Ohio, and paid tuition for countless students to attend the University of Akron; he opened his own school, I Promise School, for third through eighth graders that has produced strong outcomes; he's produced documentaries; he participated in public service announcements supporting Barack Obama when he ran for president and for Hillary Clinton in 2016.

For his efforts, Fox News's Laura Ingraham in 2018 told James to "shut up and dribble" when he and fellow NBA star Kevin Durant discussed the challenges of being Black in America after James's home in Los Angeles was defaced with a racial slur.

James did not shut up. He stepped up. Ingraham, meanwhile, represented a bloc of people who are threatened by Black leadership. "The best thing [Ingraham] did was help me create more awareness," James said at the time. "We will definitely not shut up and dribble...I mean too much to society, too much to the youth, too much to so many kids who feel like they don't have a way out."

James's activism was inspired by the Black Lives Matter founders, and while his worldwide popularity did not validate BLM, it helped expand its growth.

"There is a whole area called the 'psychology of celebrity' that speaks toward this," Atlanta forensic psychologist Dr. Christopher Bass said. "In this area of work, which is a healthy behavior, those with extraordinary gifts (especially physical) speak louder, speak with much more confidence, and in many cases have a voice that others relate to because of their gifts/skill set.

"LeBron James has consistently positioned himself throughout his career as a leader," Bass added. "He has shown leadership on the court as well as integrity in the community. In times like these where many people feel hopeless, his reputation as a leader becomes very attractive. The idea of a well-rounded LeBron James represents the very best of who we could possibly be. Therefore, the average citizen will gravitate towards him and his words when we have no words of our own.

"Ingraham represented the few who continue to hold on to the belief that leadership qualities cannot transfer outside of the given area. This is not the belief of the majority. We, as a community, recognize that athletes are not merely one-dimensional. The average citizen believes that leadership skills are transferable."

It took Michael Jordan longer to get there—thirty years, to be precise. In 1990, when a Black North Carolina candidate for Senate, Harvey Gantt, ran against Republican and devout racist Jesse Helms, Jordan refused to endorse the Black Democrat. Instead, he cracked:

"Republicans buy sneakers, too," effectively labeling himself as a selfish star who had no connection or commitment to the community from which he came, or to helping elect someone who had the ideals of making life better for the Black people of his home state.

Surely, the depiction of a standoffish billionaire who cares little about his people ate at Jordan. In 2020, he gained some social credibility by committing $100 million over ten years to organizations "dedicated to ensuring racial equality, social justice, and greater access to education," he said. Following Jordan, the Brooklyn Nets committed $50 million, and the Boston Celtics another $25 million, to bolster social and economic initiatives in their communities.

All the money thrown at the problem could not be described as a bad thing. But players and fans alike wondered if the gestures were sincere. There were rampant reports that some owners were unhappy that "Black Lives Matter" was painted on the court. And NBA commissioner Adam Silver made a point of saying that the phrase would not be on league courts the following season and that players' names on the backs of jerseys would return over social justice messages. But the prevailing feeling was that the players' position and appetite for activism had exponentially increased, and they were prepared to take a stand—or sit—when necessary.

It was the same with the WNBA, where Black players were in the majority. Notably, a strong stand was taken by the Atlanta Dream, which was co-owned by Kelly Loeffler, the Republican who lost a critical Senate seat in a contentious runoff against Reverend Raphael Warnock, who became the first Black senator of Georgia.

Loeffler criticized BLM, and her players pounced, defying her edict not to wear Black Lives Matter messages on their uniforms and calling for her to sell her portion of the team. In February 2020, Loeffler caved and sold the team to an investment group that included former Dream player Renee Montgomery, who had been vocal in her disapproval of Loeffler. The sale hammered home a point across the athletic landscape: athletes—men and women, Black, white, and brown—found a voice through Black Lives Matter.

CONSCIOUS DECISIONS

As part of their "Overlooked" series, the *New York Times* printed, for the first time, the obituary of Nancy Green, better known as Aunt Jemima, who was born into slavery in 1834 and died in 1923.

Green lived near Lexington, Kentucky, and worked in Chicago as a housekeeper and nanny. She was recruited in 1890 as the pancake company's original face. Green was killed in a car accident in 1923, but her image lasted on the box for ninety-seven years after her death—until Quaker Oats in 2020 decided the brand was built on racial imagery.

The *Times* wrote Green's obituary, which included this from her great-great-great nephew: "She would want the real story to be told of her and the ladies that came after her."

In September 2020, in a "major and extremely rare" occurrence, Dictionary.com updated more than 15,000 entries on its website. One of the changes was using an uppercase B when referring to Black people. According to a statement from the website, "capitalizing Black confers the due dignity to the shared identity, culture, and history of Black people. It also aligns with the practice of using initial capital letters for many other ethnic groups and national identities, e.g., Hispanic."

This symbolic gesture created a stir in some circles but not much of one in others. But it was born of the times.

Also symbolic was the painting of "Black Lives Matter" on America's streets. The first was in Washington, D.C., in black and gold bold letters, on the street, renamed Black Lives Matter Plaza by D.C. Mayor Muriel Bowser, that leads to the White House. That was intentional.

At least seventy cities followed suit as "Black Lives Matter" became the most used phrase in the world. Signs popped up in store windows, front yards, and on bumper stickers. Substantive or not, there was a substantial shift in public consciousness on the issues that mattered to Black people.

Additionally, there were countless financial commitments from companies, professional sports leagues, philanthropists, individuals, and government agencies to address the racist policies that had existed forever, but in this movement became targets of change.

Science company giant Thermo Fisher Scientific developed the Just Project—named after Dr. Ernest Everett Just, an African American biologist and educator of the early 1900s who ascended to prominence with his revolutionary work in the physiology of development in reproduction. The project provided free COVID-19 testing and equipment and staff to the students of America's 101 historically Black colleges and universities. It was a $15 million commitment that was lauded for efforts to minimize the impact of the pandemic on HBCU campuses.

JP Morgan Chase committed to hiring 4,000 HBCU graduates by 2024 and ramped up its Advancing Black Pathways Career Readiness program, an online program for recent graduates of historically Black colleges and young professionals of color.

Countless companies, from Amazon to American Express to Home Depot to…you name it, have pledged their support and financial backing to address the country's social justice issues, fairness in the workplace, and the public health crisis.

Reddit co-founder Alexis Ohanian resigned and urged the board to fill his seat with a black candidate. MSNBC named its first Black woman, Rashida Jones, as president, the first to head a major television news network.

Additionally, thirty-seven companies formed a consortium called OneTen, which includes among others Nike, Target, Verizon, Comcast, American Express, and Bank of America. They joined forces and committed to help 1 million Blacks who did not have four-year college degrees to secure and sustain jobs in the effort to close the gross diversity issue and growing wealth gap. OneTen was created to be a "comprehensive system" that merges skill-building organizations with local education to invest in their success in the job market. Black people were twice as likely to live below the poverty line, which explains the telling numbers: African Americans made up just 8 percent of white-collar professionals and 3.2 percent of executives or senior-level officials and managers, according to a report by the Center for Talent Innovation.

IBM committed $100 million in the form of guest lectures, curriculum, digital badges, software, and faculty training to two dozen HBCUs as part of its Skills Academy Academic Initiative in Global University Programs. And the computer behemoth chose Morehouse College and Clark Atlanta University, among others, to participate in a separate program called the IBM+HBCU Quantum Initiative. The initiative gives students and faculty access to quantum computers, which are so advanced they solve problems differently than the average desktop, laptop, smartphone, or IBM researcher.

Morehouse and Spelman College were awarded $40 million as part of a donation from philanthropists Patty Quillin and her husband, Reed Hastings, co-founder, chairman, and CEO of Netflix. The United Negro College Fund (UNCF) will also receive $40 million, pushing the total award to $120 million.

Philanthropist MacKenzie Scott lavished dozens of HBCUs with their highest-ever donations. She bestowed $50 million to Prairie View A&M University, $45 million to North Carolina A&T State University, and on and on.

Some call it "throwing money at the problem." At the same time, money speaks loudly. And having money makes it possible to do things, close gaps, cross bridges. It also amplified an undeniable fact: Black lives began to matter, at least on the surface.

Getting policies in place to curb long-standing systemic racism and reforming police procedures would be the ultimate measures to show progress. But the BLM movement sparked corporations across the country to hire diversity and inclusion officers to address the gross imbalance in the workplace.

Consciousness was raised to the point where images or statues erected across the country of owners of enslaved people, known racists, and Confederate leaders were pulled down by BLM groups or others offended by their presence. In some cases, city officials took the initiative to remove the statues themselves.

It was an uprising, so to speak. In Portland, statues of Abraham Lincoln and Theodore Roosevelt were toppled. Around the world, protesters upset long-standing statues or symbols of oppression.

In almost every case, they were representations of white dominance. The movement for Black lives empowered and elevated the need for those symbols to go. And with consciousness raised around the globe, many of them fell.

At the same time, the thirst for knowledge about Black history elevated. In Charleston, South Carolina, Joe McGill was among a team of experts with the National Trust for Historic Preservation hired to oversee the restoration of several buildings at the Magnolia Plantation and Gardens property.

They weren't just buildings. They were once the homes of enslaved people.

McGill was excited to work on the project when it formed ten years ago for two reasons: One, he is a descendant of slaves and, two, he knew that far too often slave dwellings had been ignored and decimated over time. Not only did McGill restore them, he asked for and received permission to sleep in the cabins.

"It was important for me to spend the night in those cabins," he said. "I got to see more of what these plantations were not doing. They were not telling the stories of the people from whom I derive my DNA. It was upsetting. It angered me.

"But instead of using that anger for evil, I knew I could use it for good."

And so McGill launched the Slave Dwelling Project, which started out as his idea for a sleepover on the plantation, but elevated into an "immersive experience." McGill leads thoughtful, informative discussions on the legacy of slavery with those who visit the plantations.

Through the coronavirus pandemic, McGill conducted the presentations, including at the Evergreen Plantation in Louisiana, via social media platforms or the Zoom virtual conference app.

McGill's efforts stood in stark contrast to a movement that gained some momentum to eliminate or minimize the teaching of the true history of slavery in schools. Not that American history accurately covered the authentic elements of slavery, Reconstruction, the Jim Crow era, or the civil rights movement. But to have many, including Trump, call for an elimination of teaching even the insulting, sanitized version of slavery was an unacceptable form of suppression.

Some people would rather the plantations not exist, the atrocities that took place there so piercing and long-standing to Black people. Many times the true stories are not told because some of the sites had not been preserved, McGill said. But he considered the sites a teaching opportunity.

In the decade since McGill began his crusade, so to speak, others have expanded his work. In Washington, Georgia, historian Kimberly Clements researches the lives and families of seventeen people who were enslaved on the Robert Toombs House Historic Site. She is building an exhibit space on the property that will feature artifacts believed to be those of the enslaved family. She is also creating a file for each enslaved person, hoping one day to have a dedicated room where the public can do research on other enslaved people from the area.

"The turbulence we have witnessed [in 2020] has created a greater consciousness about these issues," said Dr. Bernard Powers, director of the Center for the Study of Slavery in Charleston. Powers pointed out that it is important for the tour directors and docents to share more information about the lives of the people who were enslaved over focusing on the abuse and oppression that were their plight. Share about how the Africans resisted slavery and indentured servitude, he said.

"People don't want to learn they were mere victims," he continued.

The advocates for teaching Black history in a robust way agree. Lauren S. Brown, a teacher and contributor to the MiddleWeb website, which focuses on education, wrote: "We must remember that African American history is not all about slavery, but that slavery had a profound impact and reach that continues today.

"We must remember that when we do teach about historical slavery. We must teach students about the enormous impact of slavery on the story of America from its very beginnings. And when we wrap up our units on the Civil War and Reconstruction, we can't ignore Black history until Rosa Parks. None of us—no matter our race or the race of our students—can afford such a distorted view of history.

"If we are intentional about doing the work that social justice advocates are talking about right now, we will be busy."

Too often reports come out of teachers across America being called out for wearing Black face or having slavery simulations in their classrooms—misguided attempts to educate.

Pulitzer Prize–winning journalist Nikole Hannah-Jones said: "The color line, beginning with slavery, has informed every aspect of our history. Slavery is *the* fundamental contradiction in our country's history. Our nation's founding principle—a dedication to the proposition that all men are created equal and endowed with certain unalienable rights—is in direct conflict with slavery.

"Our country was built with slave labor. We went to war over slavery, and we have not yet made good on the promissory note Martin Luther King spoke of in 1963."

Hannah-Jones asked a profound question: "What if America

understood...that we [African Americans] have never been the problem but the solution?

"While our country espouses the ideals of democracy, liberty and equality, we haven't lived up to them, and yet ironically, it is Black Americans who have been the foremost freedom fighters in our history. Understanding this contradiction is one of the keys towards understanding the history of the United States of America."

Hannah-Jones's work, which earned her the Pulitzer Prize for Commentary, appeared in the *New York Times Magazine*'s inaugural installment of its 1619 Project, which is its ongoing initiative that launched in August 2019, the 400th anniversary of the beginning of American slavery. Its goal is to "reframe the country's history by placing the consequences of slavery and the contributions of Black Americans at the very center of our national narrative."

In her eloquent prose, Hannah-Jones at once delivered an engaging history lesson and a sweeping condemnation of slavery's causes and effects that resound today.

"No one cherishes freedom more than those who have not had it," she wrote. "And to this day, Black Americans, more than any other group, embrace the democratic ideals of a common good. We are the most likely to support programs like universal health care and a higher minimum wage, and to oppose programs that harm the most vulnerable. For instance, Black Americans suffer the most from violent crime, yet we are the most opposed to capital punishment. Our unemployment rate is nearly twice that of white Americans, yet we are still the most likely of all groups to say this nation should take in refugees.

"The truth is that as much democracy as this nation has today, it has been borne on the backs of Black resistance. Our founding fathers may not have actually believed in the ideals they espoused, but Black people did. As one scholar, Joe R. Feagin, put it, 'Enslaved African-Americans have been among the foremost freedom-fighters this country has produced.' For generations, we have believed in this country with a faith it did not deserve. Black people have seen the worst of America, yet, somehow, we still believe in its best."

BLM'S ACCOMPLISHMENTS

The grassroots organization founded on emotion grew into a tapestry of dreams responsible for substantive change in America. The name started as a catch phrase and blossomed into a sort of anthem for justice and social transformation. The elevation BLM ascended to is unquantifiable, but an idea can be gleaned from the reality that almost everywhere on the planet "Black Lives Matter" has been spoken and paid attention to by the citizenry.

In Charlottesville in 2017, white supremacists converged on the city to counter protesters who were set to remove a statue of Confederate general Robert E. Lee. Chaos ensued, as the white supremacists and militia, carrying torches and chanting racist ideologies, clashed with the peaceful protesters, causing mayhem that resulted in three deaths.

With an opportunity to quell the discord, Trump said, "There were good people on both sides," a comment that will linger in history as a dog whistle to the anti-Black groups that he was on their side.

It did not stop the BLM efforts. In fact, it illuminated why their position was paramount to changing the country, and they pressed on.

All of what Black Lives Matter inspired was a follow-up to the civil rights movement of the 1960s, led by Dr. Martin Luther King Jr., which was a follow-up to the abolition movement led by Frederick Douglass in the 1800s.

Douglass, a former enslaved person, used his autobiography to shed light on the horrors of slavery. After escaping slavery, he joined the movement to end America's original sin. The 1857 decision by the Supreme Court rejected African Americans as full citizens, which squashed the Missouri Compromise that had forbidden slavery in the West, but it galvanized Black leaders instead of deflating them and led to Abraham Lincoln, the Republican anti-slavery candidate, winning the presidency, and the Southern slave states' secession to form the Confederate States.

Did Lincoln set out to end slavery? No. But the pressure mounted by the abolitionists combined with understanding the value of Black soldiers in the Union Army facilitated the end of slavery with the Emancipation Proclamation in 1863.

In the 1960s, King led the nonviolent attack on America, brilliantly, relentlessly, and bravely speaking out on injustices and leading boycotts in the South that rallied Black people—and, at times, crushed the white economy. His movement was national news, but the focus was on the South, where vicious racist practices persisted.

There was much opposition to the movement, but King and his band of courageous soldiers were undeterred. King would ultimately pay with his life.

It was with this history in mind that Black Lives Matter moved forward and initiated change in America, doing it their way, which was as a radical, unapologetic movement that spread via local chapters across the country, deftly leveraging social media apparatuses.

However, with its success, as with other movements, came challenges. Local BLM chapters expressed disenchantment, laying out a variety of issues near the end of 2020 over power and money.

Ten chapters issued an open letter that addressed their concerns—and cast uneasiness on the movement's future. The letter, in part, read:

We became chapters of Black Lives Matter as radical Black organizers embracing a collective vision for Black people engaging in the protracted struggle for our lives against police terrorism.

With a willingness to do hard work that would put us at risk, we expected that the central organizational entity, most recently referred to as the Black Lives Matter Global Network (BLMGN) Foundation, would support us chapters in our efforts to build communally. Since the establishment of BLMGN, our chapters have consistently raised concerns about financial transparency, decision-making, and accountability. Despite years of effort, no acceptable internal process of accountability has ever been produced by BLMGN and these recent events have undermined the efforts of chapters seeking to democratize its processes and resources.

In the spirit of transparency, accountability, and responsibility to our community, we believe public accountability has become necessary.

They questioned Patrisse Khan-Cullors's elevation as the sole board member and executive director of BLMGN without most chapters' knowledge, and the formation of BLM Grassroots that effectively separated the majority of chapters from BLMGN without their consent and interrupted the active process of accountability that was being established by those chapters.

The most significant part of their grievances was concern about financial support and receiving more of it.

The discord was not much different from what happened in the 1960s. In the South, King was the clear stalwart, preaching nonviolence and boycotts in the quest for justice and equal rights. Black women were powerful in the movement, including Ella Baker, who was the catalyst for the Student Nonviolent Coordinating Committee, which in many ways is echoed by the Black Lives Matter organization, which initially encouraged input and ideas from the body.

But some grew tired of the nonviolent position King and others took and favored Malcolm X's "by any means necessary" approach, which meant fighting violence with violence, if need be.

In the end, measurable gains were derived from the abolish slavery movement, more steps made through the civil rights movement, and still more via the Black Lives Matter push. The inner tumult was frustrating and disappointing to BLM members, but it did not minimize their thirst for justice. So they continued the fight, one born of desperation and hope.

"BLM and the Movement for Black Lives has really created an ecosystem where people know and feel like they can take action now," Khan-Cullors told *Essence* magazine. "To challenge the system that has oppressed communities for so long. And what we've created is part of American democracy to stand up and fight for what's right.

"It shows the power of our work. The work we've done for seven years inside of Black Lives Matter, but the work we've done for hundreds of years as Black people to keep trying to steer this ship in the right direction—the ship being America.

"While seventy-three million did vote for a white supremacist, a bunch of us did not. And we're going to have to work to heal the pain of racism. But I believe we can."

Its efforts to "defund the police" amounted to police reform, where local agencies regroup, revise, and reimagine how law enforcement should work, specifically when it comes to African Americans. The phrase was so provocative that political pundits believe it cost the Democrats seats in the House of Representatives and Senate; Republicans used scare tactics, with commercials featuring 911 operators not answering emergency calls, to intentionally mislead on what "defund the police" meant.

Still, incremental change was made. There was a push in California to bar district attorneys from accepting money from police unions, which present the impression of favoritism when it came to pressing charges or at trial. Los Angeles mayor Eric Garcetti said he would "seek to identify $100 million to $150 million in cuts from the LAPD," with the surplus directed toward education, health care, and jobs.

In Louisville, Kentucky, the practice of "no-knock" warrants, which led to the tragic shooting death of Breonna Taylor, was abolished. Officers who did not wear required body cams when they shot and killed Black businessman David McAtee were fired. So was the police chief.

In Minneapolis, the ostensible epicenter of the 2020 BLM push, the police department's 2021 budget was cut by $19 million, including $8 million in direct reduction to the police department. The majority of those funds were earmarked for the Office of Crime Prevention, with another $11 million put in a reserve account that would need council approval before use.

Also in Minneapolis, police officers in June 2020 were required to intervene when they witness unauthorized use of force by a fellow officer—which was monumental, because three officers aided and abetted Derek Chauvin as he killed George Floyd, none interceding because they said Chauvin was the veteran officer on the scene. The New York City Council also voted to ban the deadly choke hold that killed Eric Garner in New York in 2014.

In Vermont, North Carolina, and other states, police reform was on the ballot, something not ever considered before Black Lives Matter.

Still, the popularity of Black Lives Matter, after reaching a summit, diminished as the images of George Floyd faded and the coronavirus impact emerged, according to Pew Research, in the summer of 2020.

"For the larger American public, especially and including the white American public, the spectacle and the violence and the horror of George Floyd's death really touched something deep within them and had them think and meditate on and deal with at least this one death, and what it meant," Peters, the professor who focuses on politics and social politics and society, said. "And for a while, this was the most important thing that was happening, when people were thinking about politics and people thinking about what does it mean to be in America and what is America? But I think over time, over the news cycles, the fact that there were new threats to white America's physical security and financial security, that the coronavirus had really come front and center in how we live our everyday lives [impacted BLM's popularity].

"That is not blaming or not saying, 'Oh, if coronavirus never happened we would have this great magical change.' But it's more saying that the types of feelings that people have in the face of such violence and the types of reflection that they have in the face of such violence is in some ways very momentary. And the things that sustain consciousness of these things are political movements, are arguments, are politicians talking about things, are different ways of re-centering and reframing things."

Peters was thinking about Ida B. Wells and the flag that flew outside the NAACP headquarters in New York that read "A MAN WAS LYNCHED YESTERDAY" or "A MAN WAS LYNCHED BY POLICE YESTERDAY," when there was a slaying.

"That was a reminder to anybody who would see it, that this was an ongoing thing," Peters said.

"And the fact that the flag was flying has been to tell us and to keep in people's consciousness the types of violence that was happening in America at that moment and is still happening," Peters continued. "We have to remember that for every statement for the value of Black lives, there are so many different lies, so many different fear-mongering tactics to undermine not only that statement, but everything that would go along with it."

The anti-BLM contingent pounced on the optics of burning or damaged buildings during some protests, attributing the destruction to members of the organization. Never mind that Black Lives Matter's position consistently was peaceful demonstrations that did not include defacing or vandalizing property.

But the ranking of property over Black people, while insulting, has been a consistent part of America's fabric from the outset. That this devaluation of African American life continues, and shows up blatantly in various ways, is troubling.

"In the United States, the value of property is oftentimes [viewed as] much greater than the value of human lives," Peters said. "It's clear that to have a critique of why Black lives have not mattered in the United States is to have a critique of how the United States values money and property over the lives of its citizens.

"Crimes against property, burning something down, is somehow a great no-no," Peters added. "But the mass incarceration and the killing of other people are somehow acceptable. And I think it's likely true that people, that many Americans, saw the Black Lives Matter activists or commentators or people commenting and not condemning the burning of property, many Americans saw this as, 'Oh, my goodness. They don't uphold the same values as us. How can they allow this to happen to these businesses, even though those businesses are insured?'

"So, for me, the rock and a hard place is: You can either condemn people for doing something to an object or you can't. And if you condemn those people, then you're saying property is the most important value, right? That whatever happens to property, we should always pay attention to this, more so than paying attention to what is actually the real cause of this, which is the over-policing and the carceral state and the actual death of people at the hands of the police. Those are really profoundly bad faith arguments and arguments that are meant to inculcate fear in people so that they vote and so that they support this larger structure that is killing Black people, incarcerating Black people and people of color at alarming and very visible rates."

THE BLACK CARNAGE OF THE CORONAVIRUS

BY CURTIS BUNN

COVID-19: A SURVIVOR'S STORY

In early March 2020, before coronavirus-induced stay-at-home orders and other safety measures went into effect, Val Guilford traveled from his home in Connecticut to New York to see the Broadway play *To Kill a Mockingbird*.

While waiting for the performance to begin, a woman sitting a row behind him coughed. Guilford, a divorcé who was vice president of the Stamford, Connecticut, Urban League, was aware that COVID-19 had become a worldwide concern and grew uneasy.

"It wasn't a normal cough. It was one after another and it sounded different. A dry cough. It was constant. And I was not comfortable."

He left his seat to meet his friend, who had picked up the ticket he had left for her at Will Call. But the coughing bothered him.

"I'm thinking, 'Damn, she's coughing right behind me with COVID-19 out here.' I'm also, I'm thinking, 'I won't be able to hear the play if she's coughing like that the whole night.'"

When the play started, Guilford said he did not hear more

coughing, either because he was so enthralled in the show or because the woman had stopped.

A few days later, on Friday evening, he ordered pizza from a popular restaurant in Stamford, near his home. When he arrived, a crowd of people had gathered. Again, he grew uneasy.

He had to negotiate a narrow passageway full of people to pick up his order. "It didn't look like a good situation. But I was hungry. So..."

Guilford picked up the food but looked at the stack of pizza boxes that were laid out and wondered how long they had been exposed to whoever came by.

A week later, "I got this cough."

Must be allergies, he thought.

The coughing lasted a week, though, and by the following weekend, Guilford began to feel lethargic.

"My energy was way down."

But his temperature was way up—to 102 degrees.

Panic began to set in. He set up a virtual appointment with his doctor. "I told her I had a cough, trouble breathing and a fever."

Almost immediately, she diagnosed him with the coronavirus.

Oh, shit.

Not sure what to do, he contacted his daughter-in-law, who was a respiratory specialist, who told him, "Whatever you do, do not go to the hospital."

By then COVID-19 had emerged with a furor, and hospitals were overrun with sick people. "Your immune system has been compromised, so the last thing you need is to be in a hospital around so many sick people," she said.

Guilford, who was on blood pressure medicine, followed her advice and holed up at home. His daughter-in-law provided him an inhaler and an incentive spirometer, a device that measures lung functionality and teaches how to take slow, deep breaths; it is usually used when a patient has pneumonia.

His doctor prescribed "a bunch" of medicine for his cough and Tylenol to reduce the fever. None of it mattered much. The coronavirus had taken over.

"I started getting headaches, but to the tenth power. I got flu symptoms. When I did take a shower, I was in there with the water running on me, exhausted. I literally had to wait and talk to myself: Okay, now reach for the soap.

"I would be in bed at night gasping for air. I became so exhausted I could not pick my head up off the pillow. I was super weak, like something was weighing on me so heavily that it was holding me down. My fever stayed for a week.

"To go to the bathroom was about a fifteen- or twenty-foot walk. It took everything in me to get there. Then, I would have to hold on to the wall for five minutes to catch my breath. And I never could. I couldn't breathe."

That last sentence was a variation of the same phrase that George Floyd would manage to get out about two months later as Minneapolis police officer Derek Chauvin buried his knee into Floyd's neck as he lay on the ground, hands cuffed behind his back, helpless.

America in general and Black America in particular was gasping for air, for life, under the force of a pandemic that zeroed in on the underserved and a tessellation of police brutality against people of color.

As a Black man, Guilford lived with the threat of police overzealousness daily, so much so that it was routine for him to feel anxiety when a cop car pulled up behind him on the street. He knew how to comport himself to mitigate an escalation. Living with COVID-19, however, was the more fearful and deadly threat. There was no playbook on how to survive it.

He barely ate—partly because his appetite diminished and also because he did not have the energy. The virus attacked seemingly all parts of his body to the point of his feeling defenseless against it.

"It was a blessing to have good friends. People used apps on their phones to order me food and have it delivered. I appreciated it big time, but I could hardly eat it. Not that I wasn't hungry. I couldn't chew. It took too much energy."

After another week of struggling to breathe so desperately that he felt like he was in an ocean, without a raft, with weights tied to his ankles, Guilford faced a harsh possibility: that he would die.

"I started getting my affairs in order—when I had the energy. I seriously did not think I was going to make it. The breathing was so constricted that I felt like I was drowning. I couldn't catch my breath to save my life. It was crazy. It was horrible.

"It was so bad and I was so exhausted and the psychology of it all…I said, 'Fuck it. I'm tired.' I started checking on my life insurance and making sure everything was in order. It was that bad. I was ready to check out."

For a former Wall Street executive who had traveled extensively, lived in London, appreciated the arts, loved attending sporting events around the world, laughed heartily, appreciated his family, and had more to embrace…preparing himself to die illuminates the physical and emotional despoliation the coronavirus had inflicted.

But as he lay on his back, at home alone, ready to release himself from the trauma, Guilford thought about his three grandchildren.

They need me. They are worth living for.

And in that moment, Guilford did not so much fight back as he did not give up. His eleven-, eight-, and seven-year-old grandkids inspired him.

Guilford's battle with COVID-19 continued another two weeks before he finally began to feel a breakthrough. He had lost about twelve pounds but he gained some energy—and his breathing was less constricted.

He felt optimistic when he went for a coronavirus test, the swab to the back of the nose. It was positive, and he was devastated.

It was depressing.

Although he felt better, he still slept most of the day. He was psychologically spent, especially after weeks of quarantining. Each day was like the previous day.

Six weeks after his ordeal began, Guilford's COVID-19 test was negative.

With it came relief. He had survived—but he was hardly okay. His legs and back had atrophied, so he had to undergo muscle reactivation therapy—after his legs were taken out of the casts that were placed on them for weeks.

His throat was sore from all the coughing.

But he was alive.

"My doctor told me to consider myself lucky. I didn't feel lucky going through it. But by the death count, I understand it. I was...you know, I was close. It beats you up physically and beats you up psychologically. You start to think about your mortality.

"I'm still not 100 percent. My breathing isn't the same and I get tired quicker than usual. But I'm here.

"This thing, the coronavirus made me think about my life, what's important, who's important. There was a time when my career defined who I was. Now? Fuck that.

"Now, I think about how to be a better friend, a better person. All the Gucci shoes and Zegna suits and material things...they mean nothing. It's an American phenomenon to have a big house and all the fancy stuff. If I die, some people may grab some stuff, the rest will be thrown out or go to Goodwill.

"But I have to leave behind more than that. That's why relationships mean more now than ever. I reach out to my friends who are older to let them know what they mean to me, how important they've been in my life. I'm okay telling another man I love him.

"I was by myself, afraid, and at peace with dying. Through the good and bad, I was at peace. But I found something to keep me going:

my grandkids. After this, I'm going to love on them and watch them grow up.

"And I am going to do things that matter, and be around people who matter. I'm going to double down on life. I'm going to Africa. I always wanted to go and had planned to go in 2020. But COVID-19 shut that down and almost took me out.

"I don't know if my health will be compromised the rest of my life. I am not 100 percent recovered. I am back at work, but it's still there, the effects of it. But I'm alive."

RACISM CAN MAKE YOU SICK

In the parlance of the African American community, "the rona" was a disease that was not as tough as poverty, substandard schools, joblessness, or other forms of discrimination that have plagued their existence.

Their history of battling centuries of oppression made Black people impervious to the coronavirus.

That was the word spread via social media—half jokingly, half seriously—in the early days of the worldwide pandemic. A face had not been put on COVID-19, and the prevailing thought was that white people and other non-Blacks were the primary victims.

That was spectacularly wrong.

Soon, the musings and nicknames stopped when a disheartening and frightening realization emerged: "the rona" attacked African Americans more prolifically and fatally than any other race.

Worse, it was harder on Black people than other ethnic groups because of underlying health issues tied to some of the same elements they had joked prevented them from contracting the deadly disease.

The disparity of the outbreak became more evident with the release of data each week. By the time the coronavirus reached a peak in May 2020, the devastation on the Black community was palpable.

"When white America catches a cold, Black America catches pneumonia," Steven Brown, a researcher at the think tank Urban Institute, said.

The numbers were telling.

Even though Black people make up around 13 percent of the American population, they were infected with COVID-19 and died at rates three times that of whites, according to the Centers for Disease Control and Prevention.

For Black people in the United States, the coronavirus was a crippling juggernaut.

It was as if the pandemic did an MRI on the United States and exposed the drastic systemic inequalities rooted in racism that dated to the first ships carrying enslaved Africans across the Atlantic Ocean. That "original sin" of America created a history of white supremacy, manifested, centuries later, by, among other things, expansive health disparities.

These disparities had always been there. The coronavirus illuminated them.

These inequalities were the results of several facts: food deserts, environmental disadvantages, poor patient care, and the influence of medical myths among them.

Food deserts provide limited availability of fresh fruits and vegetables in African American communities, leaving residents no recourse but processed foods or options full of sodium, fat, and unhealthy chemicals. Those unhealthy alternatives promote high blood pressure, obesity, and diabetes, among other chronic illnesses.

In some places, such as Flint, Michigan, and Newark, New Jersey, clean water remained an issue. Residents, mostly African American, in Flint were saddled for seven years with contaminated water—it flowed muddy brown out of the faucet in some cases, sparking tears, outrage, empathy, and sympathy—but still no drinkable water. At least a dozen people died, and eighty were sickened.

In a twisted piece of irony, the people of Flint paid some of the highest monthly water bills in America, upward of $200...for water they could not drink. Then, in 2019, when the water was declared lead-free and drinkable by the Michigan Department of Environmental Quality, most Flint residents opted for bottled water from somewhere else. They had been without clean water for so long they did not trust that issue had been fixed.

"The anger, the lack of trust...it's all justified," Michigan state senator Jim Ananich said.

In January 2021, the Michigan governor, Rick Snyder, who presided over the state while Flint suffered and did not stop the suffering, was indicted (and has pled not guilty), along with eight other state officials, on forty-two criminal charges related to the Flint water fiasco, including willful neglect. The likelihood of guilty verdicts for Snyder and Co. may have been low, but the acknowledgment that they were woefully negligent provided a modicum of satisfaction.

The next month, a federal judge in Michigan gave preliminary approval of a $641 million class action suit against the state for the water travesty. Judge Judith Levy wrote in her ruling: "There may be no amount of money that would fully recognize the harm the residents of Flint have experienced, including their anxiety, fear, distrust, and anger over the events of the last seven years...This litigation—however it concludes—need not be the final chapter of this remarkable story."

Remarkable, but not unfamiliar. In a town called Coal Run, Ohio, an unincorporated community, the government denied public water service from 1956 to 2003. Why? Because most of the town's citizens were Black.

Federal funding built waterlines up to and around the town—but not in it—forcing residents to retrieve water from nearby Zanesville or collect rainwater and store water in containers, risking contamination. In court in 2008, a jury awarded the citizens of Coal Run $11 million for "pain and suffering" because the government violated state and federal civil rights laws by not providing access to public water the same as provided for the white residents in neighboring towns.

Fair housing advocates and organizations around the country insisted that kind of discriminatory practice could return under a Ben Carson–proposed plan that would diminish housing discrimination protections laid out in the 2015 Affirmatively Furthering Fair Housing (AFFH) mandate.

Carson, the head of Housing and Urban Development (HUD) at the time, advocated for producing more affordable housing, while simultaneously eliminating regulations and accountability, thereby allowing the potential for even more segregation and discriminatory practices.

The AFFH mandate was designed to correct discriminatory housing practices and the lasting impacts of government and privately sponsored residential segregation. It provided an effective planning approach to aid program participants in taking meaningful actions to overcome historic patterns of segregation, promote fair housing choices, and foster inclusive communities that were free from discrimination.

"Dr. Martin Luther King Jr. was instrumental in creating the Fair Housing Act. It was a direct gift from Dr. King to the nation," said Lisa Rice, president and CEO of the National Fair Housing Alliance. "You could say he gave his life for this. It was a key part of his dream."

HUD's proposal came as the number of housing discrimination complaints reached a record high in 2019.

Diane Yentel, president and CEO of the National Low Income Housing Coalition, said Carson displayed "willful ignorance of racial policies. Increasing the supply [of public housing] would not result in fair practices or access to [Black and brown] people protected under the FHA. Our nation has expended an incredible amount of resources creating the disparities that plague our communities. What we need are resources, commitment, resolve, and a strong rule to promote fair housing."

Five words that were startling but revealing: "Our nation...creating the disparities."

Trump committed to abolishing the program, saying that Black people moving to the suburbs would decimate home values and increase crime. His and Carson's suggestion of more public housing amounted to a new wave of segregation: Keep disenfranchised Black people in subsidized housing, which are always located in food deserts or environmentally deficient areas, thereby causing two crises in one—housing and health.

A study called On the Path to Health Equity by Enterprise, a nonprofit that focuses on America's affordable housing crisis, said that 80 percent of an individual's health and social and environmental conditions are determined by where they live.

"Everyone deserves to be healthy," Oktawia Wójcik, PhD, senior program officer at the Robert Wood Johnson Foundation, said. "But now that involves much more than health care—it needs to be inter-mingled with other sectors, like community development, to really create healthier, more equitable communities."

"It's another reason I marched with Black Lives Matter," said Trevor Nigel Lawrence, an entrepreneur in Oakland. "The George Floyd horrific tragedy brought light to more than the issue of police brutality. We are now addressing housing and the environment, which is important to me. It addresses the criminal justice system and health and wellness. It's all connected."

The coronavirus in 2020, though, crippled the country. The Trump administration's inept response to COVID-19 intensified the devastation of the disease. The White House COVID-19 Task Force amounted to a vaudeville show of inconsistency and misinformation, which led to confusion about what information to process and what to dismiss. Purportedly established to work in unison, the task force became a sideshow for Trump's dissemination of falsehoods and self-promotion. A cohesive, coordinated national response plan was never devised.

Rather, Trump, focused on the economy, sacrificed lives by contradicting the science, and Republican governors—ostensibly functioning as puppets—walked in lockstep with the president's misguided direction.

All of this played out on cable news shows, with experts and specialists sharing data that reiterated the point: Black people were pounded by COVID-19.

But they often failed to delve into the heart of the matter. Factually, they were correct. But why did COVID-19 drastically strike people of color? To listen to them, the impression could have been extrapolated that the color of one's skin made a person vulnerable to the coronavirus. This gnawed at African American health professionals such as epidemiologist Linda Goler Blount, president of the Black Women's Health Imperative, the nation's only organization focused solely on the well-being of African American women.

"We have a problem with how we talk about data," she said. "People in my profession, the public health arena, and media tend to talk about data in ways that are conflated and gives the listener, reader, viewer, the impression that what they are talking about is because of race, because they're Black.

"COVID-19 was not devastating to Black people because we're Black. There's no biological determinant for getting COVID-19.

"It devastated us because of the lived experiences of people who are Black that puts us in this predicament," Blount said. "And it's the effect of chronic, generational toxic racism and gender discrimination and what that does to our body, to our immune system, that raises our risk for many things, like diabetes, hypertension, cardiovascular disease, and COVID-19."

The wreckage of the coronavirus has been about racism, not race.

From Africans' arrival to the United States, Black people have suffered from health inequities that cause chronic disease—and false narratives about their vulnerabilities. When the 1918 influenza epidemic began, African American communities were already beset by many public health, medical, and social problems, including racist theories of Black biological inferiority, racial barriers in medicine and public health, and poor health status. To address those issues, African Americans established separate hospitals and professional organizations and repudiated racist scientific theories. Black people were forced to set up hospitals because of racism, too. Whites wouldn't care for them.

Influenza actually had a less devastating impact on African American communities by the numbers, but it overwhelmed their limited medical and public health resources, so Black people got sicker and stayed sick longer. The recognition that the rate of influenza in African Americans was not higher than whites did not derail racist theories about the biological inferiority of Black people or overturn conceptualizations of Black people as disease threats to white people. When the epidemic ended, the major problems that African Americans faced remained.

Long before that, Black people endured health crises and myths that caused havoc. Case in point: the 1793 yellow fever epidemic in Philadelphia was the largest in the history of the United States, with more than 4,000 people dying. That summer, powerful citizens such as George Washington, Thomas Jefferson, and other government figures fled.

Benjamin Rush, a Philadelphia civic leader who signed the Declaration of Independence, called on Black people to assist and treat sick white people, claiming, without any evidence, that Black people were immune to the deadly illness. Rush was also a doctor, which lent credibility to his inaccurate positions.

Determined to prove their worth, the African American community worked in various capacities with the sick: as grave diggers, nurses, drivers, etc. Of course, Rush's contention was patently racist and wrong—and 240 Black people died trying to help white people.

Further and insultingly, after the disease subsided, a Philly native named Mathew Carey, who had fled the city, distributed a pamphlet accusing Black people of profiting from the outbreak by pillaging sick people's homes. Richard Allen and Absalom Jones, freed Black men, were outraged and published an eloquent denial of Carey's claims called "A Narrative of the Proceedings of the Black People." In it, they vehemently denied the charges, but mostly made the case of Black people's standing as equal humans capable of good:

The judicious part of mankind will think it unreasonable, that a superior good conduct is looked for from our race by those who stigmatize us as men, whose baseness is incurable, and may therefore be held in a state of servitude, that a merciful man would not doom a beast to; yet you try what you can to prevent our rising from the state of barbarism you represent us to be in, but we can tell you, from a degree of experience, that a Black man, although reduced to the most abject state human nature is capable of, short of real madness, can think, reflect, and feel injuries, although it may not be with the same degree of keen resentment and revenge that you who have been and are our greatest oppressors would manifest if reduced to the pitiable condition of a slave.

Their eloquence resounded. But, of course, by then, the damage had been done.

PSYCHIATRY AND THE PANDEMIC

Dr. Jessica Isom, a young African American psychiatrist who works at the Codman Square Health Center in Boston, calls herself a "Racial Health Equity Champion," "Community Psychiatrist," and an "Unapologetic Advocate for Black Mental Health."

The coronavirus forced her to wear all of her hats, sometimes simultaneously, as the pandemic—with quite a bit of assistance from the Trump administration—turned America into a virtual dystopian society.

Patients seeking psychiatric help suffered from mental illness that caused paranoia, extreme mood swings, excessive fears, confused thinking, an inability to concentrate, withdrawal from friends and family, among many other concerns.

Though many African Americans have traditionally looked at professional treatment with disdain or as a last resort, Isom saw "no shortage of Black patients" in the throes of COVID-19.

For her patients, the pandemic placed them in the center of a parallel universe that Isom had to help them navigate, a task made more complicated by the social-distancing and stay-at-home orders, limiting her to over-the-phone treatment.

"One thing we learned through this for Black people is that if therapy is offered, many of them will come," Isom said. "A lot of them may come hesitantly at first. A lot of them secretly see me because they believe they will not get the reactions from family that they want to get…It was a revealing time."

It also was revealing—and disturbing—to Isom that the coronavirus exposed not only the country's lack of preparation to handle the pandemic, but also the lack of calculation on the "psychological toll and the emotional toll of being a member of a group that's disproportionately getting impacted by and dying from a pandemic. And you can't talk about that unless you're prepared to talk about racism," Isom said.

"How could you have a conversation about grief and loss related to this virus and not talk about racism and how it produced those vulnerabilities in Black people?" she asked. "So, I haven't seen anyone—and I have been around a whole lot of psychologists and therapists—who has talked about being prepared for that collective grief."

Ironically, that lack of preparedness illuminated a larger concern, one different from the racism that caused the underlying conditions that made African Americans more susceptible to COVID-19. In the medical profession, a history of racism exists that baffles, particularly doctors of color, and contributes to the health inequities and unfair treatment that African Americans experience.

"Everyone wants to be anti-racist, but they don't understand how racist many institutions are," Isom said. "In medicine, there are resources that systematically describe racial differences, biological racial differences in the minutia. So, I'm talking Black teeth versus white teeth. Black eyes versus white eyes. Black body parts versus white body parts. Black skin, Black nerves. Black everything.

"This is the history of medicine that was 'scientifically' investigated—and I am using 'scientifically' sarcastically. That's what's been done. That's the history."

To Isom's point, according to the American Association of Medical Colleges, half of young white doctors believe Black people have thicker skin than whites or have less sensitive nerve endings so they can take more pain and that African Americans' blood hardens faster than whites.

A study performed by *Proceedings of the National Academies of Science* found that 40 percent of white medical students in their first two years embrace the preposterous thicker-skin notion. At the same time, the 2016 study indicated Black patients were not administered the appropriate pain medicine because their white doctor believed African Americans were not as sensitive to pain as whites.

"Of course, young white doctors will think that way because they read it in *JAMA—Journal of American Medical Association*, the *American Journal of Psychiatry*," Isom said. "They describe those beliefs. That was science at a time and even though people will explicitly state, 'Of course, Black people's skin is not different,' subconsciously they have already absorbed the racial structure. So, their thoughts are rooted in conscious statements that were written and talked about freely.

"I did a presentation and asked the audience [of doctors], 'Have you absorbed any ideas of racial differences in Black and white people?' and 100 percent said, 'Yes.' There was nothing else for them to say because it's the truth."

These perpetuated false narratives often led to Black patients receiving substandard treatment when they sought medical attention. This damaging ideology played out at the end of 2020 in distressing fashion.

Susan Moore, a Black physician in Indiana who had contracted COVID-19, died five days before Christmas and two weeks after she made public her concerns about treatment via a viral video that stated her unidentified white doctor dismissed her complaints of pain and requests for medication. She recorded and shared the clip on Facebook to expose the long-discussed (with little change) Black professionals' concerns of deleterious treatment from white health care workers.

Moore, an internist, was able to deftly communicate in medical terms with her physician at University Health North at Indiana University what she required based on her knowledge as a doctor. But she said in her video that the doctor told her, "You're not even short of breath."

"Yes, I am," Moore said she told him.

He made this assessment having "not even listen[ed] to my lungs. He didn't touch me in any way."

She said she eventually received a scan of her neck and lungs, which revealed issues: pus in the lungs and disease of the lymph nodes, she said. It was then she began receiving more opioid pain medication, after having been left for hours before a nurse gave her the dose.

The white doctor, meanwhile, raised the notion of sending her home. "This is how Black people get killed, when you send them home and they don't know how to fight for themselves," Moore said.

"He made me feel like I was a drug addict. And he knew I was a doctor."

She contended that she had to virtually make a scene, as much as could be made in her condition, to finally be "adequately treated." She was eventually discharged from IU North, but was admitted to another hospital after just twelve hours. Two weeks after that, she died. The hospital said they would conduct an external investigation into Moore's claims. Indiana University Hospital president and CEO Dennis M. Murphy essentially blamed the victim, describing Dr. Moore in a press release as a "complex patient" and said the nursing staff "may have been intimidated by a knowledgeable patient who was using social media to voice her concerns and critique the care they were delivering."

"I put forth and I maintain if I was white, I wouldn't have to go through that," Moore said in the video.

Isom said she was listening to NPR on her car radio when an addiction psychiatrist was interviewed.

"I was driving so I couldn't Google her," she said. "This doctor was an addiction psychiatrist. The interviewer said to her, 'Help me understand why persons of color are experiencing more addiction issues' or some kind of question like that. And I was waiting for this person to say 'racism.' But she didn't say anything like that. She didn't know how to answer the question—and she was an 'expert.'

"I know addiction psychiatrists who would have answered that question by acknowledging structural racism, disproportionate vulnerability to disease because of racism, and all the other factors that contribute to increased stress, which contributes, or at least drives, substance abuse.

"So sometimes they were asking the questions, but the people they gave the platform to answer the questions weren't prepared to give *real* answers. There's no conversation where you can't say anything about racism...but she managed to do it."

Isom believes—*hopes*—vast awareness is on the horizon.

"The root of that understanding is appreciating that it's not a biological cause," she said. "That simple, simple root is elusive, though. If understood, it could open the door to understanding so many things about Black people's experience. So, it's like an invitation."

BLACK STRESS MATTERS

It is not enough that at most every turn there is an element of life that causes stress for Black people. That stress results in trauma. That trauma leads to health issues.

That unseemly pattern has played out so prominently there is a term for it: racial trauma.

It has been examined at the Institute for the Study and Promotion of Race and Culture at Boston College. Racial trauma describes the psychological and physical indicators Black people endure after being exposed to a racially charged or stressful experience. And those experiences do not have to be a direct hit. The mere notion of racism can infuse stress or trauma in the Black body.

The institute released a report in 2015 that read, in part:

Regardless of a person's previous understanding of racism, many people of color may find themselves struggling to process their reactions to the deaths of Michael Brown, John Crawford III, Eric Garner, Aiyana Stanley-Jones, Yvette Smith, Walter Scott, and Freddie Gray, as well as the lack of indictments of the police officers involved in several of these deaths. Anger, sadness, fear, feelings of helplessness, exhaustion, rage, and the desire to act may emerge at unpredictable times in an unpredictable manner.

Dr. Terrell Holloway, a psychiatrist at Yale University, has studied the impact of stress and racial trauma on the Black population.

"It's fascinating because we think of trauma and stress with soldiers in a combat situation," Holloway said. "But what about the stress of living in the inner city of Chicago or New Haven, for that matter, and worrying about being caught up in some kind of violence going to school that day? Or at school you're worried about being singled out by a teacher that reinforces you might not be as smart as your classmates? You experience these things over your lifetime and due to this physiology response, it leaves you more vulnerable to heart issues and diabetes because it modulates your digestive system through secreting cortisol, which impacts how you release your digestive enzymes.

"It all co-relates with the health disparities we hear about COVID-19. So, you're more prone to infection and you're going to get sicker from it."

If there is something Black people lead America in, it is in getting sick. The Racial Trauma Is Real report said:

When people of color experience racism, it brings to mind both their own previous experiences with racism, as well as their awareness of the longstanding history of racism directed toward similar others in the U.S. Historical race-related events play a significant role in shaping how people of color view racism.

For many people of color, early racial socialization experiences often include listening to their parents' and grandparents' stories of living through different periods of racial tension in the U.S., including the Civil Rights movement, Jim Crow laws, and for some slavery. While the passing down of these stories is an essential part of educating and socializing the younger generation about race and racism, the transmission of racial trauma is often carried across multiple generations as a result. The cumulative emotional effects and psychological wounding that is transmitted across generations is also known as intergenerational trauma, and can result in higher rates of mental health and physical health issues within communities of color as well.

Significantly, despite centuries of evidence, there has not been a concerted movement to address the confirmed conclusions, and the report added:

Many mental health professionals and scholars have called for the recognition of racial trauma as a mental health concern. Too many accounts from student trainees, colleagues, and professionals demonstrate a lack of awareness, knowledge, and the practical skills necessary to competently address racial trauma in mental health settings. This obliviousness exists despite a pervasive body of literature that explicitly states that a clinician's awareness of race and racial factors (e.g., racism, racial discrimination) often determines clients' of color ability to seek, continue, and benefit from mental health interventions.

Dr. Holloway processed that information for Black people like this: "Understanding that the inflammatory system works based on how you perceive the world—and that you perceive the world based on racism—COVID-19 will do damage."

Generally, those most impacted by the coronavirus—and racism—were unaware they were caught up in a four-tiered system of racism that impacts health, Holloway said, and he notes that internal racism is based on experiences.

"The thought that, if I'm going to an event with a predominantly white population, I'm worried about how my hair looks and will I be accepted by this group of people I don't know," Holloway explained. "It's about how you process a situation that impacts you. But the fact that Black people have those kinds of thoughts speaks to the prominence of racism."

Then there is interpersonal racism, he explained, "where you were discriminated one-on-one, say, at a restaurant where I got poor service or no service," Holloway said. "Or being followed around in a store. It's the direct experience of racism that one experiences."

Additionally, Holloway lists institutional racism, those policies or laws that marginalize or put people of color at a disadvantage, such as public housing platforms and prison sentencing guidelines.

Lastly, there is structural racism, which represents systems that maintain the hierarchy of supremacy.

And it gets worse. "Black people experience all four levels of racism, either simultaneously or interchangeably," Holloway explained.

Which means African Americans are saddled with racism virtually every day of their lives, whether they realize it or not. And one's temperament informs how one feels about the daily experiences in his or her life.

One Black person could see being denied a seat at a restaurant because her nine-year-old wore shorts and a T-shirt as a racist incident, especially when there is a white kid around the same age wearing virtually the same thing dining in the venue. That was the case in the summer of 2020 at a Baltimore Harbor restaurant. It was captured on video.

A worker and then the manager told an African American woman that she and her son could not dine in the eatery because the child violated a dress code policy—when twenty-five feet away a white kid dressed virtually the same in T-shirt and shorts ate with his family.

The video went viral, outrage ensued, and the workers eventually were fired. But the damage had been done. The nine-year-old boy had experienced interpersonal racism. "With the Black population, it doesn't matter how old you are, you can have a racist experience that stays with you," Holloway said. "No doubt that kid will remember that the rest of his life, and it will create a certain reaction in him when something similar happens."

It not only will be a factor for the child, but he could pass it on to his children, Holloway said. That process is called epigenetics, which, essentially, is how an individual's DNA changes based on experiences.

"Africans in 'Wakanda' never experienced racism of any kind, so they would have a different epigenetic outcome. Of course, 'Wakanda' isn't a real place," Holloway said. "In real America, various studies that show the Black population's immune system and stress response can be passed on via epigenetics.

"Look, my parents were ten when they got civil rights," he added. "What does that say about *my* vulnerabilities? Their parents were sharecroppers. And their parents were slaves. So, it's not as though it has gotten better over time. It's just different."

Considering these levels of trauma that Black people endure daily, the devastation of the coronavirus was predictable to those who understood the underlying conditions that reside within the race.

"African Americans on average will live six to eight years less than the national average," Holloway said. "They are prone to be diagnosed with psychotic disorders compared to mood symptoms. And a part of that is biased by the people who are evaluating, and another part is from the racism we experience in this country.

"With COVID-19, if you are expressing these vulnerabilities over time, you're more prone to get sicker. Your immune system is already primed to react, and the inflammatory response is so severe in your lungs that you can't breathe and [eventually] die from it."

The damage of the relationship between law enforcement and the Black community extends beyond the officer-involved shootings or brutalizing people of color that sparked the nationwide protests. In some cases, simply coming in contact with police causes stress that impacts health.

Contrast that with this: Myriad videos on social media in 2020—amid the array of shootings of Black men—showed white people's volatile encounters with law enforcement, where they attack officers at worst, and issued profanity-laced tirades at best...with no physical consequences. No stun gun. No choke hold. No shooting. In one case, a white man refused to lie on the ground as commanded at gunpoint, assaulted the white officer, who *ran away* from the person he was attempting to arrest. The man jumped in his car, drove off, whipped a U-turn, and intentionally crashed his vehicle into the police cruiser. He lived to tell about it, without a shot being fired.

With Black people, the idea of asserting themselves verbally, even for questionable traffic stops, is not a possibility. There is no doubt that assaulting an officer would amount to a violent reaction. Understanding this, tension arises in people of color when the lights of a police car flash in the rearview mirror.

"If you're worried about getting pulled over by the cops and getting shot by police—like you see on TV every day—when you interact with authority figures you're going to have a much more significant stress response than someone who doesn't relate to that experience," Holloway said. "Stress is not based on how an event may have actually happened, but on how you *perceive* it to happen. And so, in regards to racism and how people experience it, there are effects of chronic unpredictable stress that the Black population has because we see ourselves or our family members or friends when we see George Floyd or Trayvon Martin and so many others."

As a result, numerous studies, including a 2019 report by the Centers for Disease Control and Prevention in Atlanta, show that though African Americans have gained in education and wealth over the last decade and are living longer, their life expectancy on average is seventy-five years, which is the lowest among all ethnic backgrounds in the United States. It also is six years shorter than whites'.

Doctors are able to measure one's aging through the study of telomeres, which are sections of DNA found at the end of each chromosome. They protect the DNA by allowing replication without damaging chromosomes. When aging occurs, the telomeres shrink. And when they become too short, they cannot serve their purpose, and chromosomes can no longer replicate and reach a "critical length."

At this stage, cells die, and apoptosis, also known as programmed cell death, occurs. Anything with "death" in its title is not a good thing. And as a result of daily racial trauma, Black people's telomeres diminish at a faster rate than those of whites and other races.

"With Black people, the telomere you'd expect to be a certain length at a particular age is often shorter than it should be. And it's completely related to the amount of stress and racism they [experienced]," Holloway said. "There are two types of aging: chronological and cellular. Your cellular age is determined by the length of telomeres. And every time a cell divides, those telomeres shorten. So, you can measure telomeres to extrapolate how much stress someone has experienced over time. In Black people, telomeres tell the story."

The stress level—and health concerns—for Black people during the era of the coronavirus and the social justice demonstrations told a story of compounded stress exacerbated by the consistent inflammatory behavior and rhetoric of President Trump. His questionable response to COVID-19 helped the virus to reach pandemic levels in America. And his inability or unwillingness to attempt to offer a conciliatory voice to calm the racial discord pumped stress into Americans as if through an IV.

He called African nations "shithole countries"; he called Black athletes who took a knee in opposition of police brutality "sons of bitches"; he said there were "very fine people on both sides" of the Charlottesville, Virginia, rally where white supremacist militia members chanted racist threats and ideology; he Tweeted that several Black and brown members of Congress—Representatives Alexandria Ocasio-Cortez (D-NY), Ayanna Pressley (D-MA), Ilhan Omar (D-MN), and Rashida Tlaib (D-MI)—are "from countries whose governments are a complete and total catastrophe" and that they should "go back" to those countries—a common racist trope, among other affronts.

The *Washington Post* reported in 2017 that the U.S. population's stress levels were the highest in the world, eclipsing Iran, a country rife with war. A study by a medical resource website Care Dash on Trump's impact on people's heath six months after the 2016 election revealed that much of the country dealt with many Trump-induced health concerns: anger, resentment, depression, weight gain, insomnia, suicidal thoughts, relationship distress, and anxiety—and that people exhibited "negative behaviors" like drinking alcohol, smoking, making poor food choices, or arguing with loved ones.

There's more. Two Harvard physicians published an article in the *New England Journal of Medicine* that crystallized how it came to be that Black people's stress levels were heightened since Trump's election. Two paragraphs bring home the point:

There has been an increase in racial resentment, animosity, and political polarization in the United States in recent years. The election of President Obama played a key role: research indicates that Obama's election led to increases in the rate of belief among white Americans, especially conservatives, that racism no longer exists. At the same time, in the wake of his election, one third of white Americans indicated that they were "troubled" that a black man was President, the Tea Party movement emerged with anti-minority rhetoric, resentment toward Democrats increased, support among whites for the Democratic Party declined, and white support for addressing racial inequities decreased. Obama's election also led to a marked increase in racial animosity expressed in social media: there was a proliferation of hate web-sites and anti-Obama Facebook pages, with the widespread use of historical racial stereotypes that are no longer seen in main-stream media.

The presidential candidacy of Donald Trump appeared to bring further to the surface preexisting hostile attitudes toward racial and ethnic minorities, immigrants, and Muslims. In a national (nonrepresentative) survey of 2,000 elementary and high school (K–12) teachers, more than half of respondents said that since the 2016 presidential campaign began, many of their students had been "emboldened" to use slurs and name calling and to say bigoted and hostile things about minorities, immigrants, and Muslims. Not surprisingly, 67% of these teach-ers reported that many U.S. students (especially immigrants, children of immigrants, and Muslims) were scared and worried and had expressed concerns or fears about what might happen to their family after the election. Even some native-born black children whose ancestors have been in the United States for centuries expressed concerns about a return to slavery or being sent back to Africa.

For Holloway, the study points out how differently Black people and non-Black people live in America.

"It's another way, a significant way, that stress hurts Black people in ways other races do not have to deal with," Holloway said. "Living in perpetual fear that the man [Trump] is going to Tweet or do some-thing that's going to put you in danger... or during the pandemic, seeing people constantly dying that did not have to die—family and friends... It's stressful. His position on race and divisiveness puts Americans in general and African Americans in particular at risk, on edge. That's stress that others in this country don't have to deal with—on top of the daily levels of racial trauma we experience. And then you throw in that Black people so often—because of structural racism—were the 'essential workers' who had to go to work during a deadly pandemic that attacked them the most, and it's a lot. It's all interconnected."

Joseph B. Hill, the principal of JBrady5 Consulting, a diversity and inclusion consulting firm in Atlanta, said he noticed a change in his health during Trump's term. "I can honestly say that there came a point where just hearing his name created tension and anxiety in my body," he said. "I had to stop watching the news because at times I literally felt sick to my stomach. My heart rate increased. That's stress.

"His rhetoric incited his base—and created so much stress for our communities—to the point that you could not feel safe as a Black man or woman in America, even more so than we already felt. That's extra stress. So, we have stress just from walking out of our front door into a world that puts and keeps us at a disadvantage. Stress. We go to work and deal with issues on the job that are too often race-related. Stress. You want to buy a house, but are charged higher interest rates. Stress. Our schools are troubled so we worry about how our kids are going to flourish. Stress. And on and on.

"But then you have him, the president of the United States, seemingly every day doing or saying something that either rouses up his base or insults African Americans—in both cases, it is stressful and unhealthy for us."

THE SHAME OF INFANT MORTALITY

Seven years ago, Dr. Rachel Hardeman wrote an article in the *New England Journal of Medicine*, "Structural Racism and Supporting Black Lives—The Role of Health Professionals," that called America's racism "a public health crisis" and used the phrase "white supremacy" in explaining her position. It was the first time those expressions were printed in the most prestigious medical publication in the world.

For her daring, Hardeman—a reproductive health equity researcher and tenured associate professor at the University of Minnesota in the Division of Health Policy and Management—received emails that questioned and challenged her argument, all from white doctors who failed or were unwilling to see beyond their internal biases. Her peers placated her.

She said: "Some said, 'Oh, that's nice. The Black girl studying racism.' There was a lot of disinterest and blank stares. 'I don't get it.' So, certainly there was some backlash: 'This is not a medical issue. This is not a health care issue. This is not a public health issue. Why is the top medical journal in the world publishing this sort of thing?' It was all so predictable."

But Hardeman continued to publish as she established herself as a foremost scholar on race, gender, and health. She studied and researched reproductive health, an area that illuminates the disheartening infant and maternal mortality rates that are higher among Black babies and Black mothers.

"There was not a single moment that drove me to my emphasis," Hardeman said. "I've been building toward this my whole life. I've always been interested in public life based on watching my parents and grandmother in particular struggle with a health care system that very clearly was not serving her in a way that it should have. As a result, she had a premature death.

"I actually had a good birthing experience. What it made me realize is that it is possible for a Black woman. We see all the horror stories and know the statistics around infant mortality and maternal mortality for Black women. I am an example of what can be done the right way. So I have been focusing on how we can transform the structures to make that a common reality for everyone else."

But the struggle was real, as they say. Elements of being a woman that whites did not consider dogged her.

"I could not find a Black OB-GYN," she said. There was a sense of sadness in her having to articulate that dilemma.

"I searched for a Black doula and eventually found one," Hardeman said. "That's one piece of the issue. Not enough Black doctors—and it's particularly hard in places like Minnesota [where the Black population is low]."

Just as in education, where Black students in public schools thrive better when taught by Black teachers, it stands to reason that Black mothers-to-be would fare better under the care of Black physicians.

"Some of the research has looked at the power of a racially concorded relationship," Hardeman said. "And what we need, not surprisingly, is that when you have a provider who shares your lived experiences, you get better care and are more satisfied with that care and are more likely to comply with the plans that have been laid out for you."

With such a small percentage of Black doctors in America, that critical concorded relationship for Black mothers is unlikely—and it contributes to the increase in deaths at birth.

"It's important to note that the United States is the only industrialized, well-resourced country that has a rising maternal mortality rate," Hardeman said. "And it's driving up because Black women are three to five times more likely to experience maternal mortality in comparison to their white counterparts."

Why is this so? Black doctors break it down this way: There has been and continues to be a lack of access to competent primary care that would prevent the chronic conditions that cause maternal deaths. Those conditions include high blood pressure, diabetes, and obesity, among others, that increase the danger of pregnancy for Black women.

An effective primary care program could manage or mitigate those issues. But the so-called most advanced nation in the world has a health care system that does not provide equal care for *all* women. Experts consider this failing one of the primary distinctions between America and other advanced nations that have commitments to improve the maternal mortality concerns with a universal health care system that evenly manages patients, despite race or economic standing.

According to myriad studies, women in the United States without insurance are four times more likely to die of a pregnancy-related complication compared to their insured counterparts. Worse, the country seems to be moving further away from universal health care, which was a premise of the Affordable Care Act, the insurance plan available for all Americans enacted by former president Barack Obama that had been under attack by the Trump administration for four years.

"Infant mortality data dates back to slavery," Hardeman said. "Overall, across centuries, America's infant mortality rate isn't great when compared to other industrialized nations, but it has improved. What stayed the same is that Black and Native Americans are twice as likely to experience infant mortality than whites.

"It's one of those markers of community health. Frankly, if we can't keep our most vulnerable healthy, then we have big issues. The two populations of people most historically marginalized and disenfranchised in our history are at the greatest risk for infant mortality. Very disconcerting."

The work drives Hardeman, though, as she anchors her work in history, hoping that context will resonate and influence treatment…eventually.

"Structural racism is a fundamental cause of the inequities we are facing in reproductive health," she said. "Part of my work is to help people connect the dots to the historical reality of how racism has manifested and persists in our society and how it drives what we've known about racial disparities today.

"All those racist narratives were created to perpetuate slavery and they have become so deeply engrained in how people are taught to practice medicine. And it's killing us—babies and mothers, too."

The lack of commitment has created another health issue in mothers that serve as a precursor to infant mortality. Deeper, the cause and effect of policing in communities of color have taken a physical toll on citizens, including Black babies.

"Preterm birth, before thirty-seven weeks, leads to Black babies dying. Black women are more likely to give birth before thirty-seven weeks, and that has a whole series of health implications for the child," Hardeman explained.

Those implications include a little-known fact: Pregnant Black women who have interactions with law enforcement can face threatening health challenges.

"Police contact on preterm birth—looking at what it means to live in a community that is disproportionately exposed to police—is significant," Hardeman said. She used her hometown as an example.

"Minneapolis has some incredibly segregated neighborhoods, so Black women are most likely to live in Black neighborhoods, and those neighborhoods are more likely to have police presence, patrolling the neighborhood for various reasons," she explained. "And we see that there is a greater likelihood of preterm birth among women living in those neighborhoods because of the stress involved with those encounters."

As a Minneapolis native, Hardeman's proximity to the Black deaths at law enforcement hands of Jamar Clark in 2015 and Philando Castile a year later inspired her to be vocal about racism in medicine. It was then that she wrote her memorable piece in the *New England Journal of Medicine.*

The article focused not only on the tragic shooting deaths of Black men by law enforcement, but also the health impacts of police presence in communities of color—something hardly anyone considered.

She wrote:

The term "racism" is rarely used in medical literature. Most physicians are not explicitly racist and are committed to treating all patients equally. However, they operate in an inherently racist system. Structural racism is insidious, and a large and growing body of literature documents disparate outcomes for different races despite the best efforts of individual health care professionals. If we aim to curtail systemic violence and premature death, clinicians and researchers will have to take an active role in addressing the root cause.

Structural racism, the systems-level factors related to, yet distinct from, interpersonal racism, leads to increased rates of premature death and reduced levels of overall health and well-being. Like other epidemics, structural racism is causing widespread suffering, not only for Black people and other communities of color but for our society as a whole. It is a threat to the physical, emotional, and social well-being of every person in a society that allocates privilege on the basis of race. We believe that as clinicians and researchers, we wield power, privilege, and responsibility for dismantling structural racism.

Hardeman's article created a buzz—it was discussed, argued, supported, refuted in countless circles—but there was not substantial action in response to it. And therein lies the problem.

"The public health system has not sat down and reckoned with the history of racism in this country and how we do things today," she said. "And until we do that, we're not going to change anything. We'll just retrofit or shove 'health equity' into the back of something that was not meant to achieve equity in the first place."

When George Floyd was killed in Minneapolis, Hardeman was simultaneously incensed and pained. She was also inspired to co-write for the *New England Journal of Medicine* an article, "Stolen Breaths."

In it, she wrote:

The truth is Black people cannot breathe because we are currently battling at least two public health emergencies, and that is a conservative estimate. One of every 1,850 Black Americans has lost his life in this global fight against a novel virus that could have harmed anyone. And yet—because of racism and the ways humans use it to hoard resources and power for some, while depriving others—it has killed an enormous number of Black people.

Please—I can't breathe.

And Black people are three times as likely to be killed by police as white people. Both these realities are acutely threatening Black lives right now. But prevailing gaps in maternal and infant mortality have long threatened our survival beginning before we are even born.

Disturbingly, Hardeman is among a legion of health experts who consider the racial health inequities a result not of a broken system, but rather of a system functioning as it was intended. Altaf Saadi, a Muslim-American physician at Harvard Medical School, sees the inequities and yearns for change. And she believes it should start with doctors.

"We, as physicians and society more generally, must realize that the struggles of one marginalized community are struggles of all of us," she said. "My fight as a Muslim-American doctor to serve my patients without fear of racism, and the fight of an African American patient to be treated with dignity and respect, should also be your fights."

Hardeman advocates for a revamped health care system developed by the people it will help the most.

"In order to fix it, we need a new system, and they need to be fixed by the people who are closest to the pain," she said. "That means we have to desegregate the health care work force. And it's not just about having more Black physicians, but also thinking about health care systems as the economic drivers of many communities, and there are many opportunities there to employ people and insure they have a livable wage and access to health care that can support the local tax base and counteract gentrification and other social issues."

Part of that revamping has to be about upgrading the training of young doctors to include education on racism, how it rears its head in the medical profession, why it is pervasive, and how to deal with it.

"We need to make understanding and mastering the health effects of structural racism a professional medical competency," Hardeman said. "Med students and rising physicians are training without understanding any of this. Just like you wouldn't allow a student to graduate from medical school without knowing all of the nerves in the body, understanding the impact of structural racism has to be a part of the core competency of medical education.

"Health systems have to mandate and measure equitable outcomes. Hospitals are required to fulfill all sorts of quality indicators to get accredited to serve patients. Part of that has to be quality indicators that are tied to equity.

"Hospitals are there to protect and serve, and sometimes they have to show up for patients and be part of a community that feels safe and trustworthy."

Hardeman's optimism on her ideas becoming reality change often, she said, depending on the news of that day, her mood, or what she sees or hears. The impact of the BLM movement has caught people's notice, making it perhaps the prime time to at least begin the process of implementing new criteria to reverse some of the long-standing concerns around racism in health care.

"There is power in that people are listening in 2020 and, hopefully, willing to learn and put resources behind this work," she said. "Some of that, though, requires that people decide to see the humanity in someone who does not look like them or have a shared lived experience.

"It's funny because the people who would shrug their shoulders [seven] years ago, when I said racism was a public health crisis, are now shouting it from the rooftop that we have to do something. That's cool. But how many jumped on anti-racism because they read a fantastic book and all this other scholarship, and work that has been done is out there and it is the 'it' thing to talk about? But will you be there next year involved in the same discussions?"

Those who embrace the "false beliefs about race" make them more likely to possess biases—unconsciously or otherwise, Hardeman contends. And that makes much of this issue about the dignity one person sees in another.

"I don't think anyone should have to beg for their humanity or to be seen," she said. "So I'm cynical today. I'm not hopeful today."

But in her heart, in her core, and in her desire for effective change, hope abounds.

"Other days, I think there are a lot of people across the country doing incredible work and that change is coming slowly, incrementally. We're looking at new leaders and a whole population of young people who are asking for change and not taking 'no' for an answer. But it also should not just be *their* job. It has to happen on the policy level, too: Having racism listed as a public health crisis, making sure measuring racism is showing up in policy-making. It's what we do with it in the next year that will determine where we go."

The core of Hardeman's work comes down to having racism established as a public health crisis. That acknowledgment would engineer action, she believes.

"Racism is making us sick. It saps the energy and the resources; we all lose when one race is in play. So, from a policy perspective, it's important to name it," she said.

"Most people were afraid to say it. You can't change hearts and minds; that takes a long time. But by putting some sort of policy that creates language that says 'this is what we are striving for'...we have a chance."

Hardeman is the mother of eight-year-old Leila, which drives her passion.

"Everything I do is 100 percent all for her," she said, "because she deserves better. I'm determined to leave things a little better for her."

THE NEED FOR HBCUs AND BLACK DOCTORS

Four historically Black medical schools have long wanted to be involved—*more* involved—in the efforts to minimize the health disparities that have plagued Black communities. The coronavirus outbreak was the event that pushed them to the forefront.

Black doctors make up about 5 percent of the physicians in America, meaning there have not been enough doctors of color to treat the Black population, which is all the more problematic when studies show the Black doctor–patient relationship produces better health outcomes.

With the pandemic, many health care entities like the National Institutes of Health and the American Medical Association understood the value of having Black doctors on board in the race to create an antiviral drug and vaccine, to go into communities of color where they would stimulate trust and construct pathways to develop more Black doctors—and solicited their assistance or partnered with them.

The Expanding Medical Education Act of 2020 was proposed on Capitol Hill to commit $1 billion to bridge multiple gaps in the health care system through a grant from the Health Resources and Services Administration. The funds would be split among Meharry Medical College, Morehouse School of Medicine, Howard University

College of Medicine, and Charles R. Drew University of Medicine and Science.

The bill, presented by Virginia senator Tim Kaine, was drafted as a vehicle to "tackle the lack of representation of rural students, underserved students, and students of color in the physician pipeline," it said, with the ultimate goal of increasing the Black doctor talent pool. Schools would use the money to make medical school less arduous and more affordable. The rationale: The more Black doctors there are, the more willing they will be to serve underserved communities and help break the established mistrust of medical institutions.

The mere idea of the legislation excited African Americans in medicine, like Donald Alcendor, a microbiologist and associate professor and scientist at Meharry, who said: "There simply are not enough doctors who look like the patients in the underserved communities. And this systemic distrust, the disparity communities have for the medical system, is something that is long-standing and has at least a chance of being overcome with Black doctors' presence to create a better patient–doctor relationship. So, if this bill would create more Black doctors, then great."

As exciting as the prospects were for what that bill would do, it had to make it through the new Congress that took office in 2021. A Democratic-advantaged Senate would support the bill, which was one of many reasons the Georgia runoff Senate victories of Democrats Raphael Warnock and Jon Ossoff in January 2021 were so vital.

Meanwhile, Morehouse School of Medicine received a $40 million grant from the Department of Health and Human Services specifically to do work in communities of color around the coronavirus pandemic. It is support that was a long time coming.

Dr. John Maupin, who has the distinction of having served as president of Morehouse School of Medicine and of Meharry Medical College, and who is considered a deity in the medical profession among African Americans, embraced the support, however late.

"This is a huge moment," Maupin said. "But bigger than that, it's a huge moment for health care in our communities during a crucial time in our history with this pandemic."

The program, the National COVID-19 Resiliency Network (NCRN), serves as a ground attack on the coronavirus in the Black, Native American, and Latino communities, with Morehouse School of Medicine personnel teaming with local organizations to make inroads in treatment, care, and other aspects of public health.

"A lot of this comes down to trust," said Dr. Dominic Mack, professor and director of the National Center for Primary Care at Morehouse School of Medicine. "We have been at the forefront in underserved communities during crisis before, like Hurricane Katrina. It's our base. So, having a trusted source to treat and educate on testing and vaccinations, etc., can help overcome some of the distrust Blacks have with medical institutions.

"We know the history, and we know the lack of trust is real. But we will partner at the community level to assure we are reaching and helping the people we need to help."

Maupin considered the grant a tipped hat.

"It speaks loudly to the value of HBCU medical centers and the value of having individuals of science and institutions that come from trusted places," he said. "We have to have greater engagement of the minority communities in various kinds of scientific studies that give us new knowledge on how to manage and handle things.

"The efficacy of the scientific work is dependent on the people involved so you understand how things impact those in one community versus those in another community, those with one background versus those with another background.

"So, this enables a group of profound scientists and dedicated individuals who have always believed in serving the underserved to do important work where it is needed. So, this speaks highly of the work being done by Dr. Valerie Montgomery Rice [president, Morehouse

School of Medicine] and her team. And it speaks loudly about what we really need to happen when we think about the future of health care in America."

Dr. Mack simplified it. "This gives HBCUs a moment of confidence," he said.

That confidence was increased when former presidential candidate Michael Bloomberg's organization, Bloomberg Philanthropies, committed $100 million to the four HBCU medical colleges, with Meharry receiving $35 million.

"Graduates of Meharry overwhelmingly choose to go into primary care so that they can make the largest impact on their communities," Dr. James Hildreth, president of Meharry, said. "But primary care, particularly in rural areas, does not provide the same level of financial security as other medical specialties. This transformative gift will significantly ease the burden of debt for our students, allowing them to make decisions about where and how they practice based on their passion, not a paycheck."

For Dr. Pierre Vigilance, adjunct professor of health policy and management at George Washington University School of Public Health and founder and principal at HealthUp Strategic Advisors, the pathway forward is clear. Well, maybe.

"The assertion often made that these Black doctors will go back to the community they serve also makes the assumption that they come from low-income communities," he said. "That's true for some, but not all. Sometimes the money to work in specialized training away from these areas is influential in where a Black doctor may work.

"In the end, though, there are two imperatives: to make opportunities for more doctors of color and to build teams that are diverse because teams that are diverse create better solutions to challenges or problems. If you diversify that health care provider group or health system, and if you're truly about this notion of population health and community wellness…you have no choice but to diversify the provider pool."

And for good reason. "Teams that are diverse create better results," Vigilance added. "If you have only one type of demographic in physicians, you will get a certain set of outcomes. But if you have a diverse team that is willing to go into distressed areas, you can address some of these concerns, you can break barriers, and you can improve outcomes."

According to a National Bureau of Economic Research study, the trust that comes with a Black doctor–patient relationship would exponentially increase preventive screenings of Black men. The researchers calculated that a workforce with more Black doctors could help reduce cardiovascular mortality by 16 deaths per 100,000 per year—resulting in a 19 percent reduction in the Black-white male gap in cardiovascular mortality and an 8 percent decline in the Black-white male life expectancy gap.

Additionally, participants in the study assigned to Black doctors were more likely to have their blood pressure and BMI measured than those who saw non-Black doctors. And for invasive tests, *only* men who saw a Black doctor agreed to utilize more services than they had initially selected. A participant who saw a Black doctor was 20 percentage points (47 percent) more likely to agree to a diabetes screening and 26 percentage points (72 percent) more likely to accept a cholesterol screening than those who saw a non-Black doctor.

Blacks in the medical field find it frustrating to have to break down this information.

Holloway, the psychiatrist, insisted it is necessary, though.

"This is about structural racism and bias and having more inclusion," he said. "At Mount Sinai, for example, every time we needed a pathology [the study of cause and effect of disease or injury], it was on a Black body. But every time we needed to humanize someone, it was a white body from the Upper East Side.

102

"So [white doctors] have this racialized sense that people from rich families who abuse, say, cocaine are given a pass, but it is a completely different mindset when the person who comes in from East Harlem was smoking crack cocaine. That's a divergence point on the quality of the care you get. So, you have to train doctors in culturally competent care. You have to allow for people who tend to be unemployed compared to the national average to get health care insurance to address those issues. And you need more Black doctors who have built-in sensitivity that eliminates these issues."

THE ERADICATION OF PUBLIC TRUST

Dawn Baker, a television anchor in Savannah, Georgia, who graduated from Howard University, was the first person in the United States to volunteer to participate in human vaccine trials for the coronavirus. The *first*.

Many hailed her as courageous. But Black people swiftly and unrelentingly unleashed a barrage of insults and admonishments that left Baker disappointed.

"I was called all kinds of names, and some were downright nasty. It's one thing to be upset, another to be nasty," she said. "I was told I wasn't 'woke.' It got to where I couldn't read the comments anymore. I couldn't live and die with them. The hurtful part was that the negative comments, the vast majority of them, came from my people."

Then she showed her dismay by saying: "I am a Black life."

Baker found the contempt ironic because Black lives mattered to her, and that was the reason she stepped up.

"As a news anchor, I reported every day on the coronavirus and how it devastated Black families," she explained. "It was so sad, heartbreaking. So, when I learned there was a need for people to participate in the trials, *our* people, I thought it was the right thing to do."

Also, her family doctor of thirty years was the chief investigator for Moderna, the pharmaceutical company that ran the trials, she said. "He assured me it was safe," she said. "I knew that some people would have a problem with me joining the trials and would not understand. But I just wanted to help.

"A lot of thought went into the decision. And I certainly did not discount the horrible things done to us in the past. But you can't live in the past like that to make for a better tomorrow."

The past medical malfeasance against Black people is extensive and documented—and the reason why Black people overwhelmingly rejected any notion of trusting medical experiments.

The most widely known is the Tuskegee Study of Untreated Syphilis in the Negro Male. Infected black men were solicited to be a part of a forty-year study (1932 to 1972) to treat the disease with penicillin and were offered free medical exams, free meals, and burial insurance.

But they were not given the drug, and twenty-eight of the original 399 black men died of syphilis, one hundred died of related complications, forty of their wives were infected, and nineteen of their children were born with congenital syphilis. That atrocity is the most-cited reason by Black people to pass on medical experiments.

There was also J. Marion Sims, the malevolent physician who was misguidedly considered the "Father of Modern Gynecology" for his advances in that field. The problem was, he practiced medicine at a time when treating women's reproductive organs was considered repugnant and rarely done.

He invented the vaginal speculum, a tool used for dilation and examination. He also pioneered a surgical technique to repair vesico-vaginal fistula, a complication of childbirth that was common in the nineteenth century, in which a tear between the uterus and bladder causes constant pain and urine leakage. He performed the experiments that led to these discoveries on enslaved Black women, and *without* any anesthesia.

Working in rural Jamaica, John Quier, a British doctor, freely experimented with smallpox inoculation in a population of 850 enslaved people during the 1768 epidemic. Inoculation, a precursor to a vaccine, involved inducing a light case of the disease in a healthy person in hope of immunizing that person for life.

He used the vulnerable enslaved people to explore questions that doctors in Europe dared not. He wanted to know, for example, whether one could safely inoculate menstruating or pregnant women. Additionally, he wanted to know if it was safe to inoculate newborn infants or a person already suffering from dropsy, yaws, or fever and the like.

Quier was employed by slave owners and would inoculate for smallpox with or without the enslaved person's permission for his scientific experiments. Importantly, slave owners had the final word. There was no issue of slave consent or, for that matter, often physician consent. Yet Quier did some inoculations repeatedly on the same person and at his own expense. He took risks beyond what was reasonable to treat the individual patient. Throughout his experiments, when pressed, Quier followed the science and not necessarily what was best for the human being standing in front of him.

Recently readers and viewers have been introduced to Henrietta Lacks, an African American woman who was betrayed by scientific history, leading to her story being memorialized into a best-selling book and adapted into a film starring Oprah Winfrey. Her cancer cells are the source of the HeLa cell line, the first immortalized human cell line and one of the most important cell lines in medical research. An immortalized cell line reproduces indefinitely under specific conditions, and the HeLa cell line continues to be a source of invaluable medical data.

Problems remain because Lacks was the unwitting source of these cells from a tumor biopsied during treatment for cervical cancer at Johns Hopkins Hospital in Baltimore in 1951. George Otto Gey cultured the cells, creating the HeLa cell line. No consent was given by Lacks to culture her cells. Additionally, neither she nor her family were compensated for the extraction or use of the cells.

Harriet A. Washington, a science writer, editor, and ethicist who authored the eye-opening 2007 book *Medical Apartheid*, said: "But why have the things that I've written about, which were not difficult to find, received so little attention?"

About two hundred miles north of Savannah, near Atlanta, Ashley Nealy was unfamiliar with Dawn Baker's story, but she was aware of some of the past crimes against Black bodies. Still, the thirty-two-year-old Black woman decided to participate in the COVID-19 trials, unaware of the reaction she would receive from the Black community.

"The moment for me was when I heard Dr. Fauci [of the National Institutes of Health] say at a congressional hearing that a vaccine cannot be produced without African Americans," Nealy said. "That sat with me. I immediately signed up when he mentioned the COVID Prevention Network website. I wasn't nervous at all originally. I just felt like it was my duty to make sure we were represented. I was so excited that I posted about it on Facebook that day that I signed up. It only received two 'likes.'

"One of those 'likes' was from a nurse, which was proof that none of my network, who primarily looked like me, was interested in this at all."

News outlets learned of Nealy's commitment and tracked her down, knowing that locating a Black person willing to participate in the trials was a rare find. She was excited to provide details of her journey, hoping it would influence other African Americans to join her—or at minimum change people's ideas about the importance of the development of a vaccine that would be effective with the Black population.

"After sharing my story with a local news station in Atlanta, I felt really good. Someone found me on Instagram and messaged me, thanking me for my participation because he lost an aunt to COVID," she said. "I went to bed that night on an emotional high and woke up with that same feeling because I felt like my story was making a difference."

That euphoria was fleeting.

The news station posted the interview with Nealy on its Facebook page.

"Perhaps it was naïve of me to think so, but I was not prepared for the backlash that I received," she said. "I read the first set of comments, which included a meme saying, 'DUMB YOU ARE,' that I was 'a puppet,' and that I 'don't speak for this divine race.'

"My heart just sank. I didn't want to read any more, and I told my friend that they were 'dragging me' in the comments. She went in and started defending me and encouraged other people to do the same. Someone also said, 'She must not know about the Tuskegee (Experiment).' It really hurt and felt like I was committing myself to a cause no one believed in. I did have a good share of positive comments that helped, such as calling me a hero, but out of the six hundred comments or so, most of them were negative and discouraging."

The response to Baker's and Nealy's altruism reflects the erosion of public trust in the medical community and in America at large from Black people. It is not steeped in paranoia. It is illuminated by history, in every walk of life.

From the outset of life in the United States to the modern, technological age of 2020—Black life has been mired in actions and events that have destroyed trust in the institutions that are, they have come to believe, designed to oppress, damage, and destroy them.

"It's not paranoia," Rodney Coates, the sociologist, said. "When African Americans came out of slavery, they immediately began to build businesses, expand their communities, and began to assert not only their freedom, but their willingness to join in the quest for the American dream. Thriving communities were the result in places such as Atlanta, Greenwood [in Tulsa, Oklahoma], Chicago, Rosewood, Washington, D.C., Knoxville, Tennessee, New York City, and my hometown in East St. Louis.

"Then in less than a twenty-year period (from 1906 to 1926) all were destroyed by angry, frustrated, and jealous whites. During the same time, lynching and differential access to finance devastated both the Black farm and the urban landowners. Racist social, political, and governmental policies ensured that no significant Black community would come into being for the next thirty years. Separate but equal, red-lining, disparate economic prospects, the war on crime/drugs, and the creation of the cradle-to-prison pipeline has assured that this process continued long into the future."

Nealy chalked up the vitriol she received to ignorance. "I realized they were all just due to a lack of understanding about the clinical trial process and what has been ingrained in our community with the mistrust in medicine. I definitely understood where they were coming from, but it didn't make the comments sting any less."

She and Baker had similar responses to their first injection to initiate the trial.

"A light cold, nausea, fever, mild body aches, headaches through the night," Baker recalled. "At first, I was like, 'Get this poison out of my arm. What have I done?' But I knew what I went through was nothing compared to what it could mean in helping so many African Americans. That was my sole focal point."

They are among a relatively small percentage of Blacks across the country who would participate in the two-year study, taking injections, undergoing examinations, charting their health.

"It's all been very overwhelming," Baker said. "Overwhelming with the criticism; I never expected the harsh backlash. Overwhelming with the praise; my mom made me cry one day when she told me how proud she was of me and my compassion. Overwhelmed with all the pain and death the coronavirus caused. And overwhelmed with the responsibility we all needed to take in order to get past COVID-19.

"The lack of trust in medical trials is rooted in real issues. I know that. I knew that when I joined the trial. After I took the vaccine, it hurt my heart more that we are not further along when I continued to see the numbers of death and sickness rise, especially among Black people. But despite the trust that so many people don't have in the system, I had to do something."

While her commitment was admirable, Black people received with far less enthusiasm than the rest of the country the news that two coronavirus vaccines were approved by the Food and Drug Administration, even as the pandemic raged at the start of 2021.

But there was hope on the other side—antiviral drugs that would help cure those who contracted COVID-19. That medicine would come from coronavirus patients who possess "super" antibodies in their blood that can be used or processed to create medicine that wards off the disease. Antibodies are the Y-shaped protein used by the immune system to identify and neutralize foreign objects such as pathogenic bacteria and viruses.

John Hollis, a Black former sports journalist, was among the fewer than 5 percent of COVID-19 patients in the U.S. who possessed the so-called "super" antibodies that has "propelled new science," said Dr. Lance Liotta, a George Mason University pathologist who led the school's antibody study.

Hollis's case of "super" antibodies was unique. While others with the coveted blood found that it lost its strength after sixty to ninety days, his maintained 90 percent of its effectiveness ten months after he contracted the coronavirus.

He was overwhelmed to learn that his blood would be a part of science to help stem the worst pandemic in America in more than a hundred years. "To say this whole surreal experience has been tough to digest is an understatement," Hollis said. "On the one hand, I am eternally grateful and feel blessed beyond measure to still be healthy and somehow have this rare natural protection against a deadly virus that is making people sick and killing African Americans at such a high rate.

"But, on the other hand, it makes me ask: 'Why me? Why have I been spared when so many others weren't?'

"But I've long preached to my son, Davis, that we all share a responsibility to make the world a better place than it was when we arrived. Never in a million years could I have envisioned this being how I might help do just that."

DEALING WITH POLICING IN AMERICA

BY KEITH HARRISTON

DOROTHY C. ELLIOTT WAS home in suburban Maryland, about fourteen miles east of the White House. It was a Friday in June, and her year teaching high school business classes was just about over. Earlier that day, she had shopped for bed linens and purchased paisley sheets, a masculine pattern that she knew her sons would like. She was getting ready to go see a movie with the younger of her two sons, John Elliott. He was eleven years old.

About the same time, her older son, Archie Elliott III—or Artie as friends and family called him—was heading home from his construction job in the nearby northern Virginia suburbs. Artie had had some hard turns in life, including once being shot and wounded outside of a D.C. nightclub, but he had taken to construction work and was sure that it would lead to nothing but good things.

"After a while working on construction, he would tell me all the time, 'I'm gonna build you a house,'" Dorothy Elliott recalled.

Somewhere along the route home, Artie had a drink or two or more. Beer or liquor. That detail doesn't matter much. The end result does. About three minutes from his family home near District Heights, Maryland, Artie was driving east on Kipling Parkway when District Heights police officer Jason Leavitt spotted the car Artie was driving, which belonged to a female friend, weaving in the roadway. Artie had just passed the huge lot of the First Baptist Church of District Heights on his right. Detached single-family homes lined small lots near the other three corners of the intersection of Kipling Parkway and Marbury Drive.

Officer Leavitt switched on his marked patrol car's flashing lights and pulled Artie over. It was about five p.m.

By then, Dorothy and John had exited their home on a cul-de-sac and settled into her car. All these years later, she's fuzzy on what movie they had planned to see. But before she started her car, John had to go back inside to use the bathroom. They got out, re-entered their home. The telephone rang.

"It was some police department," Dorothy Elliott remembered. "They kept asking me, 'Are you related to Archie Elliott III?'" She hung up, thinking it was a prank call or something of the sort. The phone rang again. The caller asked the same question: Are you related to Archie Elliott III? "And then the person said, 'We're coming over.' Right away I asked, 'He's dead, isn't he?'"

Hearing one side of that exchange, John's guts heaved, and he started vomiting. Dorothy remembered screaming and walking out of her home aimlessly on the cul-de-sac. Neighbors who had been watching early local news that late afternoon already knew. Artie was, indeed, dead, killed in a barrage of twenty-two bullets fired from the department-issued handguns of two police officers.

Artie died with his hands cuffed behind his back, sitting in the front seat of the marked District Heights police cruiser. Fourteen bullets in all pierced his chest, back, buttocks, right arm, and right hand, according to the autopsy by the Maryland Medical Examiner's Office. He was twenty-four years old. And Black.

Artie's death in 1993 at the hands of Officers Jason Leavitt of District Heights police and Wayne Cheney of the Prince George's County, Maryland, Police Department is a reminder that the phenomenon of a disproportionate number of Black men and women dying after encounters with police officers didn't start with the death in 2014 of Michael Brown in Ferguson, Missouri. It wasn't spiraling upward with the tragic death captured on video of George Floyd in Minneapolis, Minnesota, though the deaths of both men launched ongoing protests and campaigns for racial justice. However, it can seem that that is the case, especially when video captures the killings, as in the case of Floyd.

That thinking is reinforced by the near-daily media reports of Black people shot to death by law enforcement officers—226 killed by police gunfire in 2020 alone.

Rayshard Brooks, twenty-seven, was shot and killed by an Atlanta police officer. Brooks fell asleep in his car in a fast-food restaurant drive-through. An officer shot Brooks twice in the back after Brooks grabbed the officer's Taser and tried to use it on the officer before turning to flee. That, according to police body cam footage, was when the officer shot Brooks twice in the back.

Daniel Prude, forty-one, was naked and experiencing a mental health episode in Rochester, New York, when police responding to a call encountered him in the middle of the street. Officers restrained him and placed a plastic hood over his face. (The hood is meant to avoid spit.) One officer used his weight to hold Prude down against the street. Prude died, according to an autopsy, due to asphyxiation and acute intoxication.

Breonna Taylor, twenty-six, was shot eight times in her apartment in the early morning in Louisville, Kentucky, when officers executing a no-knock search warrant entered the apartment. Taylor's boyfriend, thinking a break-in was happening, fired his registered handgun, injuring one of the officers. Taylor died after being shot eight times when officers returned fire.

Jamarri Tarver, twenty-six, was killed in North Las Vegas, Nevada, after he led police on a chase in an allegedly stolen car. Two officers fired twenty-four shots at Tarver after police say he had used the stolen vehicle as a weapon against officers. He died at the scene.

Tyree Davis, twenty-six, was Tasered and then shot by Chicago police officers after they say he failed to drop a knife when cornered by officers after allegedly stealing something from a dollar store.

Brandon Roberts, twenty-seven, was shot and killed by Milford, Delaware, officers who responded to his home for a domestic disturbance. Officers said Roberts yielded a large knife in a threatening manner, though his fiancée disputes that account.

Kwame Jones, seventeen, died after being shot by a police officer in Jacksonville, Florida. Officers said Jones would not stop the car he was driving and had an exchange with officers before he was shot.

Albert Hughes, forty-seven, was fatally shot by officers in Lawrenceville, Georgia, after he attacked an officer with a chair in a fast-food restaurant. The fatal shot was fired, police said, after a Taser shot was ineffective in stopping Hughes.

Samuel Mallard, nineteen, was killed by Cobb County, Georgia, SWAT officers when police said Mallard tried to drive away from his home as officers arrived to execute an arrest warrant for his alleged involvement in a number of crimes.

In 2020, police across the United States shot and killed a Black person at a rate of about one every thirty-eight hours. That is generally consistent with the number of fatal shootings of Black people by police annually since 2015, according to data compiled by the *Washington Post*. Police shot and killed 5,960 people since 2015, according to the *Post* data, and Black people accounted for about 36 percent of the victims who were unarmed and about 25 percent of the victims who were armed—largely disproportionate considering that Blacks make up about 13 percent of the U.S. population.

Of course, the *Post*'s data would not include Floyd, who died in the emotionally draining nine minutes and twenty-nine seconds that Minneapolis police officer Derek Michael Chauvin pressed his knee down on Floyd's neck. And it would not include any other man or woman, Black, white, or other, who died by any method other than gunshot. And even the shooting numbers are not complete. Why? There is no federal requirement that law enforcement agencies report to the federal government incidents of use of excessive force by officers.

Artie Elliott isn't included in the *Post* database, obviously, because it covers fatal police shootings only since 2015. Police shot and killed Artie on June 18, 1993—twenty-eight years ago.

How did we get to a place where a Black person is shot and killed in the United States almost once every day by law enforcement, and in a majority of those cases, no criminal charges are filed against officers who did the shootings?

Benjamin Crump, a Black lawyer who represented the family of Trayvon Martin after vigilante George Zimmerman shot and killed the Black teenager in 2012 in Florida, has become the legal representative face of relatives of victims of police shootings—including Breonna Taylor in Louisville, George Floyd in Minneapolis, and Jacob Blake in Kenosha, Wisconsin. In televised press conferences, Crump shows up with a consistent message.

"We want justice."

Exactly what that means, we don't know because "We want justice" provides a great sound bite for broadcast and cable news but doesn't give viewers any explanation. Clearly, it means more than multimillion-dollar settlements between victims, their families, and the local governments who employ police officers. There's seldom discussion about underlying forces that led to the shootings or why it was unlikely any police officer would face criminal consequences for their actions, no matter how outrageous the circumstances of the shootings seem.

Artie Elliott was "a typical teenager," his mother said. "He enjoyed having friends around the house. He loved playing video games.

When he was a young child, he was very shy. Artie wouldn't let me out of his sight."

Dorothy Elliott and her husband, Archie Elliott II, a former General District Court judge in Virginia, separated when Artie was four years old. That same year, his appendix ruptured, and Dorothy stayed by his bedside during his hospital stay. "I was so scared," she said. "It was hard looking at those tubes coming out of him filled with that green liquid. I didn't leave him. I was there forty-eight hours straight."

A mother's bond with a child—especially between mothers and sons—is strong, even when the child follows a path not preferred by the mother. She knew, for example, that after he was shot and wounded outside of a D.C. nightclub, he bought a small handgun. For protection. Since Artie's killing, Dorothy has dedicated her life to ensuring that the government agencies that employed the officers who took his life don't forget that her older son "got no justice."

It's not as if Artie could somehow fade from her memory. The living room walls of her home where she raised Artie are full of photographs of him—by himself; with her; with his younger brother, John. She's written scores of letters to prosecutors, police chiefs, council members, state legislators, members of Congress, sitting and retired judges. She's initiated petitions. Made countless phone calls. She led a twenty-five-plus-mile march from her home in the Maryland suburbs of Washington, D.C., to the state capital in Annapolis. She's testified at legislative hearings and traveled to South Africa to talk about Artie's case and police brutality.

Her demonstrations—at one point for twenty-two straight Wednesdays—seeking to reopen the case against the two officers who killed her son have drawn representatives from Amnesty International; Martin Luther King III, the oldest son of Martin Luther King Jr.; the late Dick Gregory; and activist New York City pastor Mark Thompson, among others.

There were and are frequent reminders. Shortly after Artie's death, she took two years off from teaching. "I couldn't go back," she said. "There was one young man in particular who reminded me so much of Artie." Drivers passing by the intersection where Artie was killed and where she maintains a small memorial for her son stop to ask how she's doing. And then there is one of the members of her church, St. Paul Baptist Church in Forestville, Maryland: Officer Cheney's sister. "When I first found out who she was, I said something to her in church. A little girl with her overheard me and asked, 'Is she talking about Uncle Wayne?'

"This has been my life for the past [twenty-eight] years," Dorothy Elliott said. "I don't have any choice. Artie no longer can speak for himself."

The details of Artie's shooting largely stay fresh in Dorothy's mind. If she's unsure of particulars, folders of court documents, news clippings, letters, and photographs fill her living room coffee table. Standing on the northeast corner of the intersection where police pulled him over, Dorothy points to the section of curb where passersby had seen Artie sitting handcuffed before police placed him in the front seat of the police cruiser. The lamppost a few feet away from that spot still holds up a handful of artificial flowers that she placed there more than five years ago—green stems with fading red petals. She pointed to a spot in the street several steps away. "His blood was all over there," she said.

When Officer Leavitt, who is white, stopped Artie, he said he smelled alcohol. Artie, according to Leavitt, admitted he had been drinking. A lot. It was late spring but hot, and Artie wore only under-wear, shorts, and shoes with no shirt. He failed several field sobriety tests, Leavitt said, and was having trouble walking. The officer called for backup, handcuffed Artie, and told the young man he was being arrested for driving while intoxicated. Leavitt said he searched Artie— at least he remembered searching the back side of Artie's body and shorts but could not recall whether he searched Artie's front side. He found no weapon or contraband.

The backup officer arrived. It was Wayne Cheney, a Black patrol officer with the Prince George's County Police Department. In the car with Cheney was Mark Erik Gamble, a civilian on a police ride-along—a community relations offering from many police departments for civilians interested in how the police work or who are considering policing as a career. Officer Cheney helped Officer Leavitt move Artie from a seat on the curb to the front passenger seat of Leavitt's patrol cruiser. They fastened a seat belt around Artie and shut the door with the windows rolled up. The two officers stood outside on the passenger side of the vehicle talking when Leavitt noticed movement inside the car. A more focused look, and Leavitt said he saw Artie with his finger on the trigger of a handgun that was pointed toward the officers. Cheney said he also saw Artie with the gun pointed toward them.

"Gun!" Leavitt screamed and ordered Artie to drop the weapon.

The officers said he did not. So they both fired their handguns, twenty-two bullets in all, striking Artie fourteen times and leaving quarter-sized holes in the front and rear passenger-side doors of the cruiser. Artie's hands were cuffed behind his back. His seat belt had been fastened. He was wearing only underwear and shorts, and Leavitt was sure he had checked Artie's back side for weapons or contraband. But somehow, according to the two officers, Artie was able to maneuver his hands and arms to remove a small handgun from his shorts and point it at the officers with his finger on the trigger. When the shooting stopped, Leavitt said, Artie's gun was still in his hand.

A police investigation recommended that both Leavitt and Cheney be exonerated for the fatal shooting. A Prince George's County grand jury declined to take action against the officers. Investigators determined that Artie had somehow removed his seat belt, pulled his handgun from his shorts, maneuvered his hands to the right side of his body, placed his finger on the gun's trigger, and aimed at the two officers—all while his hands were handcuffed behind his back. "All the grand jury recommended was that officers get better training on when to shoot their guns and how to better search people in custody," Dorothy Elliott said.

Apparently, a key part of clearing the officers was a sworn statement by a man who said Artie had threatened him while both were driving months before the shooting. The other motorist identified the handgun officers recovered from Artie's hand as the same gun that Artie had used to threaten him. In addition, an FBI report showed that a blue-colored fiber snagged on the gun had come from the shorts that Artie was wearing.

Dorothy wanted justice.

"Police could talk for themselves during the investigation," Dorothy said. "Artie couldn't. I shouldn't have been so naïve. I just knew somebody would be charged. But there was no indictment. No charges whatsoever."

About eighteen months later, Prince George's County officer Wayne Cheney killed again.

This time, according to police, Cheney fired a single shot that killed twenty-nine-year-old Michael Donald Reed after a high-speed chase just after midnight in February 1995. Cheney told investigators he fired at Reed, who was a passenger in the car, after Reed jumped from the car and looked as if he were reaching into his pants for a gun. Hit once in his chest, Reed died about an hour later at a hospital.

Police found no gun on or around Reed. Cheney was cleared in that fatal shooting, too.

Journalists contacted Dorothy Elliott with news about Cheney's second on-duty fatal shooting. In fact, it turned out to be Cheney's third officer-involved shooting. The first had happened in the late 1980s when Cheney responded to a domestic dispute and shot and wounded a man police said was armed with a .357 Magnum handgun.

"I could not believe it," Dorothy Elliott said. "I felt so sorry for the family. I reached out to Reed's mother. Cheney should have been in jail for killing Artie. And he should have been in jail for killing Michael Donald Reed."

"THEY SEE US AS THUGS"

Bobby Walker Sr. is a Black man who has twenty-three years in law enforcement, fourteen as a member of the Greenville, Mississippi, police department. Since 2019, Walker has been chief of the small Sunflower, Mississippi, Police Department, about thirty miles from Greenville. He comes from a family of police officers. He first wanted to join after attending an older brother's graduation from the police academy.

"That got me hooked," Walker said. He often posts on social media, including clear pro-police phrases such as "Blue Lives Matter." In midsummer of 2020, after months of protests in cities across the United States led mainly by the Black Lives Matter movement, Walker posted this on Facebook:

> As law enforcement officers, we come in contact with people from all walks of life, no matter the race, gender or creed...we don't get to choose but we do have an obligation to treat all individuals equal.

"It had five hundred likes the first day, three thousand in a few days. Now, it has more than a hundred thousand likes," Walker said. "So many Black officers want to speak out, they want to say something. They hesitate because they don't want fellow officers to look at them funny. I can do that without worrying because I am the chief here. I don't have to worry. But the same message I posted needs to come from departments' leadership. It sets the tone for the morale of the department. Officers will know what you will and won't put up with. If you let them know you will not tolerate racist actions in their encounters, they won't do that. Or at least, they won't do it often."

When Walker first saw the video of George Floyd on the pavement with Officer Chauvin's knee pressed against Floyd's neck, "My first thought," Walker said, "was how can we prevent something like this from *ever* happening again."

Chauvin was convicted in April 2021 of second-degree murder, third-degree murder, and second-degree manslaughter. He faced no hate crime–related charges. Minnesota has no hate crime statute.

Walker and other officers said race and race relations are not topics that come up in many police training academies, especially in small or medium-sized departments, though it is starting to change.

"They don't teach about it. And you cannot talk about those shooting situations without talking about race. Ask yourself this question: 'Are there a disproportionate number of white people killed by Black cops or any cops?' You don't have a lot of Black cops killing white people. A big part of the problem seems to be clear to me. We are living at a time when it must be taught how to deal with race issues, mental health issues, domestic issues."

In many law enforcement departments across the United States, Walker said, he believes the makeup of the force contributes to the rates that Black men and women are killed by law enforcement officers. "A lot of these white police officers, when they join law enforcement come from areas where they have very little or no experience being around Black people. So that white officer is already uncomfortable around Black people. In some cases, they are afraid of Black people.

They see us as 'thugs.' They are already afraid of the culture because they are unfamiliar with it."

Michelle Randall-Williams, a Black retired New York City police detective, said that systemic racism in the United States has trained the country to believe that "we are the problem. Black is bad. Then that feeds a fear of Blacks. Couple that with police numbers: Law enforcement is predominantly white. And Black people? Those stereotypes. We're bad. We're violent. We're lazy, too. That fear factor kicks in. Slave masters had the same thing. It's been the American way since Europeans arrived here."

As for Floyd, many men and women in law enforcement prefer not to speak publicly on the case, choosing public silence over damaging working relationships with their police colleagues. That isn't so with retired officers when they are asked their opinion of Floyd's death.

"It was murder," said Alton Bigelow, who retired from the Washington, D.C., police department as a deputy chief. "You don't do that. And that officer did it as if he had done something like that before. The officers watching—you don't stand there. You pull him off. I don't care if he is your field-training officer, or if you're worried about what other officers will say. It looks like a clear culture problem in that department."

Compounding that culture problem and systemic racism that Walker, Randall-Williams, and Bigelow described is the fact that, according to U.S. representative Jamie Raskin, a Maryland Democrat who chairs the House Subcommittee on Civil Rights and Civil Liberties, white supremacists have for years aimed to infiltrate law enforcement. At a prophetic congressional hearing in September 2020, Raskin released an unredacted version of a previously redacted FBI report, "White Supremacist Infiltration of Law Enforcement." The report had been released initially in 2006.

At the virtual hearing of his subcommittee, Raskin heard from several witnesses, including Frank Meeink, a former neo-Nazi; Heather Taylor, a retired police officer and president of the Ethical Society of Police, based in St. Louis; and Mike German, a former FBI agent who had worked undercover within white supremacist groups. Meeink, now an advocate for racial equality, recounted how he himself had been pointed toward joining law enforcement during his time as a neo-Nazi.

"I attended a small meeting in Baltimore, run by the National Socialist Movement and a group called SS Action," Meeink told the subcommittee. "I heard the same rhetoric there. They told us to join law enforcement, so that we can give Blacks [felony charges] so that they wouldn't be able to legally arm themselves. So that they wouldn't be able to vote."

German, who worked at the FBI for sixteen years and is a fellow with the Brennan Center for Justice's Liberty and National Security Program, described the efforts of white supremacists to join law enforcement as a matter of national security.

"If the government knew that al Qaeda or ISIS had infiltrated American law enforcement agencies, it would undoubtedly initiate a nationwide effort to identify them and neutralize the threat they posed," German testified. "Yet white supremacists and far-right militants have committed far more attacks and killed more people in the United States over the last ten years than any foreign terrorist movement, and both the FBI and Department of Homeland Security regard them as the most lethal domestic terror threat. The need for national action on the issue of explicit racism, white supremacy, and far-right militancy in law enforcement is critical."

In his opening statement at the September 2020 hearing, which was the fourth held by his Subcommittee on Civil Rights and Civil Liberties, Raskin said that the issue "is disproportionately a threat to Black and brown communities." He noted that the unredacted report points out that the infiltration of white supremacists into law enforcement has two principal issues: white supremacist groups encouraging members to join police departments; and current law enforcement officers who share supremacist racist ideas.

Raskin invited the FBI to send someone to testify at his hearing, but the Bureau passed on the opportunity.

"The Bureau declined to come," he said, "claiming they have nothing to say because they have no evidence that this is a widespread problem demanding the FBI's attention. What's more, they have attempted to disavow their own 2006 intelligence assessment, which has every sign of being an authentic document."

The unredacted portions of the FBI report also warned that law enforcement could "volunteer their professional resources to the white supremacist causes with which they sympathize."

"These are chilling conclusions," Raskin said. "But rather than clearly spell out this threat for the American people, the FBI has suppressed them from public view for fourteen years. For the first time, we can now see that the FBI believed internally that white supremacist infiltration of law enforcement departments was a serious problem, a source of potential abuse of power and authority on the street and a source of potential violence against the civilian population."

Less than six months after Raskin's hearing, in the aftermath of Trump supporters storming the U.S. Capitol, videos of Capitol Police officers went viral showing an officer wearing a MAGA hat during the riot, another officer taking time to snap a selfie with a rioter, and another video showing officers who seemed to pull back a barricade to usher rioters into the building. Within a week, at least fourteen Capitol Police officers were investigated by federal authorities for possible involvement in the riots. Within two weeks, authorities had identified about thirty law enforcement officers from several police agencies across the country as attendees at the rally prior to the riot at the Capitol. One from Rocky Mount, Virginia. A few from

Philadelphia. Another from Houston. The night of the riot, the head of the Chicago Police Department's 12,000-member union supported the mob in a television interview.

German, the former FBI agent, has pointed out in his work for the Brennan Center that law enforcement officers with connections to white supremacist far-right militant groups have been uncovered in "Alabama, California, Connecticut, Florida, Illinois, Louisiana, Michigan, Nebraska, Oklahoma, Oregon, Texas, Virginia, Washington, West Virginia, and elsewhere." Most often those officers are disciplined. Sometimes they are fired. And sometimes courts overturn those firings.

"Leaving officers tainted by racist behavior in a job with immense discretion to take a person's life and liberty requires a detailed supervision plan to mitigate the potential threats they pose to the communities they police, implemented with sufficient transparency to restore public trust," German said.

In most departments, though, those supervision plans are inadequate at best.

After the September hearing, Raskin said that the United States' "social contract" must have "fair and neutral enforcement of the laws to protect the whole citizenry against criminal violence and state violence. We must work to disentangle the police power of the state from groups and individuals that subscribe to the violent white supremacist ideology and seek to inflict harm on African Americans, Asian Americans, Latinos, Jewish Americans, LGBTQ Americans, and anyone who stands in the way of a race war and the civil war that the extreme right is calling for in America today."

Such allegations from a Democratic House committee chair about law enforcement, and the FBI in particular, might seem like just so much political rhetoric spewing from the nation's capital, where the two major political parties stake out positions at such extremes that they seldom, if ever, agree on anything. But much of what Raskin said about the FBI is backed up by the Mirror Project, a group of Black, former FBI agents who in 2020 decided to speak publicly about race problems inside the Bureau.

The group noted that in 2020 white men held the top ten FBI leadership positions, those that make the Bureau's most important decisions. It noted that Black people hold about 4 percent of the 13,000 agent jobs, numbers that have been consistent for decades. Promotions largely go to white, male agents. The lack of diversity at the FBI, the Mirror Project said, raises doubts about the Bureau's ability to fairly investigate cases of police use of deadly force in the deaths of Breonna Taylor and George Floyd, or the case of Jacob Blake, who was shot seven times in his back by a Kenosha, Wisconsin, police officer. Some of what the former agents point out are the same type of issues pointed out by Chief Walker in Mississippi.

How can the Black community rely on the FBI—the top agency in the country for investigating police actions and protecting peoples' civil rights—to fairly investigate cops when there is a scarcity of Black agents involved in reviewing those cases? As one Black former agent put it: A white male growing up in Nebraska is not going to have the same life experience as a Black female growing up in New York City.

But the issue of policing and police use of force is more complex. It isn't as simple as black and white. Take the early September 2020 case of Deon Kay. He was an eighteen-year-old Black man shot and killed by a Washington, D.C., police officer in a majority Black neighborhood in the southeast section of the city. Police said Kay was among a small group of men inside a parked Dodge Caliber who were openly displaying handguns—actions that were livestreamed on social media. When police arrived, the group of men scattered from the car, including Kay. An officer shot Kay as the young man was running toward the officer.

The shooting in the summer of 2020 sparked immediate protests, with hundreds of people, Black and white, demonstrating at the local police precinct. The next night, protests continued there. But this time an overwhelming majority of the protesters were white. What happened in that short time to change the racial makeup of the group of demonstrators? Police released body cam footage of the shooting that showed Kay pulling a handgun from his waistband as he was running toward the officer, Alexander Alvarez, who drew his service weapon and shot Kay.

Sandra Seegars, a Black community activist in that part of the city, posted the video on social media. Hundreds commented on the video, most of them—but not all—in fact offering cautious understanding for why the shooting happened.

"One thing I am sure of," Seegars said, "is that because I posted it, they respect me and they respect what I think. The video showed Deon Kay pulling the gun from the back of his waistband and running toward the officer. You cannot determine whether something like this is right or wrong based just on emotions. I am sorry the young man was killed. Everyone is. But you can't run at police holding a gun."

In late November, federal prosecutors declined to charge the officer who shot Kay, saying in a statement that the Office of the U.S. Attorney for the District of Columbia "is unable to disprove a claim of self-defense or defense of others by the officer involved, who fired a single shot at Mr. Kay within one second of Mr. Kay holding a gun in his hand and raising his arm."

Seegars has one brother who was shot and killed in 1978 and another brother serving a life sentence for murder. She believes that Kay and other young men like him would benefit from more government investment in programs such as job training and counseling services—part of what proponents of the "defund the police" movement propose.

"Defund the police" means different things to different people. A majority of its supporters say that the words do *not* mean ridding towns, cities, counties, and states of police and sheriff's departments. It means diverting money from law enforcement budgets that in some larger jurisdictions take up almost one-third of the municipal budget. For example, according to the American Civil Liberties Union (ACLU), the city of Los Angeles budget for police is $3.4 billion out of a $10.5 billion operating budget. The ACLU also cites the budget in New York City, where the city spends about $6 billion annually on policing—more than what the city spends on the combined budgets for homelessness, health services, housing development, and youth and community development.

In some instances, "defund the police" means prohibiting spending funds on military-style equipment for police forces. In others, it means ending police officers' involvement in traffic enforcement. In the broadest sense, it means to rethink the role of policing in the United States while diverting some funds from police departments to social programs that in the long run would promote safer communities. A majority of the Minneapolis City Council, in the aftermath of the George Floyd killing that sparked both peaceful protests and rioting, pledged to dismantle the city's police department and come up with a different way of policing. Details were scarce.

In December, the council ended up cutting about $8 million from the police department budget—less than 5 percent of its operating expenses. Camden, New Jersey, often is held up as the city that successfully defunded its police department. But the changes in Camden were driven by politics and economics, not desires for social justice. Essentially because of budget shortfalls driven partly by costly police union contracts, the city of Camden dissolved its police department and replaced it with a Camden County department. That new department's officers worked under a less costly union contract.

Seegars said that she disagrees with most efforts to defund police, however the proponents define it. "We need to let the police be the police. We have way more good ones than bad ones, but the bad ones get all the attention and publicity."

Maria Haberfeld, a professor of police science in the Department of Law, Police Science and Criminal Justice Administration at John Jay College of Criminal Justice in New York, has authored more than twenty books about policing. She describes herself as "pro police" and teaches many law enforcement officers in her classes at John Jay College. She said in spite of what seem like constant reports about police using deadly force, "The numbers are not trending upwards. The numbers are relatively low when you consider them in the context of the numbers of police officers in the United States and the numbers of encounters with civilians." Haberfeld noted that there are about 18,000 law enforcement agencies in the United States.

Christy Lopez is a Georgetown University law professor and a former deputy chief in the Justice Department's Special Litigation Section of the Civil Rights Division. She led the Justice Department group that conducted pattern-or-practice investigations of law enforcement agencies, including the Ferguson, Missouri, Police Department after police shot and killed Michael Brown in 2014. Defunding police is not the final answer when it comes to police reform, but the discussion is as necessary as such reforms as banning choke holds and reducing the use of no-knock warrants. "Take away police, however imperfect, and bad as it is, there always will be some people who say they'll take their police because it is better than nothing," Lopez said.

She said most people misunderstand how much communities over-rely on police for things such as traffic accident reports, drug overdoses, controlling the homeless, resolving family arguments, and, in some school districts, managing student discipline problems. "Defunding the police means shrinking the scope of police responsibilities and shifting most of what government does to keep us safe to entities that are better equipped to meet that need," she said. "It means investing more in mental-health care and housing, and expanding the use of community mediation and violence-interruption programs."

Defunding police in the thousands of law enforcement agencies in the United States is not likely to happen soon, Lopez said, so it is imperative that advocates work simultaneously on reforming police work. She points back to the fatal police shooting of Kay, the Black eighteen-year-old in Washington, D.C., in Seegars's neighborhood. "Think about how police handled that situation. There were teenagers in a car with guns. They were Black. So, police cars speed up to the car and jump out. So, of course the teenagers are going to run. If they had been white teenagers doing the same thing in a white neighborhood, you know police would have responded differently. They would have approached the car in a whole different manner," Lopez said.

If ever there was any doubt about the different ways in which law enforcement deals with white and Black communities, the Capitol riots are illustrative, Lopez said.

On the day of the riot, only unarmed National Guardsmen had been activated to help out Capitol Police. And that morning, only about one-fourth of the 2,200-member Capitol Police force was on duty. When the mob pushed against barricades to gain entry to the Capitol, officers offered little resistance. A single shot was fired, and it was fatal, killing a white woman insurrectionist. But that happened only after rioters had gotten inside the building and were forcibly trying to get further access to an area that housed congressional leadership.

In June 2020, Black Lives Matter planned a protest at the Lincoln Memorial in Washington, D.C. Scores of armed National Guardsmen were activated and deployed all over the steps leading up to the monument. And days before, guardsmen used chemical irritants and rubber bullets to disperse a BLM demonstration in a park near the

White House, a heavy show of force that included military helicopters buzzing over the heads of the demonstrators. That was all done to allow Trump to walk along that path from the White House to a nearby church for a photo opportunity.

The president of the Major Cities Chiefs Association, Houston police chief Art Acevedo, said two days after the Capitol riot that he worried that law enforcement's lack of preparedness was related to police perception of the overwhelmingly white crowd.

"They see Black Lives Matter and go, 'Oh my God, we've got to be ready.' But, hey, these people have their blue lives matter flags all over the place," Acevedo said. "And that bias and that false sense of security bit them. And it bit them in a historical fashion."

Lopez sees the law enforcement reaction to rioters as a lesson to learn. "What you saw at the Capitol is what police restraint looks like," Lopez said. "That kind of restraint in policing should happen for everyone.

"We cannot wait to make changes that will save lives and reduce policing harm now."

U.S. SLAVE PATROLS

Policing as we know it today, according to historians, dates to the 1830s in the United States in Boston, which had the first department that was fully funded by the government and offered full-time work as a police officer. But the roots of policing in the United States go back further, into the 1700s with the formation of slave patrols that were created to track runaway slaves, capture them, and return them to their owners. They were used to strike fear into slaves to deter revolt against slave owners and to help with keeping slaves in line, especially when the enslaved were outside of the direct control of their enslavers, since the slave patrols could dispense punishment at will.

In other words, slave patrols kept slaves in check, since in many areas enslaved Black people outnumbered white people, who lived in fear of insurrections by the enslaved. The National Law Enforcement Museum says that slave patrol "routines included enforcing curfews, checking travelers for a permission pass, catching those assembling without permission and preventing any form of organized resistance."

The first slave patrols came about in 1704 in South Carolina and ended on paper in 1865 when the Thirteenth Amendment abolished slavery, though groups that functioned much like slave patrols took part in enforcing Jim Crow in the South and ensuring that the Black Codes were being enforced, according to historian Keisha Blain.

We still see similar tactics used today by law enforcement in Black neighborhoods. Traffic stops. Stop and frisk tactics that were used in New York City and targeted mostly Black and Latino males. Creating reasons to question Black men and women: not coming to a complete stop at a stop sign; broken brake lights on vehicles; obscured license tags. These policing attitudes reinforce stereotypes about Black people as criminals and thugs, which factors into the implicit bias that some researchers believe leads police officers—both white and Black—to more quickly draw their weapons on Black people. In the hands of a Black person, a mobile phone looks like a gun. Food looks like a gun. Empty hands hold guns. Hands cuffed behind a Black man's back magically maneuver to his front, grab a handgun, point it at an officer with a finger on the trigger.

Aggressive policing in Black communities—officers working to control Black people instead of protecting and serving them—could be changed by the mayors, county executives, and other top local elected officials who on paper are in charge of police departments. But even those elected officials who are well-meaning fall victim to the same issues that led to the creation of slave patrols. That, said Blain, Lopez, and others, is structural, systemic racism.

"This is something that we have not actually dealt with," said Blain, a history professor at the University of Pittsburgh. "And so we keep having conversations about how we might tweak this or tweak that. Maybe we'll pass some policy that's anti-chokehold, and that sounds wonderful. But if you don't actually get to the root of the problem, then you'll find yourself in the same place over and over again, even if you pass a hundred different policies that say, don't choke a person; don't place your knee on a person's neck."

Lopez said that it is important to remember that policing "didn't invent America's institutionalized racism.

"If we were to get rid of policing tomorrow, those pathologies would remain," Lopez said. "And they would continue to be deadly. Race bias in our health care system has likely killed far more Black and Latinx via COVID-19 than the police have this year. Successful police reforms help us learn how to identify and mitigate the harms of these structural features, even as we work to remake them."

In her experience teaching many law enforcement officers, Haberfeld said, she has found that no one hates bad cops more than good cops. "They are not supporting bad behavior," she said. "They are just not reporting it."

But officers who do not intervene, who fail to step in to calm other officers whom they see using excessive force, *are* supporting bad behavior in two largely important ways—by not stopping the violent officer and by not reporting it to supervisors.

When Eric Garner died in 2014 after being put in a choke hold by a New York City police officer, Randall-Williams—the retired New York City police detective—said there was a Black female sergeant on the scene. Randall-Williams said the Black sergeant, who did not intercede to stop the choking as Garner yelled, "I can't breathe," was demoted after only a couple of months—while it took the U.S. Justice Department almost five years to determine the offending officer would not face federal charges. In her opinion, Randall-Williams said, "She should have taken some action to stop it. It's not easy. You join the force, you want to be accepted. It's a stressful job, and you don't bring that home. You talk it through with your partner. Officers play together. You do inappropriate things together. You eat together. You drink together."

When an officer does report bad behavior—or intervenes to stop it—sometimes the consequences are career-ending. Take the case of former Buffalo, New York, officer Cariol Horne. She stepped in to stop her white partner, Officer Gregory Kwiatkowski, from applying a choke hold on David Neal Mack, a Black man. The two officers were among several police who responded to reports of an argument between a man—Mack—and a woman who said that Mack, her boyfriend, had stolen her $646 Social Security check. Inside the home, officers used pepper spray to subdue Mack. That failed. Horne, her partner, and other officers worked in unison to push Mack out the front door. Once outside, Horne's partner cuffed Mack with his hands in front of his body. From behind Mack, Kwiatkowski reached around Mack and held his right forearm tight against the front of Mack's throat.

Horne heard Mack yelling, "'I can't breathe,' so I said, 'Greg you're choking him.' He didn't stop choking him, so I grabbed his arm from around [Mack's] neck."

Her partner then punched Horne in the face, knocking loose two of her teeth. But when other officers who were on the scene talked to investigators, "They said I was jumping on officers, kicking ass and taking names. But why would I do that?"

Her department investigated and said Horne's actions showed a lack of professionalism and could have had fatal consequences for other officers, as well as for Mack. The internal investigation report said that Horne's decision to intercede had made it "almost impossible for officers to have any confidence in her."

"The hearing officer said that what I did was so awful that I should be fired," she said.

Horne was found guilty in an administrative department hearing for violating several regulations and was fired from the force. She was less than two years away from being eligible to receive a pension. She continued to work as she waited for her departmental hearing. But she said other officers failed to respond to her calls for backup when she requested it. The woman who had become a law enforcement officer "to help people" had joined the Buffalo department when she was young with two sons, thinking it would be a secure, decent-paying job.

She now has five sons, fourteen grandchildren. When she was found guilty by the department, she not only was fired, she lost her pension. She's had two cars repossessed. She's been homeless, as recently as in 2019. She depended on a GoFundMe account to help make her monthly rent payments.

Years later, Officer Kwiatkowski was indicted on federal civil rights violation charges of excessive force in an unrelated case. Federal prosecutors said Kwiatkowski admitted to "forcibly pushing the heads and upper torsos of four people suspected of shooting a BB gun into the vehicle." He admitted as part of his plea agreement that his use of force against the four suspects was un-reasonable and excessive and that his use of such force deprived the suspects of their constitutional rights to be free from unreasonable seizure and to due process of law, by a person acting in an official capacity.

Prosecutors in the Western District of New York further said that after his use of excessive force against the suspects, Kwiatkowski recovered a BB gun from the vehicle in which the suspects had been riding and handed the BB gun to one of the other two Buffalo Police Department officers on the scene. Those two officers were accused of shooting one of the suspects with the BB gun while he was handcuffed in the backseat of the police car. Those two officers were acquitted at trial.

Kwiatkowski pled guilty to deprivation of rights under the color of law, was sentenced to four months in prison and one year supervised release that included four months' home detention. Prior to that, he had sued Horne for defamation and was awarded $65,000, of which he has collected about $20,000.

Her former colleagues on the Buffalo Police Department still remember Horne and her intervention. In the late spring of 2020, days after video captured Buffalo officers pushing down Martin Gugino, an elderly white man who had joined a demonstration against racism and police brutality, local law enforcement and others in Buffalo held a rally in support of two officers who were suspended for pushing Gugino to the ground and fracturing his skull. It was what Horne called "a rally for bad cops."

She showed up and used her mobile phone to take video of the officers at the rally. She said the crowd started chanting "no pension, no peace" and "fired" when they saw her. "If they did that to me in broad daylight, think of what they are doing to our kids in the dark of night," she said.

Police brutality isn't the only issue between police and Black men, she said. It's also the way in which Black communities are policed. Her description again mirrors the coercion and control of slave patrols. Constant ticketing, arrests, jailing, planting evidence.

"It's a revolving door," Horne said. "I wasn't doing it. It's a problem in the whole country. It starts at the top. As a cop, you have a go-along-to-get-along mentality instead of doing what is right."

Buffalo's Common Council, the city's local legislative body, passed a bill in September 2020 that came to be known as Cariol's Law. Signed into law by the city's mayor in late October 2020, the law requires officers "to intervene in a situation where they believe another officer is acting inappropriately or jeopardizing another person's safety or well-being."

Horne would like to see a version of Cariol's Law passed in every state and the District of Columbia. When she saw the George Floyd video, she said, "I cried for days.

"That would never happen here now. As an officer, you would not be able to stand by and watch what happened to George Floyd because officers would have a duty to intervene. It would be illegal for you to stand by and watch," she said.

She was among those who lobbied for passage of Cariol's Law, although friends and legal advisors suggested that she hold back speaking out on her case and policing issues because she's still—after almost a dozen years—fighting for her right to collect her police pension. "I want my pension, but I can't be quiet. I have to speak out. I'm trying to empower people. We need to keep speaking up about it."

A Chicago law firm, Kirkland & Ellis, whose team includes a former chief counsel to President Barack Obama, filed papers in New York state court in fall 2020 seeking to get her firing reversed "in the interest of justice," according to the court filing.

"For doing precisely what we expect and hope from our law enforcement officers…Ms. Horne was assaulted by her colleague, and her employment was terminated," according to the court filing. "In Buffalo, in America, and in the world, the public is now recognizing the cost of not having officers like Ms. Horne who are willing to intervene."

She won the lawsuit with back pay and a full pension.

Though Horne and several police officers, current and retired, view the issues of police use of excessive and fatal force through the prism of racism, it's not simply an issue of white officers versus Black men and women. Studies on police use of deadly force reach similar conclusions that Blacks and other minorities make up a disproportionate number of those shot by police, but many of those studies had opposing conclusions on whether racial bias by officers played a role. Generally, researchers say the issue is more complicated than white versus Black, and factors such as how often police come in contact with white and Black people and other criteria are not always available across departments.

One study, "Blue on Black," by Georgia State University College of Law professor Nirej Sekhon, analyzed 270 police shootings in Chicago from 2006 and 2014. The data came from the Chicago Independent Police Review Authority (IPRA). The study of what was then the third-largest police force in the United States showed:

- 95 percent of the 270 shooting victims were minority
- 80 percent of the victims were Black
- 70 percent of the off-duty shootings were done by Black officers (but more than half of the off-duty shootings in the IPRA reports involve an attempted robbery of an officer or a burglary of his property)
- 59 percent of on-duty shootings by uniformed officers were by white officers
- 48 percent of on-duty shootings by plainclothes officers were by white officers

Among its conclusions were that there was not sufficient data to conclude whether most or all police shootings could be explained in terms of individual officer's racist malice. A key reason, researchers generally agree, is that it is hard to compare police use of force incidents, including fatal shootings, across jurisdictions, because there is no single standard for departments to compile the information. Details collected in each incident vary from department to department, sometimes within the same state.

Writing in *Scientific American* in 2019, Lynne Peeples said the social science research community is debating which police incidents to track and include in studies and which details should be given the most weight, "such as whether the victim was armed or had previous contact with the police."

A key point of the Chicago study revealed that a difference

can be made by elected officials, mayors, county executives, and the like.

"The enforcement choices police make in these [Black and minority neighborhoods] may create unnecessary risk of officer-involved shootings." In other words, the manner in which law enforcement police Black and lower-income neighborhoods at least partially accounts for the disproportionate representation of Black victims of deadly police shootings.

Donald Temple, a Washington, D.C.–based attorney who led the now-defunct D.C. Civilian Complaint Review Board, noted that his experience with the review board, and as a criminal defense and civil case attorney, suggest that "not all police officers are bad, but the bad police officers are very bad."

While overseeing the Civilian Complaint Review Board, he received death threats from officers the board was investigating. "The biggest thing I witnessed over those years was the language difference. The way police [who were] patrolling in lower-income neighborhoods talked to people was very different than the way they talked to people and treated people in upper-income, white neighborhoods," Temple said. "A big language difference, and they set the tone for differences in the way officers policed in those neighborhoods. It's more than a training issue. It's more than a Black and white issue, because I've seen Black officers do horrible things to Black people."

Alexander Williams is a retired federal judge and former state prosecutor who led the Maryland Commission to Restore Trust in Policing for more than two years. The commission was formed to make recommendations on police reform after more than a dozen members of the Baltimore Police Gun Trace Task Force were charged or convicted of corruption-related offenses in federal court.

"No one who is sincere can dispute the numbers," Williams said. "The numbers have been consistent for ages. Always been a disproportionate number of Black people victimized by police excessive force, fatal or otherwise. Police have been running rampant in African American communities. Years ago, in Prince George's County, they had the Death Squad. That was the culture then and now in police departments across the country. So, this has been happening for a long time. In African American communities, police concentrate on street crimes, drug enforcement. They don't do that in white communities."

Historically, police actions—including shootings—have sparked protests and rioting in Black communities. In Los Angeles in 1965 (thirty-four dead). In Detroit in 1967 (forty-three dead). In Newark, New Jersey, in 1967 (twenty-six dead). In Miami in 1980 (eighteen dead). In Los Angeles in 1992 (fifty-nine dead). In Cincinnati in 2001 (seventy injured). And in 2014 in Ferguson, Missouri; 2015 in Baltimore; 2016 in Charlotte. In each of these instances, Black communities again were the concentration of anger and unrest with law enforcement. But those protests, for the most part, remained in the locale in which the police use of excessive force that sparked the demonstrations happened—not at all like the killing of Floyd, which launched protests and riots across the United States and around the world.

"People are more attuned to what police are doing now because of technology and social media. And the pandemic helped to focus attention. Police have to be held accountable. And, yes, I believe they are going to be," Williams said.

THE POWER OF POLICE UNIONS

On the first day of his first year on campus at the University of Maryland, College Park, Julian Ivey picked up the key to his dorm room from Annapolis Hall, the South Campus greeting center. It was the fall of 2013. His mother dropped him off. She had a severe headache that forced her to wait inside her car in a parking lot at the side of the building. Julian Ivey was inside for only several minutes.

He picked up the key to his room, grabbed a "welcome package," a Maryland backpack and a campus map. And he headed outside, figuring he'd hitch a ride with his mother to the dormitory, the place he'd live for the next nine months. No more than twenty-five steps from the front entrance to Annapolis Hall, he got an unofficial greeting to the campus in Central Maryland: Six Maryland State Police troopers surrounded him, hands on their weapons.

"They said I fit the description," recalled Ivey, who is Black. "That was enough for them to think their lives were in danger. Why else would they put their hands on their guns? I was standing there holding all that University of Maryland gear I had just gotten. But to them, it was clear that I was an 'other' on campus. I was viewed as a threat."

Still surrounded by the state troopers, Ivey used his mobile phone to call his mother.

"He said the police have me," Jolene Ivey remembered. "I bolted out of the car." She said she must have reached her son and the troopers in a few seconds. She couldn't believe the state troopers had her son surrounded with their hands on their guns. She asked what was going on, trying to keep her composure. "They kept saying he fit the description. I asked what description. I didn't get an answer. They finally said, 'You can go.'

"He was traumatized," she said.

The troopers didn't know that Ivey's father, Glenn, was a recent state's attorney—the highest-ranking elected law enforcement officer in Prince George's County, where the Maryland campus resides, and his mother, Jolene, was the chair of the county delegation to the state legislature.

The troopers never shared with Julian Ivey or his mother what the description was. By his own "description," Ivey is short, light-skinned,

141

and stocky. That day he was wearing athletic shorts. "They finally just said 'you can go,'" Julian Ivey said. "No apology or anything."

Less than thirty minutes later, the Iveys were in his dormitory room on the sprawling campus about nine miles northeast of the White House. They looked out the window and saw the same group of state troopers. "They had another Black guy surrounded. He was dark-skinned and tall. Over six feet. He was wearing khaki shorts. We didn't look *anything* alike," Julian said.

A few minutes later, from the same dormitory, his mother saw the troopers stop yet another young Black man. "Neither of them looked anything like Julian," she said. "I went outside and confronted them, told them it looked like they were just stopping any young Black man. They said they were looking for two different suspects. That was bullshit."

Later, settling in to his first night on the Maryland campus, he finally understood just how unsettling his encounter had been. His mother was a force in the state legislature and the state Democratic Party, and his father was a former federal prosecutor and twice-elected top prosecutor in their home county—but that didn't matter. "My mother was parked not even twenty yards away, but there was nothing she could do about it. I started thinking about how close that situation could have changed. Fast. If I ever thought that I was somehow privileged, that I was somehow protected…it stopped that day. I could have been shot. And my mother was right there."

That "situation," as Ivey called it, pushed him toward a calling to protest, to demonstrate, to demand change. His friends on campus encouraged him to speak out. He did. After the encounter with troopers, Ivey led demonstrations on campus protesting police profiling of Black and Latino students, as well as other "racial incidents on campus." It was a relatively easy move for Ivey, who had worked for years as a child actor, starting with Comcast commercials at age four, a role in a Shakespeare Theatre production of *A Midsummer Night's Dream* in D.C. at age six, and a role on Broadway as the young Simba in *The Lion King* at age eleven. "When we started the demonstrations at Maryland, I remember thinking, 'They have to deal with me now.'"

The demonstrations led to sporadic coverage from local TV stations, but there were few tangible changes implemented on campus by the administration—until after commencement weekend his senior year. The pockets of racism that Ivey and other students had protested about for four years became too real for the university administration when a white Maryland student with ties to white supremacist groups stabbed and killed a Black male ROTC student visiting campus from nearby Bowie State University. Richard Collins III had just been commissioned by the U.S. Army as a second lieutenant and was preparing to be deployed to the demilitarized zone between South Korea and North Korea. Collins and Ivey "weren't friends, but we knew each other, you know we had at times been interested in some of the same young women." The fatal stabbing reminded Ivey, again, how quickly "situations" can turn into tragedies. Sean Urbanski was convicted of first-degree murder, but the hate-crime charges were dropped.

Ivey entered politics after graduation, first as a member of the Cheverly Town Council, in the town where he was raised. Before leaving that elected position, he helped to uncover that the town's police department had an unwritten policy to stop Black and Latino drivers within the town's borders in a misguided effort to combat auto thefts. Now twenty-six, Ivey is a state delegate taking his fight for police reform to the legislature. During the months of Black Lives Matter protests, he repeatedly called on Larry Hogan, Maryland's Republican governor, to call a special legislative session. Ivey's main target: the Maryland Law Enforcement Officers' Bill of Rights.

In 1974, Maryland was among the first states in the country to pass a bill of rights for law enforcement officers. The legislation, pushed by unions representing police officers, in many cases set up protections for law enforcement officers that "essentially puts them in a special class of individuals," Ivey said, even when they are ensnarled in the criminal justice system. In Maryland, for example, law enforcement officers under investigation can avoid being interviewed for up to five days—delays not afforded civilians. In the same state, an officer charged with a felony or misdemeanor cannot automatically be fired from the force—because of bill of rights protections that allow officers to stay in jobs unless they are convicted, no matter the circumstances of the crime. It limits, and in some cases prohibits, access to disciplinary files of officers. It sets time and other limits on the filing of complaints against officers and requires all complaints filed to include personal information on the person making the complaint. It bans any drug tests, polygraph tests, or alcohol tests ordered as part of an investigation of an officer from being admissible in a criminal court proceeding.

Police unions "have been making deals for decades," Ivey said about the laws protecting police officers. "Now they are acting as if these 'rights' cannot be taken away."

Two states—Maryland and Rhode Island—are considered to have the most police-friendly bill of rights for law enforcement, according to Richard DeShay Elliott, a graduate student at Johns Hopkins University in Baltimore who has researched the impact of these laws across the country. Both were among the first states to enact these protective laws for officers. Rhode Island's law came in 1976.

"They started in Democratic stronghold states: Maryland, Rhode Island, California," said Elliott, whose work, "Impact of the Law Enforcement Officers' Bill of Rights on Policy Transparency and Accountability," was published on the Social Sciences Research Network website. Several states have some versions of these laws, with

Kentucky, Texas, Alabama, and Arizona the most recent states to adopt versions from the mid-1990s through the early 2000s. Unions in at least ten other states have tried but failed to pass versions of the bill of rights. "For so long, the issue of policing has been focused on other aspects, like better hiring and training," Elliott said. "However, these bills are the main impediment to accountability for police officers."

The conclusions of Elliott's study are stunning—and worrisome.

Only seventeen states and the District of Columbia have a version of the law enforcement officers' bill of rights, about 33 percent of the states. Yet, those seventeen account for a majority or near-majority of several categories of law enforcement shootings, including 54 percent of police shootings of civilians and 51 percent of police shootings of Black people. Those seventeen jurisdictions account for 80 percent of police shootings of Latinos, and 43 percent of officers involved in shootings while on duty.

"There is a clear link between states with Law Enforcement Officers' Bill of Rights and police shootings," Elliott said. Those laws clearly are "detriments to police accountability and transparency to the general public, and allow police officers to avoid scrutiny for misconduct up to and including murder of civilians while on duty."

In 2015, after the death of Freddie Gray, a Black man who died under mysterious circumstances while in the custody of Baltimore police officers, riots erupted for several days. State lawmakers looked at policing in the state, and a working group of legislators focused then on the Law Enforcement Officers' Bill of Rights.

"The only significant 'reform' was reducing the number of days that officers under investigation could delay being questioned from ten days to five," Julian Ivey said. "This time we're looking for sweeping reform, especially with the Law Enforcement Officers' Bill of Rights. When there are no repercussions for officers who do bad acts, if there is no accountability, you have removed an incentive to not commit bad acts. If they know they could lose their jobs, lose their pensions if you wrongfully use excessive force, then we might start getting a handle on the problem."

He is also seeking to establish statewide use of force standards for officers and improve training and lengthen the time recruits spend in the police academy. "We have to regain the community's trust by changing the culture of police departments."

The umbrella organization of the Fraternal Order of Police (FOP) Lodge in Maryland is more than aware that these conversations are taking place. "They are working really hard to stop these reforms," Ivey said. "The FOP is so powerful, it would take an act of God to completely repeal the Law Enforcement Officers' Bill of Rights."

The Alexander Williams–led Maryland Commission to Restore Trust in Policing in early fall 2020 was considering a range of options before making recommendations to the state on actions needed to restore public confidence and trust in law enforcement. The considerations include getting rid of the Law Enforcement Officers' Bill of Rights. "I can't imagine there will be any more Law Enforcement Officers' Bill of Rights," Williams said. "We have to hold officers more accountable. We also have to use psychological screening for hires and while on the job. And we need to get hurdles out of the way to allow the collection of data about arrests, traffic stops, and other information that gives a clear picture of how departments are policing our communities."

A lawyer representing one police union spoke at a commission meeting arguing that the Law Enforcement Officers' Bill of Rights wasn't the problem. The problem was poor management in the Baltimore Police Department, whose leadership is pushing to significantly change the bill of rights. "The true problem is the mismanagement and incompetency of the [Baltimore Police Department] to follow the law like every other law enforcement agency in the State of Maryland," Michael Davey said.

Police unions—whether the Fraternal Order of Police (FOP), the Police Benevolent Association (PBA), or some other name—have fought for years to maintain laws that protect their membership and to lobby for policy or budget changes using a similar tactic: fear. After the D.C. Council passed a package of police reform laws in the summer of 2020, the D.C. police union filed a federal lawsuit calling parts of the package unconstitutional. And they released a statement, saying that reform laws would not improve the quality of policing in Washington, D.C. "The legislation will only result in more applicants who have been rejected by other agencies as less qualified," the statement said, without providing evidence to back up its claims. "The legislation that has targeted D.C. police officers is already resulting in countless officers planning to retire from the department early or opt to resign to work in other jurisdictions."

The D.C. police union used the same fear tactic in the late 1980s, at the beginning of the crack epidemic, when then-D.C. mayor Marion Barry refused to increase the size of the city's police force as drug-related homicides and nonfatal shootings were on the rise. The union went to Congress, which had final say over the city's budget. The union said that more than half of the officers in the department would be eligible to retire in the next two to three years—an impending catastrophe the city could ill afford just as drug-related violence was exploding in the nation's capital. Congress forced the city to hire about 1,800 officers within two years, and voted to withhold the $430 million federal payment to the city in 1989 and 1990 if the city failed to hire the officers. The city complied, and the result was chaos. Without the infrastructure to properly screen and train applicants— and under a tight deadline—the city hired hundreds of new officers who, once on the force, ended up being charged with crimes ranging from rape to murder and drug dealing.

In the 2020 U.S. presidential cycle, New York City's largest police union, the PBA, endorsed Donald Trump's reelection, the first time the union made an endorsement in a presidential race in almost forty years. The head of the PBA told President Trump at an event to make the endorsement announcement that Trump had "earned" it because of his staunch support of law enforcement. In 2017, Trump even encouraged officers to rough up suspects being arrested.

In Chicago, the FOP leadership rejected a new contract in summer 2020 that came with a 10 percent raise because the deal included changes in the way the city would handle allegations of police misconduct. The proposed changes included keeping the names of those who file complaints from being disclosed until the person filing the complaint has been interviewed, allowing complaints filed anonymously to be investigated, and ending the practice of destroying an officer's disciplinary files.

When Alex Williams first ran for state's attorney in Prince George's County, Maryland, he ran on a platform to hold police accountable. He was challenging Arthur "Bud" Marshall Jr., a white man who had held the office since 1960. Police in the county had a notorious history of brutality against Black people. "Well, the FOP didn't support my campaign," Williams said. "I was an outsider. I wasn't a prosecutor." Most importantly, he pledged during the campaign to present all cases of police use of fatal excessive force to a county grand jury. That had never happened before.

"Once in office, some officers would say, 'Are you with us or against us?'"

Williams had little success bringing charges against police officers in cases where police had killed people, including the case of Archie Elliott. Generally, those cases are harder than others to get a grand jury to hand up charges, he said, even more so years ago when there wasn't widespread public videotaping. "Those are the toughest cases," Williams said. "We investigated [the Elliott case] thoroughly. I remember it. His father was a judge in Virginia, his mother was a teacher in public schools. It was an emotionally trying case. I put my lead investigator on it. I had the head of my homicide unit present the case to the grand jury. Based on the evidence we could present to the grand jury, the jury decided not to indict. His mother has worked hard to keep the case alive."

COURT CHANGES AND QUALIFIED IMMUNITY

Cynthia Lee, a professor at the George Washington University Law School and author of the book *Murder and the Reasonable Man: Passion and Fear in the Criminal Courtroom*, has had key provisions from her model legislation on police use of deadly force adopted by state and local lawmaking bodies, including in Connecticut, Virginia, and the District of Columbia. She came up with her model after observing that racial stereotypes impacted the outcome of many self-defense cases involving victims of color.

Among those were rare occasions when police officers faced charges related to excessive use of force and used self-defense—aka the justifiable force defense—as justification for their actions. She said that prior to the new laws in these jurisdictions, jurors would need only to find that officers "reasonably believed they needed to use deadly force." And because the officer-defendant would usually get on the stand and testify that he feared for his life, by and large, jury verdicts would find in favor of the officer.

"Most use of deadly force statutes require only a 'reasonable belief' that the use of deadly force was necessary to protect the officer or another from death or serious bodily injury," Lee said. In those cases that made it to trial where the victim was Black, attorneys for the officer "would focus on the dangerousness of the neighborhood and the victim's past criminal history or drug use"—a method that plays to stereotypes about Black people in general, and Black men in particular.

The new use of force laws in Connecticut, Virginia, and D.C. require a finding that both the officer's beliefs *and* actions were reasonable. They also require that all other options were exhausted, if other options were feasible. The new laws also give juries more guidance. Juries will have to consider three factors when deciding whether an officer's beliefs and actions were "reasonable":

- Whether the victim had a weapon or appeared to have one and refused to drop it.
- Whether the officer engaged in de-escalation tactics prior to using deadly force.
- Whether the officer engaged in any conduct before the use of force that increased the risk of a deadly confrontation.

"At least with respect to factors two and three, the aim is to encourage jurors to think about things they wouldn't necessarily think of on their own," Lee said. "In requiring that officers not use deadly force unless they have tried less deadly options, the newly adopted legislation hammers home that officers should not use deadly force unless it is really necessary to do so.

"Even if these changes in the law don't change verdicts in officer-involved shooting cases immediately, they might do so over time," Lee said. "The real goal here is to change police culture. And changes in the law can change culture. We've seen how changes in rape law in the 1970s and 1980s helped change the culture surrounding sex and eventually paved the way to the #metoo movement. Changes in use of force laws can have the same kind of influence on police culture.

"Prior to George Floyd's death, there wasn't an appetite to change policing laws," Lee observed. "Legislators thought their communities wanted law and order. The racial justice protests have helped push through police reform legislation that will do a better job of holding officers accountable than existing laws."

Back in 2013, Clarence Jamison, a Black man, was headed back to his home in South Carolina after a vacation in Arizona. He was driving a Mercedes-Benz convertible along Interstate 20. At some point, in Pelahatchie, Mississippi, he passed Richland Police Department officer Nick McClendon. The officer is white. Jamison's recently purchased Benz still had temporary tags, but the officer said the rear tag was "folded over" and he couldn't read it.

So he pulled Jamison over. The driver provided his driver's license, proof of insurance, and even a bill of sale for the vehicle, as the officer requested. They all were clean. The officer even ran a criminal history check on Jamison. That, too, was clean. Still, Officer McClendon asked Jamison several times for permission to search his car.

Jamison asked, "For what?"

"To search for illegal narcotics, weapons, large amounts of money, anything illegal," the officer responded.

The stop and search lasted nearly two hours. No weapons or contraband were found. And Jamison, who works as a welder, was on his way. But he later sued McClendon in federal court, claiming he was falsely stopped, detained, and searched.

At some point in the civil case, McClendon asked for summary judgment and for the case to be dismissed, saying he was protected from claims by the qualified immunity doctrine, which generally says that officers and other public officials should be shielded from civil liability claims when they act in good faith. In summer 2020, U.S. District Court judge Carlton W. Reeves, an African American, issued a seventy-two-page opinion reluctantly granting qualified immunity protection to Officer McClendon—protecting the officer from any liability for stopping Jamison essentially without cause. Reeves began his opinion listing a litany of circumstances under which Black men and women had died in encounters with police:

"Clarence Jamison wasn't jaywalking.

"He wasn't outside playing with a toy gun.

"He didn't look like a suspicious person.

"He wasn't suspected of selling loose, untaxed cigarettes.

"He wasn't suspected of passing a counterfeit $20 bill.

"He didn't look like anyone suspected of a crime.

"He wasn't mentally ill and in need of help.

"He wasn't assisting an autistic patient who had wandered away from a group home.

"He wasn't walking home from an after-school job.

"He wasn't walking back from a restaurant.

"He wasn't hanging out on a college campus.

"He wasn't standing outside of his apartment.

"He wasn't inside his apartment eating ice cream.

"He wasn't sleeping in his bed.

"He wasn't sleeping in his car.

"He didn't make an improper lane change.

"He didn't have a broken tail light.

"He wasn't driving over the speed limit.

"Thankfully," the judge wrote, "Jamison left the stop with his life. Too many others have not. Tragically, thousands have died at the hands of law enforcement over the years, and the death toll continues to rise. Countless more have suffered from other forms of abuse and misconduct by police. Qualified immunity has served as a shield for these officers, protecting them from accountability.

"Under that law, the officer who transformed a short traffic stop into an almost two-hour, life-altering ordeal is entitled to qualified immunity. The officer's motion seeking as much is therefore granted. But let us not be fooled by legal jargon. Immunity is not exoneration. And the harm in this case done to one man, sheds light on the harm done to the nation by this manufactured doctrine. As the Fourth Circuit concluded, 'This has to stop.'"

The judge, who is assigned to the Southern District of Mississippi, urged the U.S. Supreme Court to take on cases that challenge the qualified immunity doctrine. "Overturning qualified immunity will undoubtedly impact our society," Judge Reeves wrote. "Yet, the status quo is extraordinary and unsustainable. Just as the Supreme Court swept away the mistaken doctrine of 'separate but equal,' so too should it eliminate the doctrine of qualified immunity."

Dorothy Elliott encountered the doctrine of qualified immunity when she and her former husband sued the officers who killed their son Artie and the police departments where the officers worked. Like the officer in the Mississippi case, the Maryland officers sought a summary judgment to have the lawsuit dismissed, as they were protected from personal liability by qualified immunity. A U.S. District Court denied the officers' request, but that ruling was reversed by the U.S. Court of Appeals Fourth Circuit. "We reverse the judgment of the District Court, finding that the officers' use of deadly force in response to an obvious, serious and immediate threat to their safety was reasonable," the Appeals Court opinion said.

Elliott appreciates the changes in laws, the efforts to hold police officers more accountable. She keeps working to keep her son's memory alive. She has established the Archie Elliott Scholarship Fund to award financial support—already thousands of dollars—in his name to minority students who attend HBCUs. She said she's learned to live with the pain of losing her older son to a hail of bullets fired by police officers. In those moments when she wonders how we will ever get past this seemingly unending cycle of Blacks dying at the hands of police officers, Dylann Roof comes to mind.

Roof is the white supremacist sentenced to death for slaughtering nine Black churchgoers inside a Charleston, South Carolina, church in 2015. When police in nearby Shelby, North Carolina, arrested Roof, he hadn't eaten in about two days. So the officers sent out for a hamburger and other food from Burger King to feed the then-accused killer of nine innocent Black people.

"If law enforcement would just see Black people the same way they see white people, that would go a long way toward ending this problem," Dorothy Elliott said. She called on police officers to treat African Americans the same way they treated the mass murderer who fatally shot those nine Black members of a prayer group inside Emanuel African Methodist Episcopal Church. He was arrested without incident. "Just treat us, treat Blacks, the same way they treated Dylann Roof in South Carolina," she said.

LOCKING UP BLACK LIVES

BY PATRICE GAINES

ON THE AFTERNOON OF Saturday, May 30, 2020, a Black father searched for his family among the protesters gathered at Love Park in Philadelphia's Center City. It was five days after the killing of George Floyd, and Qadree (pronounced Kwa-dree) Jacobs was looking for his ex-wife, Shay, and their two young children. If he couldn't find them in the crowd, how could he keep them safe?

He had sworn to care for his new family in a way he had not been able to care for his elder son.

Jacobs served fifteen years in prison for selling drugs. He marks that time by the significant events he missed in the life of his namesake, "Lil Qad."

"I missed sixteen of his birthdays...my son losing his first tooth, having his first girlfriend. I missed the first time he dribbled a basketball and made a basket, when he rode a bike with no training wheels."

He paused to catch his breath.

"When he learned to tie his shoe. His first grade, second grade, third grade. I missed his first birds-and-bees talk. The first time he got into a fight. I missed everything."

Now Jacobs is forty-two. Lil Qad is twenty-three.

155

The first thing Jacobs did when he was released from prison was to go to his son's house and hug him.

Jacobs admits he made poor decisions. He broke the law.

But there is also this: By the time he sold crack, he had been a child who lived with addicts, experienced hunger for weeks at a time; had been molested by a relative and held a friend as he died from bullet wounds. In his world, selling drugs, or risking death to earn a living, was an acceptable antidote to hopelessness.

On that sunny afternoon of protests, Jacobs spotted Shay cuddling their one-year-old son, Sakou, while their three-year-old, SuSu, stood nearby in her pristine white tennis shoes holding a cardboard sign that said: "I Stand for Justice."

Jacobs bent his six-foot frame, lifted his son to his shoulders, and together the family marched down Broad Street.

They joined a crowd of hundreds that surely included many people like him, Black men and women who had spent years incarcerated, or some who still had loved ones locked in cages.

They marched to protest the killing by a Minnesota police officer of a man who had spent a quarter of his adult life incarcerated. In one conviction George Floyd served ten months behind bars for a ten-dollar drug deal, a conviction under review now because the arresting officer is suspected of fabricating evidence in other low-level drug cases. Like Jacobs, Floyd made bad choices, spending four years incarcerated on drug and robbery charges. He had difficulty finding work, partly because of his criminal record.

Research shows that Black men ages thirty-five to forty-four who have been formerly incarcerated have an unemployment rate of 35.2 percent. White men in that category have a rate of 18.4 percent.

The toll of being convicted is significant and, in addition to job discrimination, can include exclusion from voter rolls, and disqualification from food stamps, public housing, and student loans. Justice advocates have coined the phrase "death by incarceration" to emphasize the finality of life without parole sentences handed out regularly and disproportionately to Black people by U.S. judges.

Floyd had moved to Minnesota to get a fresh start.

Now the world knows his name.

Ben Crump, the attorney representing Floyd's family, told protesters in Louisville, "There seem to be two justice systems in America. One for Black America, and one for white America."

The difference between those two systems is horrifying. Though Black people make up just 13 percent of the population, they are 32.9 percent of the 2.2 million people incarcerated. One in five Black men is serving what are effectively life sentences. There were almost 500,000 Black lives locked away in state or federal prisons at the end of 2018.

One out of every three Black boys can expect to be incarcerated.

The criminal justice system reserves its harshest punishment for Black people. When a crack epidemic devastated some Black communities in the 1980s and '90s, the response by the government was to proclaim "war," deploy armored cars, and order raids on crack houses; and to create longer mandatory sentences for crack users, who were generally Black people. The government decided the penalty for possession of crack would be a hundred times greater than for possession of the same amount of powdered cocaine, the drug then favored by whites.

Instead of responding to the crack epidemic as if it were a public health crisis and increasing funds to rehabilitation clinics, the government increased funding to local police departments, turning them into paramilitary operations.

But when a new wave of opioid and heroin deaths hit white communities, the government responded in a more humane way. State governments increased money for rehabilitation, and the federal government began to investigate doctors who prescribed opioids. The white addict was often portrayed as a sympathetic victim while the Black addict was a criminal deserving punishment.

Jacobs wants to believe that the protesting in 2020 will make a difference. But he is weary. Black people are weary—and angry—about historically receiving the most brutal punishments in America.

They have been enslaved, sold back into slavery as "laborers" and leased as convicts to work themselves to death building wealth for white corporations. When Black bodies were left swinging from trees or beaten and mutilated, then tossed into rivers, those extrajudicial murders were called "law and order." Now, when they are shot down in a city street by police, it too is called "law and order."

To many white people, the disparity in the imprisonment of Black people just proves they are right to believe that Black people are inherently violent and criminal. Since the civil rights era, this myth has been deliberately nurtured by politicians who unabashedly use coded phrases such as "law and order" and "get tough on crime" to placate white fears and win white votes. This has not changed since a 1968 *Time* magazine article in which a supporter of then–presidential candidate George Wallace said: "Y'all know about law and order. It's spelled n-i-g-g-e-r-s."

During the 2020 presidential campaign, Donald Trump and Vice President Mike Pence mentioned "law and order" more than ninety times.

These days, as Jacobs rides in his Philadelphia Water Department truck past his old neighborhood, he sees evidence that the cycle of addiction and punishment will continue. And knows that it is the children who will suffer.

"I see people out on the streets who are on drugs, and I wonder why the government isn't doing anything, and what is happening to their kids?" he asked, recalling his own childhood.

"Every kid in the street has PTSD," Jacobs said. "You see people dying. You see big guns. You see drugs. No kid should have to deal with this. No kid should have to figure out a way to eat or how he will survive."

Jacobs knows these endangered children could easily end up in prison unless this cycle is interrupted, not necessarily by removing the children but by removing the poverty, assisting the families, and strengthening the communities. He wants to believe that George Floyd's life—not just his death—will serve as a megaphone to raise the voices of activists calling for prison reform.

If Black children's lives matter, shouldn't the life of a troubled, hungry child living in a poor neighborhood devoid of greenery and hope be saved and that child be educated at richly financed public schools? That, he said, would be far better than having prisons built with the anticipation that these children will end up there.

The questions are obvious: Can America save a Black child without locking him up for fifteen years when he becomes a man—or does America even want to? How do we dismantle a system built on structural racism that disproportionately sentences and locks up Black people? What can we build that is fair and equitable and provides substantially better public safety?

We are at the tipping point. It is time to listen to the voices of advocates who speak for those Black bodies that have been silenced, locked away in cages, made invisible, rendered powerless for years.

PHILADELPHIA: THE CITY OF BROTHERLY PRISONS

Qadree Jacobs's hometown of Philadelphia is known as the birthplace of the nation, but it is also home of its first penitentiary. In more recent days, some reports also call it the city with the highest incarceration rate of any large jurisdiction in this country.

Since 2015, the city has worked under a national grant to decrease the local jail population and reduce racial, ethnic, and economic disparities in the criminal justice system. Still, in November of 2020, non-Hispanic Blacks represented 42 percent of the city's population, but they made up 73.6 percent of the people incarcerated. NAACP researchers found the poorest neighborhoods in Philadelphia had the highest rate of incarceration and the lowest performing schools. While the government uses millions from taxpayers to keep citizens imprisoned, it seems unwilling to increase funds to educate inner-city children.

Jacobs grew up in North Philadelphia, in one of the nine neighborhoods representing a quarter of the city's population and accounting for 50 percent of all adults sent to Pennsylvania prisons from Philadelphia. Jacobs also attended some of the lowest performing schools, dropping out in tenth grade.

In 2017, Philadelphians elected a progressive district attorney, Larry Krasner, who joined the new wave of reform-minded DAs who have won offices in major cities such as Los Angeles, Detroit, and Chicago. Jacobs's father, a recovering addict also once incarcerated, knocked on doors and did some organizing to help Krasner get elected. Since taking office, Krasner, like most of the newly elected criminal justice reformers, has earned the ire of law enforcement for his changes that thus far have included diverting nonviolent offenders from prison, eliminating cash bail on some charges, and decriminalizing weed possession.

Other DAs are watching Philadelphia, which in some ways is ground zero for the fight between the left pushing for revolutionary change in criminal justice and the right, still pushing for "law and order" that will "make America great again."

Krasner, who as a civil rights and defense attorney sued police at least seventy-five times, was embroiled in a public debate with Trump-appointed U.S. Attorney Bill McSwain. As U.S. Attorney for the Eastern District of Pennsylvania, McSwain represented Trump's Justice Department, which expressed disdain for the national reform movement.

Krasner and McSwain battled over how to resolve criminal cases, with McSwain using his power to supersede Krasner's office. In one case, after the city negotiated a three-and-a-half- to ten-year sentence for a man who shot a storeowner with an AK-47, leaving him wheelchair bound, McSwain sentenced the man to fourteen years. In another case, McSwain announced federal charges against two men for gun-related crimes, saying Krasner's office mishandled the case.

Shortly after the DA's election, at the close of meetings between the two, Krasner told McSwain, "You are gonna lose and Trump's gonna lose, because history is not on your side."

The country's first prison, established as the Jail and Penitentiary House at Walnut Street, was founded in 1790 by a group of white men in Philadelphia. Their goal was to improve conditions at the Walnut Street Jail, which locked up men and women together, did not classify people by offenses or age, and allowed the purchase of liquor. The new penitentiary offered private cells, where the founders thought prisoners could reflect in solitude on what they had done wrong.

Leslie Patrick-Stamp, a history professor at Bucknell University, examined the documents of that first penitentiary, concluding, "This evidence reveals that Black people did in fact endure disproportionate imprisonment in this country's first state prison."

Patrick-Stamp noted that prior to the opening of Walnut Street Jail and Penitentiary House, the Pennsylvania legislature passed in 1780 the "Act for the Gradual Abolition of Slavery," which began the process to end slavery in the Commonwealth. The last slaves in Pennsylvania weren't freed until 1847—sixty-seven years later.

The legislation, theoretically, eliminated racially specific courts and penal practices and imposed a uniform penal code for people of all races.

Nevertheless, Patrick-Stamp found that the 3,053 Black people sentenced to the state penitentiary between May 1790 and June 1791 made up 14.9 percent of the prison's population. Black people made up 2.3 percent of Pennsylvania's population at the time.

"Urban Black people were overrepresented in the penitentiary with 85 percent of the total Black prison population sentenced from Philadelphia courts, while they constituted only 35.3 percent of the commonwealth's Black population," wrote Patrick-Stamp.

In rural Pennsylvania different means were used to control Black people, such as curfews and threats of exile and of unemployment. Just like today, Black women were incarcerated at a much higher rate (per capita) than white women, though there were more Black men in total incarcerated. White men believed Black women were immoral and lacked dutifulness to family.

When a series of fires engulfed York, Pennsylvania, in 1803, only Black people were found guilty of arson. The state's attorney general proclaimed arson "the crime of slaves and children."

Most Black people sentenced to the Walnut Street prison came from the South, likely to escape slavery. While the prison's records were incomplete, Patrick-Stamp occasionally came across some specifics: Ester Green, condemned to Walnut Street in 1796, born on the Maryland plantation of Robert Hoops, jailed for stealing goods and chattel worth $72.50; Samuel Jackson, laborer, convicted of larceny in 1814; Teeny Deal, "a Negress," born in Philadelphia and sentenced for larceny. Upon her release from prison, Deal was "pardoned and discharged by the Governor, upon condition of leaving the state forthwith not to return."

The largest group of incarcerated Black men were common laborers, such as chimney sweeps. The second-largest group provided personal services and included waiters, house servants, and barbers. The smallest group had worked in skilled occupations, such as cabinetmakers, shoemakers, and painters.

The largest group among Black women were domestics and servants.

These were poor people. The Prison Sentence Dockets showed that

83.8 percent of the 3,053 Black people committed to the penitentiary between 1794 and 1835 were jailed for larceny or for stealing tools, food, clothing, and other goods.

Speaking at a national conference of the American Correctional Association in 2005, Patrick-Stamp said: "Such numbers only confirm a long-standing belief held by many African Americans that they always have been disproportionately represented in this country's prisons. Most Black people know intuitively and experientially that racial discrimination in the criminal justice system always has existed in the U.S."

While the North often gets a pass because of the abolition movement, Patrick-Stamp said imprisonment by the state began in the North and that all the states, except New Jersey, founded their prisons after abolishing slavery.

In other words, after slavery, prison became the new method of controlling Black bodies.

"What need was there for imprisoning the black populace when there was slavery, an institution which performed functions quite similar to the prison?" Patrick-Stamp asked.

Before it closed in 1835, the Walnut Street Penitentiary became known for being the first to use inmates for labor. Western State Penitentiary opened in 1826, and a few years later, Eastern State Penitentiary in Philadelphia opened, featuring cells equipped with feed doors to minimize contact with other humans.

Eastern State Penitentiary, now a museum, describes its first prisoner this way: "Charles Williams, Prisoner Number One. Burglar. Light Black Skin... Sentenced to two years confinement with labor."

Nearly two centuries later, Black people still fill Pennsylvania prisons, and Black Philadelphians still represent a disproportionate number of those caged in the state's prisons.

THE ROAD TO PRISON IS PAVED WITH HOPELESSNESS

Brenda Jacobs was walking across the street of her North Philadelphia neighborhood, munching on fried fish, cradling her six-month-old son, Qadree, in her arms.

Her cousin waited on her front porch. Suddenly, Brenda fell. Her cousin ran to catch the baby.

Brenda Jacobs was dead at twenty-eight. She choked on a fish bone.

Years later, Qadree Jacobs would blame himself for her death after drunk relatives told him repeatedly that his mother was headed across the street to show him off. Then when he was nineteen, Jacobs finally asked his mom's cousin what happened that day, and she told him his mother was coming over to finish a conversation she didn't want anyone to hear: She was going to take her kids and move away from Jacobs's father, a heroin addict, fleeing from him and a house crowded with alcoholic relatives. If Brenda Jacobs had lived, perhaps her son's life would have been completely different, devoid of poverty, neglect, sexual abuse—and prison.

For a while, the family remained in the house Brenda had owned, a total of thirteen people in a one-bathroom house. When Jacobs was five, his father stopped using drugs and came home and told his sons, "Pack up your things. We got a house."

They put their belongings in a grocery cart and walked to another house nearby. For the first week or so the new house didn't have electricity or water, but the boys were happy because the crowd was gone, and their father wasn't using drugs.

"We painted the walls. We had candles," said Jacobs. "We made it our home."

His father worked for a city councilman and took his sons to political rallies.

"We met Jesse Jackson and Bishop Desmond Tutu—and had a car," said Jacobs.

Then things began to change again. Jacobs remembers watching four people at a time go into the tiny bathroom and stay for what seemed like hours. Eventually, after seeing his father sit in a chair and nod all day, he came to know that the people he saw were shooting up heroin in their bathroom and that his father had started shooting drugs again. The house fell apart, and his sons were neglected. Jacobs grew angry with his father.

"I thought he chose drugs over us. But now I think: He put a roof over our heads and taught us to not let anything come between us. I don't know what his demons were."

Jacobs's father was born to a teenage mother and a father who was married to someone else and didn't acknowledge him. The elder Jacobs was a teenager when he met his father. He grew up with three siblings in a Philadelphia high-rise housing project, hustling—first legally—from the time he was in first grade, stocking store shelves and shining shoes, then later turning to illegal hustles, selling fake gold rings, picking pockets, and burglarizing.

But Wayne Jacobs had one experience in seventh grade that would hint at the potential he possessed and the joy it could bring him. He joined a local civil rights leader in protesting at a construction site where Black people were not being hired. This was during the Black Power movement, and Jacobs was struck by the possibilities and power he possessed even as a kid when fighting for Black advancement.

But the senior Jacobs dropped out of school in the tenth grade when he wasn't allowed to wear an Afro for class photos. He increased his hustle, went to prison for a break-in. By twenty, he was hooked on heroin, and life turned into a revolving prison door.

"I got busted fifty-two times," he said.

His last stint ended in 1997. He was forty-seven and finally drug-free. He has since become a noted community activist in Philadelphia and has worked in some successful political campaigns. He co-founded X-Offenders for Community Empowerment with his friend

Steve Blackburn, also a formerly incarcerated person. The nonprofit group works to empower convicted people to become "change agents" and helps them in securing pardons from the governor.

But when Qadree Jacobs was growing up, it was the block he called "family" that fed him.

"I used to go to our neighbors—get bread from one, sugar from another," said Jacobs. "Oatmeal from another. Butter. Another lady, her husband worked at the Slim Jim factory and she gave me Slim Jims.

"I'd get up and hustle—go to the store for people, dig pennies out the street tar and go to the store and get penny cookies for a meal," said Jacobs. "I went to school for breakfast and lunch. I went to school for heat."

But his father taught him that they were doing better than some neighborhood people because they were clean. It didn't matter that they washed their clothes in the bathtub or put cardboard in the bottom of their shoes when they had holes. Most of the other kids in the neighborhood were doing the same.

It was his North Philly community that was saving the Jacobs boys. The adults held block party talent shows, made a stage, hired a deejay, and served food, featuring toddlers modeling in a fashion show and performances by the youth of the community. Qadree Jacobs and his friends formed groups to sing R & B songs and dance.

It was the neighborhood ice-cream man, who used to give Jacobs free ice cream for watching his truck, who finally called child protective services about Jacobs and his brothers being hungry all the time and their father being on drugs.

Qadree always understood that the neighbor was doing what he thought was right to help him and his brothers.

Another neighbor tipped off his grandmother, who came to get the boys, who did not want to be separated, and take them to her house.

He moved a lot after that and went to three schools in sixth grade. At times he and his brothers had to split up between relatives. His father had another son and a daughter by a woman he dated, and Jacobs and his brothers considered them siblings.

But Jacobs was lost, falling into hopelessness despite the help of the adults in his community. He began to act out in school.

"I just wanted attention from my father," he said.

When he was twelve, Jacobs and five other friends chipped in money, which they had earned hustling, shooting dice, and running errands, to buy a .22 automatic pistol. Jacobs had already sneaked and held his oldest brother's gun and played with it a little bit. The first night he and his friends had their .22, one friend shot another friend they all considered a bully.

"The gun was in a brown paper bag on a tire, and we were shooting dice," Jacobs recalled. "My friend, the shooter, had the dice and the guy was talking trash, saying stuff like, 'I heard you got a gun. I'll make y'all eat that gun.'"

When the trash talker turned his back, the other friend got the gun.

"The guy turned, and he tried to shoot him in the face, but the gun didn't go off."

The victim fell, though, and when Jacobs's friend shot again, he hit the guy in his shoulder. Wounded, the boy nevertheless got on his bike and left with the shooter chasing him and still trying to fire the gun. Jacobs never saw that gun again, and the bully stopped bullying.

"A few years later my friend with the gun got shot in the head by someone who tried to shoot him in the chest, but he had on a vest. He had become a menace by that time. He had shot other people."

Witnessing one friend shoot another didn't scare him, Jacobs said. It was more like watching a cartoon or something that wasn't real. Eventually, carrying a gun and witnessing shootings became normal.

He was arrested for the first time after being caught with a gun at school. He was fifteen. He had taken his uncle's .38 Long Smith

& Wesson Police Special, an old service gun, and planned to use it to threaten a kid who had stolen money from a cousin. But he didn't get past the school's metal detector. He was expelled and sent to a detention center.

Once back home, he tried to return to school, but he just didn't have the discipline or desire to attend classes anymore. He dropped out in tenth grade, just like his dad. To provide regular meals for themselves and to buy popular expensive sneakers and clothes, the Jacobs boys began selling crack.

"The decision to turn to the streets hits kids in some neighborhoods at a certain age," Jacobs said. "Before that, a kid has dreams. Once they lose their dreams, that's it. They look outside and see poverty. At some point, I had no hope."

In *The Fire Next Time*, James Baldwin wrote of the summer he was thirteen: "Crime became real, for example—for the first time—not as a possibility but as *the* possibility. One would never defeat one's circumstances by working and saving one's pennies; one would never, by working, acquire that many pennies, and, besides, the social treatment accorded even the most successful Negroes proved that one needed, in order to be free, something more than a bank account. One needed a handle, a lever, a means of inspiring fear. It was absolutely clear that the police would whip you and take you in as long as they could get away with it, and that everyone else—housewives, taxi-drivers, elevator boys, dishwashers, bartenders, lawyers, judges, doctors, and grocers—would never, by the operation of any generous human feeling, cease to use you as an outlet for his frustrations and hostilities."

That was the summer Baldwin chose to become a child preacher, which surely gave him a sense of purpose and power. He later chose writing. But neither of those choices is available to every child suffering from hopelessness.

Jacobs said, "It felt good to be able to buy food and clothes." Soon he knew the cops who worked his neighborhood, and they knew him. He didn't find them particularly racist because he'd experienced Black cops lying and planting guns and dope on people in his neighborhood.

The Jacobs brothers also became neighborhood "Robin Hoods," giving money to kids, elders, and other neighbors when they needed help.

He was eighteen when his girlfriend got pregnant. Jacobs stopped hustling for a brief time and went to night school to get his GED and tried working as a dishwasher at Olive Garden. But he was used to making way more money selling drugs, so he returned to the streets.

He admits he was running the streets and hustling on the day his son, nicknamed Lil Qad, was born June 19, 1997. Qadree was nineteen. A relative called to tell him he was a father.

A couple of years later, early one afternoon, Jacobs walked out of the house, headed toward the block, where some friends stood. He heard what he thought was banging from construction at a nearby store.

Then somebody said, "No, that's gunshots. Weasel just walked that way."

Weasel was a friend, somebody Jacobs used to share conversations with about what they were trying to do for their families. He'd drop off Weasel at home and on the way, they'd smoke weed and talk.

Now he saw Weasel lying in the street. Jacobs fell to the ground, grabbed him, and held his head in his lap. He talked to Weasel, saying, "Keep your eyes open. Keep your eyes open. Talk to me."

Another guy opened Weasel's shirt.

"I saw blood coming out of bullet holes in his chest. He had a pager in his hand.

"I kept talking to him. I said, 'Weasel, you all right. Breathe! Breathe! Keep your eyes open, man.'"

Weasel's hand opened. The pager fell.

"I knew he died at that moment," said Jacobs.

It was the first dead body he'd seen in the street; it wouldn't be the last.

Jacobs and the two friends with him ran, but the cops caught him and took him to the station for questioning.

"They said, 'How do you know Walter Bryant?' I said, 'I don't know no Walter Bryant.'"

That's how he found out Weasel's real name.

"That was a rough time," he said of the period after Weasel was killed. "I had a few friends from North Philly get killed."

He started drinking cough syrup and popping pills to escape. Then on June 5, 2000, police charged Jacobs and his brother with running a crack cocaine operation. Jacobs maintains they were lone street dealers and not part of a large drug organization, and that co-defendants lied to get themselves better deals.

"In the streets, you already have it in your mind you're going to prison one day," Jacobs offered. "We had accepted that this is part of life. I knew there was a chance I'd get killed or go to prison. But there's also the real slim chance you can make some money and get out of the game. Everybody is counting on that real slim chance."

Some of his co-defendants were sentenced to life. Jacobs received thirty-five years. His middle brother, Rashid, was sentenced to thirty-one years, and his elder brother, Mark, got thirty-three years.

For some of his sentence he was incarcerated with Rashid in FCI Allenwood Medium in Allenwood, Pennsylvania. He would not see his older brother for sixteen years.

From prison, Jacobs did everything he could to continue fathering his son.

His son Qadree Jones, "Lil Qad," said, "He sent me money, poetry, taught me lessons and sent cards."

The son said he didn't understand where his father was until second grade.

"I realized I wouldn't see him for a while," said Jones. "It was tough because he called me every day, and I wanted him to be there with me."

Though it was against the rules to have a cell phone in prison, Jacobs had one that he used to call his kid. In prison, inmates were given 300 minutes a month on a pay phone, "which is nothing when you are trying to keep your family together and maintain a bond," Jacobs said.

Eventually, the prison discovered his cell phone, and his punishment was severe: Jacobs was transferred from Pennsylvania to a prison in Minnesota. He wrote letters to his son, called when he could, and sent him money earned on his prison job.

Both father and son called this their hardest time. Lil Qad spent a lot of time with his fraternal grandfather, which helped him. From prison, the father organized a tenth birthday party for his son.

"It was the birthday that I missed him most," Jones said. "My grandfather's house was decorated, there was a cake from him [his father]."

In Minnesota, as part of his punishment, Jacobs was also put in solitary, but he had inherited his own father's love of books. While "in the hole" he read voraciously and wrote poetry. Though his father was Muslim, Jacobs had not practiced the faith. In prison, he read the Quran—in one facility even serving as imam, the leader of the Muslim worshippers.

While the brothers were away, their youngest half-brother, Solomon, was killed at nineteen. He was caught between two worlds.

"He was always going back and forth from college to North Philly," said Jacobs quietly. "He wanted to make his own name. He started hanging around guys we used to hang around with."

Jacobs was freed on August 11, 2015, after fifteen years. He was the first of his siblings to return home. At thirty-seven, he was vastly different from the young man who entered prison at age twenty-two.

He calls his release day "glorious but bittersweet" because he left his brother Rashid in the prison and his older brother also still incarcerated. And he was scared without them. Since childhood, they had depended on one another.

One of his best friends picked him up. Jacobs walked outside and got on his knees, bowing to touch his forehead and nose to the ground in a Muslim prayer position.

"On the way to Philly I was looking at everything," he said. "I was in the mountains and behind a wall so long, and all I saw was green grass, trees, windmills, and open land. Now I saw abandoned houses, trash everywhere, drug addicts, desolation. I saw poverty all over again. I saw what I was returning to."

His first stop was to visit Lil Qad. "When I walked in and hugged him for the first time as a free man I cried," said Jacobs. "He was eighteen. I admitted to him I fucked up. I never wanted him to think me not being there had anything to do with him.

"He said, 'We all right, Dad. We all right.'"

Even today, Jacobs's eyes fill with tears when he recounts that visit.

"For him to not hate me and see me as a role model, someone to look up to, that's a major thing to me.

"That took a weight off me."

Unlike thousands of returning citizens, Jacobs had a place to live and people to support him. A cousin gave him a place to stay. His father, drug-free and working for his own nonprofit, told him to take a year to adjust instead of going directly to work.

Still, there was a lot to get used to, like walking past a group of young guys and not carrying a gun for protection.

"I was viewing life from how I used to be," said Jacobs.

He got into a fight with his son's stepfather, a violation of his parole. He faced a return trip to prison, but the judge considered his efforts to create a new life for himself and sentenced him to three months of confinement at a halfway house.

He found a job at Avis Car Rental, where he was given a chance despite his record. A year later, he went to work for the Philadelphia Water Department as a repair helper, going deep into the ground to fix water main breaks.

Mark got home in 2016. One of the best days of his life was when his last brother, Rashid, came home in February of 2017. Finally, the brothers were together again. That April, for the first time ever, they went to the mosque together to celebrate Ramadan, fasting together, sharing prayers and meals.

Now, each day, at least one of the brothers checks on their father and they meet as often as possible to share a meal with him.

Jacobs believes he had to serve at least fifteen years to learn to think differently and straighten out his life. But Jacobs could not answer this question: If he were institutionalized in a system that focused on rehabilitation, would it have taken him fifteen years to change?

"In some way the young guys on the street are mentally in prison before we go into institutions," he said. "I don't blame prison for anything that has happened to me. I'm grateful in a way...I would have been dead, or my brother Rashid would have been dead. It gave me a chance to grow up, to see life differently."

But, of course, Jacobs has had to make sense of his life. Perhaps justice advocates are the ones to ask this: Should any child grow up in a country where he looks to prison as a place to save his life?

THE INJURED CHILD THOUGHT: "AT LEAST THE DRUGS AND MONEY WERE SAFE"

Reverend Michelle Simmons remembers being a little girl standing on the red leather bar stools in her father's dark, smoky bar. Patrons repeatedly dropped coins in the jukebox to play "Misty Blue," a song about a woman grieving a lost love. And always, strangers came over to her to compliment her with things like, "What a cute little girl."

Her mother and father never married and did not live together. Even as a child, Simmons thought the bar scene and hanging with her father was much more exciting than staying at her mother's house. But she had no way of knowing that she'd become hooked on her father's "fast" life, as well as on drugs, or that her relationship with her father would become abusive and cause her to nearly destroy her own life.

It was Simmons's aunt Jean, her father's sister, who used to take her to the bar. Simmons lived with her single mom in Germantown, where she was the middle of three siblings. But on her father's side, she was a rarity, a girl, adored and spoiled. Her dad had twelve sons— and she was the baby—and only girl.

He lived in a duplex in Mount Airy, but he went to the projects a lot to do business.

"I loved going down to those projects," Simmons said.

She would find out as she got older that her father was selling drugs there.

She treasured hanging with her brothers also.

"They taught me to gamble. I learned to shoot dice on an ironing board," Simmons recalled. "I remember taking home my first dice and shooting them in my own neighborhood when I was twelve."

By fifth grade she spent most of her time at her father's house. She loved riding on the back of his motorcycle. So one afternoon when he headed out to make a delivery to the housing projects, she grabbed her helmet and hopped on the back of the bike.

Her dad seemed to be in a real hurry. She kept patting his back and saying, "'Slow down. Slow down.' I held onto him tight with my head against the back of his leather jacket," she remembered.

As they drove up a hill to the projects, a kid in a go-cart was headed down. The bike and the go-cart hit each other. Simmons flew through the air but got up and brushed herself off.

Before she could fully recover, her father whispered to her, "Take this down to Miss Shirley's house." Simmons walked the short distance to the house and gave Miss Shirley a two-pound bag of marijuana. An ambulance and police car arrived at the scene of the accident. On her walk back, Simmons felt pain in her knee and sat down on a wall. Her father saw her and sent over a paramedic.

"The go-cart handlebar went through my kneecap. I had on jeans," said Simmons. "My socks were red."

Both she and the teenage go-cart driver were taken to the hospital right across the street. In her book *Keep It Movin'!* Simmons wrote: "I remember thinking, at least the drugs and money were safe."

She was hospitalized for six months with a compound fracture of her kneecap. When she got out, she had on a cast that covered her hip and leg on one side. Because her mother, a psychiatric aide, was working and not at home all day, her parents decided Simmons would stay with her father.

She was happy and envisioned watching TV in bed and eating everything she liked.

"Instead, that was the first day I was sexually abused by my Dad," Simmons said.

She was twelve years old. She didn't tell anyone.

When she was on her feet again, she began to smoke weed and drink alcohol. Her brothers taught her how to package and sell a "nickel bag," or five dollars' worth of marijuana, to make money.

She sold joints at school. She was popular, played softball, ran for "Miss Pickett Middle School," and was called "Missy" by everyone.

In eighth grade an assistant principal caught her with marijuana in her pocketbook, took her to the office, and called the school police. An officer handcuffed Simmons and walked her down the halls to the police car outside.

"I felt embarrassed. The halls were crowded. I could hear people saying, 'Dag, look at Missy.' 'They locking Missy up.'"

But once outside, Simmons said, "I wasn't scared. I thought getting arrested was cool and didn't matter."

She got kicked out of school. Her mother picked her up from the police department.

"She was mad, but she couldn't say much 'cause she smoked weed, too," Simmons said.

At home, she was still being sexually abused. At age fifteen, she had what she thinks was a "mental breakdown." She didn't speak for forty days and was placed in a children's psychiatric center and diagnosed with depression.

She didn't utter a word about her sexual abuse. "I guess I was numb to everything," Simmons said. "What shook me out of my depression was I had a roommate who was pregnant by her dad. Her baby died, and she lost her mind. One night I woke up and that girl was dressed in my clothes and standing over me saying, 'You killed my baby! You killed my baby!'"

The incident terrified Simmons, who decided to leave the facility. She started talking—except she still didn't speak about her own abuse.

"My pop would give me money and drugs. I had the finest clothes and jewelry," Simmons said. She felt guilty for accepting gifts from her father and enjoying them. While other teenagers drove used cars, she drove a new Cadillac he provided. "He would give me things and say if you want to go to the mall, come do this and that. I stayed high."

For a while, she delivered drugs and carried money back from the South for her father. She tried college, spending a semester at Cheney University. But she was too mentally damaged to be disciplined enough to follow rules or attend classes. At home, the incest continued until she moved to Los Angeles at age twenty-seven.

By this time, she had fallen in love and had a daughter, a child she left with her favorite aunt Jean, voluntarily giving up her parental rights. Her daughter's father eventually joined her, and the two worked for a company selling magazines and books.

But Simmons had a bad cocaine addiction—and got pregnant again. She returned to Philadelphia alone and gave birth to her second daughter in January of 1994.

She tried being a hands-on mother, taking her daughters to Los Angeles with her. But that lasted just a few months. She was still an addict and unable to work, so in desperation she returned the children to her aunt in Philadelphia.

Finally, in 1996, all her demons caught up with her, and Simmons was arrested in Los Angeles and charged with possession of narcotics with intent to distribute. She became the statistic she'd avoided for so long, the increasing number of women imprisoned, especially for drugs, a number that had increased at twice the rate of men since 1980.

She was sentenced to six years at the Central California Women's Facility in Chowchilla, California.

"I was all alone," she said.

A cellmate told her to try God, something Simmons had avoided. After all, she wondered, how could God allow her to be abused by her father? But she started going to church and she said after one particular gathering she felt "saved."

"There was a woman and she told us how she had been molested by her dad and used to shoot drugs," Simmons said. "Her story just touched me, and I wanted to be saved, too."

She returned to her cell and started praying, just as the chaplain had suggested.

"I prayed and cried. There was a small window—and I saw a light in the window," Simmons said. She also saw a bright light shining down the hallway of the jail.

"That was my first experience of knowing God," she said.

She turned from the circle of friends who gambled and smoked to the group that went to Bible studies. A chaplain advised her to go straight into a drug rehab and mental health program called His Sheltering Arms once she was released. Normally, during her shorter stints in jail, Simmons would arrange for a drug dealer to meet her outside the facility upon her release, but not this time.

She walked out of prison on October 23, 1999, and entered His Sheltering Arms, staying for six months. While there, she revealed for the first time that her father had sexually abused her. She was motivated by listening to other women tell their stories.

"People were very honest," said Simmons. "One girl told how she was on drugs and allowed her son to be sold for drugs and had so much guilt and shame. Her honesty made me be honest."

Simmons put up her hand to speak, and before she knew it, she had blurted out her secret.

"I had promised I would keep that secret the rest of my life. I shocked myself," she said. "A counselor pulled me aside and said, 'Thank you for your bravery. We're getting you some counseling.'"

She received counseling and initiated communication with her daughters. At first her mother and her daughters did not believe she was drug-free. But in time, her mother accepted Simmons had changed and even helped her pay court-ordered fines so she could come home.

In Philadelphia, Simmons fought her aunt Jean in court for custody of her children. It took time, but she proved to the court she had taken parenting classes and drug and alcohol treatment and had a full-time job. On March 15, 2003, she won custody of her girls.

"I was excited and nervous—and they were, too," she said. "We stood at the bus stop and I called my mom and said, 'I got the kids and we're coming home.'"

In early December she moved into her first home, which she secured through Habitat for Humanity. Later that month, she and the girls had what Simmons refers to as her "first clean Christmas." They decorated the Christmas tree and hung blinking multicolored lights on the banister leading upstairs to their bedrooms and around the doorway to the kitchen.

On Christmas Eve they left cookies out on a plate for Santa. While the girls slept, Simmons sneaked out to get two bicycles hidden in her car, thankful to the social service agencies that had donated gifts to the girls.

"I remember looking at the bikes, the cookies, and lights and crying," said Simmons. When the girls were younger, Simmons would take the Christmas toys to the drug dealer to exchange for crack. By the time the girls woke on Christmas Day, most of the toys were gone. Sometimes Simmons pulled out old toys, wiped them off, wrapped them, and placed them under the tree. "This year, I wasn't selling their toys for crack."

And on the first "clean" Christmas, she watched the joy on two faces and enjoyed the laughter that filled the house, and she knew her old life had ended and a new one had begun.

Her youngest daughter, Traynesha Allen, has fond memories of that period.

"It felt normal because we had our own bedroom," Allen said. "It was safe and clean and comfortable."

Her mother missed the first seven years of her life and the first nine years of her sister's. Allen remembers that both she and her sister took advantage of their mother's feelings of guilt.

"My sister came from a place of anger, so a lot of stuff she got was because she was angry. For me, I was happy to get the stuff, but it was like my mother was saying, 'I'm giving you this stuff because I wasn't there.'"

Allen believes her sister suffered the most from their mother's absence because she did not always live in a healthy environment and was not always treated well. Once the family was reunited, she said her mother also worked ten hours a day, which she now believes was an attempt to catch up for time missed building a career.

"We got up and got ourselves dressed and went to school and she was working," Allen said.

Life was peaceful in their new home except for the constant arguing between her sister and mother. Her sister moved out when she was fifteen. The two still have a strained relationship. "My sister definitely still has a lot of hurt," said Allen, who is twenty-six and a social worker. "I think I've learned to cope and maybe mask any pain, so I don't re-traumatize myself."

But Allen wishes she, her mother, and sister spent more time together, and she believes prison or the "time away" helped create barriers in her family. (Simmons's oldest daughter did not want to be interviewed for this project.)

Simmons has two granddaughters: Traynesha is mother to one, and her sister had her first child this year. Allen said the baby helped soften the relationship between her sister and mother, but the tension and discomfort between the two persists.

"My mother is very focused on what she is doing. She is a huge support and role model on the professional side," Allen said. "She will give you money, but I would prefer time together."

She thinks her mother's view of family is "tainted." But it must be difficult for Simmons to have an understanding of family that isn't sullied by sexual abuse. Both of Simmons's parents are alive, yet she has never talked to them about her sexual abuse. She has only told her daughters her story.

"I wouldn't say I have a good relationship with my father. I don't hate him. I'm just neutral," Simmons said.

She believes her mother now knows about the abuse, but they haven't spoken of it.

"My [life] coach keeps saying I need to talk to my parents about it, but I haven't had the heart," said Simmons.

Once, when Traynesha was young and going over to Simmons's father's house to visit, Simmons did threaten her father, saying, "If you ever touch one of my daughters, I'll get you locked up."

In 2015, Simmons received a full pardon from the then-governor of California, Edmund G. "Jerry" Brown, which meant restoration of all citizenship rights.

She has also authored a book offering encouragement to others working to overcome addiction, *Why Not Prosper? The Decision Is Yours!* She helps other women build new lives, operating Why Not Prosper, a nonprofit she founded that helps women returning home from prison to find jobs, become mentally healthy, and stay drug-free.

She has earned a couple of undergrad degrees, as well as a master's in clinical and counseling psychology and a doctorate in ministries. She lied about her criminal record on entrance applications, knowing some colleges will not accept convicted felons. Today she has $160,000 in student loans. While in general, federal financial aid is available to all but a small subsection of people who have been convicted of felonies, Simmons followed the advice of school counselors and applied only for financing in which her criminal record would not matter.

By her own account, Simmons has helped 1,000 women through Why Not Prosper. She provides housing for twenty-five women at the three locations of her program, knowing some landlords will not lease to a person with a criminal record, even though they may collect and retain application processing fees. Also, her women need a permanent address so they can receive other benefits for which they are eligible.

Simmons wants the U.S. criminal justice system to offer more diversionary programs that treat people with addictions as people who are ill and need healing.

"If the judge knows Sally keeps smoking crack and stealing, then the judge needs to listen to her story and put her in rehab. Test her every week and put her in a program," she said. "Treat her in a restorative justice way instead of using punitive justice."

Meanwhile, Simmons said she is seeing more mental illness among women, especially since COVID.

THE GROWTH OF PUNISHMENT

During the eighteenth century as the proliferation of prisons expanded in the North, white slave owners in the South tried and sentenced enslaved people in plantation "courts."

Few Black people ever made it to a prison.

At one point, Virginia punished free Black people convicted of serious crimes by selling them into slavery.

At first, Southern legislators hesitated to establish prisons for fear of creating a white criminal underclass, something that had initially also concerned Northerners. And Southern governors did not want racial mixing—even in their prison systems.

They also wanted prisons to be profitable, which spurred the use of inmate labor to produce goods. Jails even charged some city slave owners to "store" or punish their enslaved people.

But most enslaved people met their fate at plantation trials and were punished, in horrendous ways, at the discretion of slave owners. Prisons and asylums were for foreign-born and poor whites. Then in 1865, the Thirteenth Amendment abolished slavery, except "as a punishment for a crime whereof the party shall have been duly convicted."

To maintain control over the 4 million newly freed people, Southern states drew up Black Codes, limits on the movement of Black people. Codes included restrictions such as "walking without a purpose" or "walking at night." These codes evolved into Jim Crow legislation, laws that institutionalized racism, crippling the economic, social, and educational growth of Blacks, limiting them to certain jobs, banning them from sharing public facilities with whites and prohibiting them from voting—laws that have similar consequences as those enacted today against people with convictions.

Jim Crow laws were aggressively enforced, which meant law enforcement focused its attention on former slaves, perhaps marking the beginning of the "official" overpolicing Blacks endure today. As a result, the conviction rates for whites accused of crimes dropped substantially while the rate for Blacks dramatically increased.

The number of women in Southern prison systems also increased in the postwar years, and virtually all of them were Black.

Without slavery, the South needed laborers, and so Black people were arrested on flimsy charges, such as vagrancy, and sentenced to hard labor. For decades after the Civil War, state judges sentenced offenders to work on chain gangs on county roads, railroads, or other local improvements. Convict leasing, which had become popular in the North by that time, was adopted by Southern states. But in the North prisons only contracted out the prisoner's labor, while in the South the state government basically turned over the prisoners to former plantation owners and companies that leased them. These southern contractors, responsible for the total care of prisoners, set up their own "penitentiaries." Some 90 percent of these prisoners were Black.

Imagine the fear of Black prisoners leased to former Confederate officers, some of whom were also Ku Klux Klan members.

Convicts worked in the most dangerous and unhealthy conditions in phosphate mines, on railroad operations, and in turpentine plants. In *Slavery by Another Name: The Re-Enslavement of Black Americans from the Civil War to World War II*, author Douglas Blackmon tells the story of Green Cottenham, the son of a formerly enslaved couple, arrested for vagrancy in 1908 and sentenced to six months' hard labor. His original sentence was three months, but the "convict" was required to pay a fee to the sheriff, the judge, and other local officials. When he could not pay the $38.40, three months were added to his sentence.

Cottenham was leased by Shelby County, Alabama, to a U.S. Steel subsidiary, where he served in shackles alongside more than 1,000 convicts, digging coal with a pick in the dark and damp mines. In five months, Cottenham died of tuberculosis and was buried with mine debris.

The mining company had leased him for twelve dollars a month. The deputy who arrested Cottenham received a fee for delivering him to the mine. In fact, this human trafficking paid the salaries of law enforcement.

Len Cooper, a writer who grew up in Birmingham and now lives in Naples, Italy, said as a child his grandfather, Daddy-Yo, always told him, "Mister Lincoln ain't freed no slaves."

In one account Cooper wrote about, from when his grandfather was seven in 1918, he and three friends ran from white men who wanted the boys to get into their new car. Cooper's grandfather made it home; the three others did not. Twenty years later, in 1938, Cleveland, one of the boys, returned home.

"Cleveland told Daddy-Yo he had been taken to the Mississippi Delta, sold into slavery and held for twenty years on a plantation surrounded by two rivers and protected by armed guards, barbed wire and dogs," Cooper wrote. "There were other plantations, all over the South, Cleveland said. Men kept under lock and key. Men were whipped for insubordination, men killed on a whim."

Meanwhile, white men and their companies accumulated great wealth from this labor, wealth they would pass on to future generations.

This practice of convict leasing was formally outlawed by the last state (Alabama) in 1928, but it persisted in various forms until it was abolished by President Franklin D. Roosevelt in 1941.

In 2018, construction workers uncovered a mass grave with the skeletal remains of Black prison inmates, estimated to be from fourteen to seventy years old, in Sugar Land, Texas. The area had been home to an infamous web of sugarcane plantations and prison camps. Archeology experts determined that the people had muscular builds but were malnourished with bones misshapen from backbreaking, repetitive labor.

Convict leasers could work convicts to death and ask the state for a replacement. Like slavery, it served as a stepping-stone toward mass incarceration.

"Slavery gave America a fear of Black people and a taste for violent punishment. Both still define our criminal-justice system," civil rights attorney Bryan Stevenson wrote in an essay in the *New York Times Magazine*.

"It's not just that this history fostered a view of Black people as presumptively criminal. It also cultivated a tolerance for employing any level of brutality in response," Stevenson said.

This brutality included lynching, a public act of torture used to punish Black people considered guilty of "crimes" cited by whites. In 1895, William Stephens and Jefferson Cole were lynched in Texas after they refused to abandon their land to white people. In 1916, Anthony Crawford was lynched in South Carolina for refusing to accept a low price for his cotton. In 1933, Elizabeth Lawrence was lynched near Birmingham because she chastised white children who were throwing rocks at her.

When thousands of Black people left the South for the North as part of the Great Migration, racial disparities in prisons in the North doubled.

"NEVER GOING HOME AGAIN"

Shariff Ingram was fifteen when he was arrested and jailed and thirty-eight when he came home. He has been home three weeks.

Some people think he is doing amazingly well. He has a car and a construction job and lives in a nice Philadelphia suburb with his sister, Dara.

But they don't see the million little things he has to adjust to daily.

On his third day home, he got dressed for his family's welcome-home party. Before leaving the house, he stopped in the downstairs bathroom. The last thing he did was wash his hands. It was about eleven a.m.

He and his sister returned home about nine-thirty that night. His sister went into the downstairs bathroom and found the water still running from the faucet.

"In prison, the water is on a timer," explained Ingram, who made the same mistake several times.

"Now I don't leave home without checking the faucets in the kitchen and the two bathrooms I use," he said. "People think I've made an amazing adjustment, but I have to be mindful of everything. I can't even make little mistakes other people can. My number one goal is to not go back or to put myself in any situation where something bad can happen."

Black youth are more likely to be tried as adults than white youth. In 2018, when Black people made up 14 percent of all youth under eighteen, they represented over half the youth transferred from juvenile to adult court, nationally. The number is often much greater in some states when the discretion is left up to prosecutors. Meanwhile, criminal justice systems in some European countries rely less on the incarceration of young offenders, diverting them instead to educational and rehabilitative programs, even those guilty of serious crimes.

Ingram was sentenced to life after he killed a drug dealer who had threatened him. His life sentence was reduced after justice advocate and attorney Bryan Stevenson represented a plaintiff in a landmark case in which the Supreme Court ruled it was unconstitutional to give mandatory life sentences without parole to children under eighteen.

"Bryan Stevenson is my hero," Ingram said.

His mother is his hero also. He was diagnosed with depression while in elementary school.

"She went to everybody, every professional and agency to try to find ways to help me," Ingram said.

He received some counseling and was in and out of mental hospitals. He was a good student through most of elementary school. Then, when he was eight years old, two young cousins who he said "were like a sister and brother to me" died in a house fire.

He remembers their father visiting him and his mother after he was released from the hospital. Ingram stared at the burn marks on his uncle's skin as he explained how he tried to go back into the house to get his children, but it was just too hot.

"I was trying to visualize what he was saying," said Ingram. "I thought he should have died trying to save them."

Shortly after the tragic fire Ingram set his mother's mattress on fire. In prison, he got access to his old mental health medical records and read that he told a doctor, "I set the fire because I thought if I died that way, I would see my cousins."

Less than a year after the fire, his father, with whom he had a loving relationship though his parents had separated, died of cirrhosis of the liver.

Ingram continued to receive counseling and was occasionally hospitalized. But his behavioral problems continued. By age eleven, he was selling drugs and stealing. He was transferred from one school to another. He failed three grades before a teacher skipped him from sixth to ninth grade, commenting in class, "You're the only one here with a beard."

Ingram, unable to understand the schoolwork, dropped out. He could now be considered a child on the "school-to-prison pipeline." The pipeline, normally formed by expulsion from school for disciplinary reasons, feeds the disproportionate incarceration of Black youth.

Ingram fit the profile: He was already labeled a discipline problem; he was used to institutions—in his case inpatient mental institutions—and he was now a dropout.

In another attempt to save him, his mother sent Ingram to live with his uncle Odell and his girlfriend in Richmond. But unbeknownst to his mother, Uncle Odell was a drug addict. Ingram found himself in a house without food or adult supervision.

"I used to go into the grocery store and steal bread, lunch meat, whatever I could eat," he said.

When he told his mother two months later, she sent him to her other brother, whose name was Ray Charles, who lived in another part of Richmond. The living situation was better, but one day the police came to the house to arrest him for robbing a white woman who worked at the laundromat where Ingram washed clothes. He spent thirty days in a juvenile detention center before the case was thrown out of court after the woman admitted that all Black people looked alike to her.

Still, Ingram was selling drugs and hanging out with an older crowd of troublemakers. One night they robbed a 7-Eleven with a water pistol painted black. Ingram got caught and was sent to a juvenile facility for three and a half months. He was sentenced to two years of probation. But he violated his probation on the second day and went on the run, sleeping under people's beds, in abandoned houses, and in stolen cars.

"We don't understand we have other options," he said of the youth he hung with on the streets. "We see people working out there, struggling. The drug dealers have money and clothes and girls. They drive through and the street gets quiet. It's like LeBron James went through."

He was on the corners selling crack when he got into a dispute with a street dealer. When he stopped acquiring his cocaine from that dealer, the dealer got angry, threatened him, and one night shot at Ingram.

On another night as Ingram stood in a phone booth, he heard loud music coming down the street and turned to see the dealer's burgundy Grand Cherokee with tinted windows driving closer to him.

"He was shouting, 'Where's my money?!'" Ingram recalled. He saw the window going down.

Scared, he shot at the truck and ran. He was arrested two days later. Ingram said he pled guilty, explaining that he shot in self-defense. The judge sentenced him to life.

"My lawyer had all but guaranteed me I would not get life," Ingram said. "I took a judge instead of a jury because of his advice. He felt the judge would not find me, a kid with my circumstances, guilty of a killing. But my lawyer never presented any evidence either."

Ingram, sixteen when sentenced, was devastated. "It was an indescribable feeling, knowing I was never going home again. I felt like my life was over."

He was assigned to an adult prison. "We [juveniles] had single cells, but whenever I went out of my cell I was with adults," he said. "I showered with adults, ate with adults."

Still, he was determined "to thrive, not just survive."

He focused on educating himself, reading books—first the Bible and Quran, then novels. He chose to hang with people who had been in prison a long time and yet seemed mentally healthy and spiritually positive.

"I picked their brains. I wanted to know how they made it with dignity, sanity and morals," he said. "I found a lot of people were closing their minds or taking medication to escape. The prison is quick to offer you psychotropic meds. There were people walking around who were out of it. When the prison offered me drugs, I refused them."

He became a Muslim and dedicated himself to learning more about Islam. He worked out regularly, which he said helped release stress.

"I used to speak to my mom all the time," Ingram said. His mother and his sister, Dara, visited him every week when possible. Other family and friends came, too.

"That gave me a sense of connection and motivation, knowing I had people who rooted for me and wanted me to survive," said Ingram.

He took the GED every year for seven years until he passed it. But he was disappointed to learn there were no other classes offered to lifers.

"They think it's a waste of time," Ingram said.

In 2005, he began filing grievances to get into classes. In 2012, after the Supreme Court ruling opened the possibility of getting his time reduced, the prison allowed him to take classes.

Although the first Supreme Court ruling regarding juveniles was in 2012, it took years of other rulings, discoveries, and negotiations before he was freed.

Meanwhile, his mother and sister were excited about the new progressive district attorney in Philly, Larry Krasner. However, when Ingram's case came before Krasner for resentencing, the DA offered the youth forty years. Ingram turned down the offer. Next, Krasner offered twenty-nine to life, but the judge refused it, saying, "It's too low."

Ingram told his lawyers to contest the judge's decision.

"All my lawyers said, 'You won't get a better deal than this,'" Ingram recalled.

He went before a judge in April 2019 with character witnesses that included prison guards and administrators. The judge gave him time served.

"My lawyers cried," he said.

But when he went to the parole board after his resentencing, they denied parole, citing incidents he had been involved in while in prison. They told him to return to the board in a year and that if he remained free of misconduct incidents he should be paroled then.

He was in the State Correctional Institution at Fayette, a remote area southeast of Pittsburgh, when George Floyd was killed. He and the other incarcerated men followed the case on television, watching the protests spread across the world.

"I was thinking how sad our society is that we are going through this in 2020," he said. "I would hear guards talking about it and making excuses for the killing."

He grew up in prison overhearing white guards supporting the killing of Black people they viewed as criminals. He heard them more recently dismiss Black Lives Matter as "ridiculous" people who hate police.

"I used to hear them speaking, saying things like, 'He shouldn't have resisted. Black Lives Matter just uses these situations. What about all the killings going on in Black communities?'"

On the news, he saw one Black person after another get gunned down by police officers.

"I remember after one incident where a Black guy was killed, I heard a guard say, 'I would have let off all my clips in his ass.'"

Meanwhile, Ingram had to steel his feelings, suppress any reaction. Occasionally, he failed and got into an altercation with a guard.

"I was watching George Floyds being murdered in prisons all my life," said Ingram. "Now society was talking about the same thing I was seeing every day. People in prison were being beaten and killed by guards and nothing happened. A lot of the incidents stemmed from racism, and these guards were white people who hated us for no reason."

He called Fayette "one of the most oppressive" prisons he had been in.

"Most of the guards are white," said Ingram. "But to say most guards are white in some prisons is an understatement."

He rarely saw a Black guard while he was there, and the ones he saw seldom lasted, he said. "If you see a few Black guards you know they are likely forced to be oppressive, too."

Ingram was suspicious of the Black prison staff he met. For two years at Fayette, he avoided therapy even though the psychiatrist was a Black woman.

"After a while I realized she was one of the ones that would stand up for us and go at those white guards," he said.

One day the psychiatrist told him Fayette was a very depressing place and she didn't know how much longer she could work there. Then she told him something he'll never forget.

"She said, 'I can never take my grandchildren to the zoo anymore.'"

Ingram asked her to explain.

"Because this place reminds me of a zoo. They have you in cages—and the animals in the zoo are treated better," she said.

Ingram was released on September 24, 2020. A guard led him to the prison lobby, which he had never seen before. He stood, staring outside, until a prison employee told him he could open the door.

"I can go out?" he asked in disbelief. "It was weird. I was free and asking permission to walk outside."

His mom, now retired from the tax abatement office for the City of Philadelphia, was waiting, along with Dara, a cousin, and his mother's boyfriend.

He stepped out the door, and his mother ran to him. As he walked to the vehicle, he paused to stare at the building holding solitary confinement—"the hole."

"I was thinking how I never thought I'd be on this side of the gate," he said.

He voted for the first time in 2020. He reluctantly voted for Joe Biden, determined to vote out Donald Trump.

An estimated 5.17 million people are unable to vote and disenfranchised because of a felony conviction. Because Black people suffer from mass incarceration disproportionately, they are underrepresented in the electorate.

Pennsylvania is a state where voting rights are automatically restored to people convicted of felonies. In some states people lose these rights for a period of time, and in some others they must re-register.

Because Ingram was a juvenile when he went to prison, he registered for the first time.

"Thinking back, I believe the system failed me," Ingram offered. "I was always being arrested between twelve and fourteen years old, but there was no form of treatment available for me in the juvenile system. They locked me up—and let me out. That's all they did.

"The core of how we look at crime is wrong. We must look at the real causes and the real solutions. Imprisonment is not a solution," he said. "Those of us who come out and are better, it is not because of the system but because we beat the odds on our own.

"Look at it from the perspective of trauma. You have to treat hopelessness, poverty, despair, lack of options. These are the things that would make a major difference, rather than incarceration. When you have people growing up in poverty without hope, they don't care about incarceration or about being killed—or killing.

"We are victims before we become victimizers," said Ingram, who recalled being robbed of his beloved red Freestyle bike at gunpoint at age eleven. "People don't understand what life is like for a child like me.

"We don't call the police. We learn how to adapt and survive."

WHEN WHITE PEOPLE GET SCARED, BLACK PEOPLE GET LOCKED UP

The hard-fought civil rights movement opened new routes to success for Black people, and thousands of families moved from the cities to buy homes in the green suburbs. Meanwhile, the government shifted monies from education and social services to law enforcement, basically to "protect" white people who feared Black people, who had been abandoned in inner-city communities and left behind in poverty.

It was President Richard Nixon who coined the phrase "war on drugs" during a speech in 1971. He also increased the size of federal drug control agencies and pushed through "tougher" measures, such as mandatory sentencing and no-knock warrants.

Around the same time politicians began making their "law and order" speeches, and the prison population boomed. In 1970, the state and federal prison population was 196,441. In the 1980s and '90s, Democratic and Republican politicians battled verbally and then with legislation to prove which party should hold the title of "toughest on crime." By 1985, the state and federal prison population increased to 481,616, with a disproportionate number being young Black people.

The Ronald Reagan administration launched a media campaign to publicize the crack epidemic that had hit poor inner-city communities. The media coverage won the administration support for the Anti-Drug Abuse Act of 1986, which included new mandatory minimum sentences and far more severe punishment for distribution of crack.

In Pennsylvania, Secretary of the Department of Corrections John Wetzel recalled how this crack disparity caused the prison population to grow.

"There was a significant difference in how we reacted to the cheaply produced urban crack cocaine crises versus how criminal justice treated possession and use of cocaine, a more expensive white suburban drug," Wetzel said.

According to the Drug Policy Alliance: "Despite the fact that the chemical structure of powder cocaine and crack cocaine is nearly identical, the punishment for crack possession or sales is far greater than that of cocaine. Until 2010, this sentencing disparity was 100 to 1, which means that while just 5 grams of crack would carry a 5-year mandatory minimum, it would take 500 grams of cocaine to trigger the same 5-year sentence. While the law was changed in 2010, there continues to be a disparity of 18 to 1."

President Bill Clinton's 1994 federal crime bill included $9 billion for prison construction and expanded the federal death penalty, mandatory minimum sentencing, and "truth in sentencing" incentives to encourage states to adopt harsh punishments and limit parole. The Clinton bill also supported federal legislation denying food stamps, public housing, and financial aid to college students convicted of drug felonies.

Joe Biden was chair of the Senate Judiciary Committee, which largely wrote and shepherded the bill through Congress. While some Black leaders were dissatisfied with the expansion of the death penalty, Clinton met with members of the Congressional Black Caucus and was able to garner enough votes to get the bill passed into law.

Although mass incarceration is caused by policies enacted by both Democrats and Republicans, Wetzel said, "Bill Clinton put mass incarceration on steroids and the situation was worsened by federal monies making military equipment available to law enforcement."

Indeed, the increase in incarceration had already begun before the crime bill. The "Fact Sheet in U.S. Corrections" by the Sentencing Project said, "Since the official beginning of the war on drugs era in the 1980s, the number of Americans incarcerated for drug offenses has skyrocketed from 40,900 in 1980 to 443,200 in 2018."

The harsher sentences and mandatory minimums have also resulted in keeping people in prison for longer stretches, almost three times longer today than the average in 1986.

Half the people in federal prisons are serving a sentence for a drug offense. Most are not big-time drug dealers, and most have no criminal record for a violent offense. Drug offenses still account for the incarceration of almost half a million people, and police still make more than 1 million drug possession arrests each year, many of which lead to prison sentences. Still, when you combine prisons and jails, four out of five people are locked up for something other than a drug offense, according to the Prison Policy Initiative, a nonprofit organization that produces research to expose the harm of mass incarceration.

However, incarceration is just one part of a larger system of correctional control. The U.S. justice system controls almost 7 million people, more than half on probation. Black people are 2.6 times as likely to be on probation and nearly four times as likely to be on parole as white people.

"Today, a criminal freed from prison has scarcely more rights, and arguably less respect, than a freed slave or a black person living 'free' in Mississippi at the height of Jim Crow," wrote Michelle Alexander in her classic book, *The New Jim Crow: Mass Incarceration in the Age of Colorblindness*. In the book, Alexander further illuminates how the criminal justice system functions as a new system of racial control by targeting Black men through the "War on Drugs."

This control continues after incarceration through community supervision like parole and probation, both of which require a person to be supervised and follow certain rules and guidelines. Criminal justice advocates recommend fewer rules and less supervision for people returning home, so that they can have more flexibility to get to work, go to school, or care for family members.

And Alexander warns against the shift toward using "e-carceration" devices such as electronic monitoring and viewing them as criminal justice reform. Like other supervision, the electronic ankle bracelets limit the person's mobility.

"If our goal is not a better system of mass criminalization, but instead the creation of safe, caring, thriving communities, then we ought to be heavily investing in quality schools, job creation, drug treatment and mental health care in the least advantaged communities rather than pouring billions into their high-tech management and control," she wrote in the *New York Times*.

It is impossible to fully measure the devastation mass incarceration has caused Black communities and families. Often an employer rejects an application of an ex-offender—or the opportunity available pays less than their qualifications warrant. But those instances are difficult to show in data. Nevertheless, America's appetite to punish Black people and the structural racism that has supported this has assisted in broadening the gap in wealth and health between Blacks and whites.

For formerly incarcerated Black people the average loss in lifetime earnings is $358,900; for whites in this group, the loss is $267,000. The difference of nearly $100,000 between the two can mean a substantial difference in the quality of life; whether or not a person can become a homeowner, or how much they receive in retirement benefits or Social Security.

Structural racism, in fact, has created a system that results in Black people with no criminal record earning less annually than socioeconomically similar white people with a record.

Race remains a major factor in determining which communities become wealthy in America, and the wealth gap between Blacks and whites will continue to widen as long as Black people are disproportionately incarcerated.

FREE FROM A CAGE, BUT NOT FREE

Steve Blackburn earned college degrees, got married, raised his children, and had a successful career directing family services and running youth programs. But one day, nearly forty years after he was convicted of first-degree murder, decades after he completed his prison term, he was told his record meant he would have to be removed from the position he loved.

He was offered a new position. Blackburn didn't lose any income. But he lost the work he was passionate about. He felt disrespected.

"As unfair as it was, I took it on the chin. I had had a good run. It had been a blessing," Blackburn said.

It didn't matter to the school that Blackburn had gotten out of prison in 1991 and had not committed a crime since his release.

It didn't matter that he was a noted community activist in Philadelphia and had co-founded a nonprofit agency, X-Offenders for Community Empowerment, which assisted formerly convicted people in getting clemency.

"When I came home, I found out that freedom is not just freedom," Blackburn had proclaimed once to a local newspaper. "You still have restrictions; you still have barriers so you're not free."

Blackburn served sixteen years of a life sentence before the governor commuted his sentence. He was twenty-four when he went to prison in 1975; he was forty when he came home.

His stepfather, Clifford Shannon, whom he calls his father, and his mother, Gertrude Shannon, died while he was incarcerated. His daughter, Stephanie, was four when he left. She was twenty when he returned. In prison, he earned twelve cents an hour at a prison job, which barely made a dent in what was needed to care for his child.

He grew up in North Philly, about five blocks from Temple University, in a house his parents owned. He had one sibling, a brother ten years younger, but his mother raised three of her nephews, so there were five boys in the house.

"We were poor, but I never went hungry, even when we ate syrup sandwiches," Blackburn said.

His mother kept the family together. His stepfather was an alcoholic. He never knew his biological father, so his stepfather filled the role.

He graduated from St. Joseph's Preparatory School run by the Jesuits, but he had to navigate his way through a war zone of four different gang territories to get there.

"On any given day, those guys from the gangs came around to rob or pick on people," said Blackman.

Despite everything, he graduated in 1968 and went to Drexel University.

"It was crazy times. Civil rights. Vietnam. Hippies. Drugs," Blackburn said. "I was radicalized, anti-establishment, leaning toward Black militancy, affiliated with the Nation of Islam."

He began doing drugs—acid, pills, marijuana. He quit school after one semester. He worked "low-paying jobs."

"I got more involved with a particularly corrupt, vicious crew," he said. "We hustled marijuana and cocaine.

"I started leaning toward a more violent personality because that was my understanding of how things went. You had to be a wolf or a sheep. I didn't want to be a sheep."

A guy stole money from his crew, and when Blackburn found him the two got into a fight. He took a crew member with him, and that member brought along a friend. When the guy Blackburn was fighting ran away, the "friend" he didn't know pulled out a gun and fatally shot the man.

"I didn't shoot the guy," Blackburn said. "That wasn't my plan. I figured I'd beat his ass. I had known him for years, and it wasn't that big an amount of money."

In court, the shooter pled guilty and received a sentence of eighteen months to ten years.

"It's my first offense. They find me guilty [and] I get life," said Blackburn. He added, "My lawyer wasn't very expensive—and he wasn't very good."

Blackburn was sent to Graterford Prison, forty miles from Philadelphia. When his father died in 1986, Blackburn said his counselor came to him and said, "I got bad news. Your father had a heart attack."

"My mom was diagnosed with cancer. She visited until she got too weak and then we talked mostly by phone."

As she deteriorated, he was allowed to visit her bedside, a rare privilege for a prisoner. Blackburn was handcuffed, and a sheriff escorted him. When they got to his mother's house, his grandmother was present, and the sheriff recognized her.

"He took the handcuffs off, and I saw her at her bedside. He even took a nap while I was with my mom for an hour. It was very humane," Blackburn said.

When his mother died, the prison allowed him to attend her funeral, another unusually humane act.

To avoid depression, Blackburn said he had "to compartmentalize life and focus on one thing at a time" so that everything didn't crash down on him at once.

"In that environment you already face life or death every day," he said. "My mom was my one and only supporter. My baby brother was away attending the University of Colorado. My cousins my mother raised, a lot of them got caught up in the crack epidemic."

But he believes his mother sent angels for him. She left money to her Catholic church, and she had asked her priest to fight for her son.

"The priest and nun came to visit. The priest said, 'I loved your mother, but I wasn't signing blank checks. I needed to see what kind of guy you are.'"

The priest began to fight for Blackburn's release. Blackburn's lawyer joined them, determined to get him out, especially since the real triggerman got a much lighter sentence.

Meanwhile, he had earned a good behavior record in prison. He helped rescue a "female civilian" who was attacked by one of the inmates. He was president of the "lifers" organization; he earned an associate degree from Villanova University, and he started the Prison Literacy Project, which taught prisoners to read.

His brother returned to the East Coast and came to visit. His daughter and her mom moved back from the West Coast and began visiting him as well.

"I had always corresponded with her, mostly by mail. I sent cards and photos," Blackburn said of his daughter. "We developed a strong relationship by mail."

Then what he calls "a miracle" happened: Governor Bob Casey Sr. commuted his sentence—and Blackburn was free.

He went to a halfway house for eleven months, a period he found beneficial because he received welfare and medical insurance. His brother encouraged him to continue his education. Blackburn enrolled in Temple, majoring in social work. Someone he met in prison helped him get a job at the mayor's office.

He graduated summa cum laude from Temple in 1994. A month later he married a woman who had grown up in North Philly. And he continued college, receiving a master's degree in social work.

He has been married for twenty-six years. In addition to the daughter he had before he went to prison, he and his wife have two sons, twenty-seven and twenty-five years old.

He works for a nonprofit school in family services, supervising five case managers. He also created various programs and was on the founding coalition that created Sankofa Freedom Academy Charter School, where he is president of the board of trustees.

What he has seen as a social worker and what he experienced as a prisoner combine to influence his opinion about the country's criminal justice system.

"When I got to prison, I was an outsider," Blackburn offered. "My background was different than most of the other guys. I had a pretty good family. I didn't have the hardships they had.

"My observation was that for a majority of the men in prisons, their institutionalization began much earlier than prison—in juvenile facilities. Instead of talking about elementary, middle school, and high school, they talked about going to juvenile facilities and then to prison.

"The problem didn't start with the crime, but how that crime was handled by the system. I had a hard enough time as a grown man in prison. I can't imagine how it would affect me if I had been much younger. I am sure there is a lot of trauma young people carry for the rest of their lives."

Ironically, Blackburn said, he observed some of the younger men succeeding in prison in a way they had not been able to outside. In prison, they got their first jobs and were mentored by elders and counselors. They responded to that attention, earned a solid reputation, developed their self-esteem, and freed themselves from childhood demons.

He was aware of all he missed while incarcerated and how fortunate he was for the way his life has turned out. He said he has tried to spend his freedom doing good, despite the continued judgment by an unforgiving society.

"In retrospect, I think about the hardships my daughter had to endure, because I missed so much of her growing up. She's solid now, though. I have two granddaughters who have graduated from college. I think the relationship my daughter and I established through letters made us close on a spiritual level."

At age seventy, he said he is looking forward to the unfolding of an upcoming journey: retirement.

"I've been blessed," Blackburn said.

WE MUST BECOME MORE HUMANE

For decades, the United States has maintained a corrections system based on punishment rather than rehabilitation. This violent and brutal system has severed parents from their children and left neighborhoods void of generations of potential.

To change such a system will take time. But there must also be a will to do so, a belief that incarcerating millions of humans does not make our society safer, and, in fact, probably sets it up for even more violence.

"Where life is precious, life is precious," prison abolitionist and scholar Ruth Wilson Gilmore has been fond of saying.

There are some justice reformers who look to more progressive countries for examples of what is possible, pushing for the adoption of at least some of the simple, less costly policies that could be a beginning.

"It doesn't cost for guards to say, 'good morning' or 'thank you' or to let inmates wear their own clothes," said Elena Vanko, a senior program associate at the Vera Institute of Justice, a nonprofit and advocacy group that has sponsored trips to more progressive prisons abroad for corrections leaders, justice advocates, and journalists.

"One of the values of the prison system in Norway is normalization," said Vanko, who visited two prisons in Norway in 2013.

Normalization means that inside the facility should resemble a "normal" life outside, so that transitioning back to the community is not difficult.

Halden Prison, just outside of Oslo, Norway, has been called "the most humane prison in the world." It bears no resemblance to a U.S. prison. There are no bars. The grounds look like a campus. The people incarcerated are called "inmates," but they have their own bedrooms with a private bathroom and doors they can close. Windows give inmates a view of nature, and instead of the concrete and steel used in U.S. prisons, Halden features softer materials such as cork and wood, and other textures that help absorb sound.

In general, the longest sentence in Norway is twenty-one years, though there is a thirty-year maximum for some crimes. There is a rarely used indefinite sentence, where the person is examined every five years to be reconsidered for release. Instead of mass incarcerations, the corrections system in Norway mostly uses fines and community-based sentences.

Prison guards are expected to talk to inmates and socialize with them, play games, watch television, and hold conversations so they can motivate them and know when they are troubled and how they are progressing.

"Each person is treated as a human being with human dignities," Vanko said.

This sense of humanity was obvious in the way Norway handled the spread of COVID-19 in prisons. While the U.S. was slow to take measures to reduce or halt the spread of the virus among incarcerated people, Norway, which has a much smaller corrections system, nevertheless made some quick decisions that reduced the spread of the virus. The country released some prisoners or gave them alternative sentences, sending them home with ankle monitors. Many two-person cells were turned into single bed, one-person cells.

Meanwhile, the corrections system in the U.S. basically ignored criminal justice reformers who asked for thousands of early releases to reduce the prison population and allow people who were elderly, near completion of their sentences, or in ill health the chance to go home. By the end of 2020 at least 275,000 prisoners had tested positive and more than 1,700 had died. At one point, one in five state and federal prisoners had tested positive. And, of course, this highly contagious disease spread from prisons and jails into communities.

COVID-19 disproportionately impacts Black people, who are also disproportionately incarcerated. These two facts have added to the endangerment of life for the entire Black community.

In Norway, prisons have become more rehabilitative, while U.S. prisons have maintained their punitive nature: sentencing children and mentally ill persons; handing out life without parole sentences; locking people in crowded and unhealthy prisons; removing the right to vote and adding other restrictions; and allowing the burden of mass incarceration to continue to fall disproportionately on Black people and brown people.

In 2013, John Wetzel, Pennsylvania secretary of corrections, went with a group to tour prisons in eastern Germany. He had an unforgettable exchange, he said, with the minister of justice.

"I asked her how Germany got where it is, and she said, 'When you kill and lock up your own people, the notion of freedom is different.' She was talking about the Holocaust," Wetzel said. Instead of responding punitively to a history of violence, Germany chose to be more creative.

In Pennsylvania, Wetzel said, the push for change that he has seen more recently came about when opioid and heroin addiction spread through white communities. He did not, however, see as much concern from the federal government or our country's health agencies when crack addiction spread through Black communities.

"I would argue that the use of heroin is what has reduced calls for incarceration," Wetzel said of Pennsylvania. The governor even signed an opioid disaster declaration that allows the state to loosen regulations and work outside typical procedures to expedite aid and initiatives to fight the opioid and heroin epidemic in the state.

"We saw individuals in every zip code being impacted by heroin, and these new people affected saw the system up close and personal and didn't like what they saw," said Wetzel. "You saw prosecutors say, 'We can't incarcerate our way out of this.' Hell, we couldn't incarcerate our way out of the crack epidemic," said Wetzel.

"What the Holocaust did in Germany and heroin did here in Pennsylvania is it made us and them disappear and it became we," said Wetzel, who in 2018 reduced his state's prison population by 1,000, the largest yearly decrease on record.

Most justice advocates agree that decarceration in the United States is necessary, and some states have already been successful in reducing prison populations by using strategies such as offering alternatives to sentencing, better mental health treatment, parole reform, and early releases.

But prisons and the punitive thinking behind them are embedded in this country's history. Some reformists, including abolitionists, are not satisfied to consider only the tweaking of corrections.

"Abolition is not a better kind of punishment," prison abolitionist Gilmore explained in a September 2020 interview on radio station KQED in San Francisco. "What abolition is, is figuring out how to live in a world where prison is not necessary."

Gilmore has expressed a belief repeated by other abolitionists, which is that we can't just address the harm caused by our current prison system but that we must "change everything."

Noted abolitionist Mariame Kaba has explained in her writings: "Prison industrial complex (PIC) abolition is a political vision, a structural analysis of oppression, and a practical organizing strategy. While some people might think of abolition as primarily a negative project—'Let's tear everything down tomorrow and hope for the best'—PIC abolition is a vision of a restructured society in a world where we have everything we need."

Kaba wrote: "Some people may ask: 'Does this mean that I can never call the cops if my life is in serious danger?' Abolition does not center that question. Instead, abolition challenges us to ask, 'Why do we have no other well-resourced options?' and pushes us to creatively consider how we can grow, build, and try other avenues to reduce harm."

And when we look at those countries cited as having the most progressive prisons—Germany and Norway, Sweden and the Netherlands—there are gnawing questions unspoken by some: "Do those countries have a significant number of Black people? Would they operate those systems the same if they did?" asks MiAngel Cody, an attorney who says she "picks locks to human cages" because she has won freedom for at least forty prisoners sentenced to life for drugs.

Cody's questions are legitimate. Cultures and history and how governments react to them determine the answers they give to the questions that shape a corrections system.

Vanko agrees, but also thinks we might still learn something from the prisons she has seen. "In Norway, sentences are not politicized and people don't worry about sentences. They don't want them to be punitive. And Norway does have a welfare state, so even in prison you could argue that the level of living conditions are better than it is for some people who live in poverty here in this country."

Longtime justice advocate Dr. Divine Pryor also noted cultural differences and said the most memorable experience he had in the Netherlands occurred in Amsterdam outside the prisons he visited.

"I went into a variety or grocery store. I was looking around, and the owner seemed irritated," said Pryor, who is president and CEO of the People's Police Academy, a community-based problem-solving public safety laboratory at Medgar Evers College.

As a Black man in America, Pryor had been a victim of racism, subtle and blatant.

"The owner was by himself. I assumed his irritation was racially motivated," Pryor said. "I asked him with attitude if there was a problem. He said, 'No, no. No problem at all. I was on my way out when you walked in. But don't worry. When you get what you want, just leave the money on the counter, and lock the door.'"

With that, the man left. "Of course, it could never happen here [in the U.S.]," Pryor said.

His head filled with questions about how people who trusted their fellow humans—including a Black man—that much might make different decisions regarding prisons. Although he was quick to note that he also talked with Black people in Amsterdam who made it clear "they are not treated the same as white people. They said it may not be as evident as in the U.S., but they definitely have a class system, and it is mired in race."

Wetzel, the Pennsylvania secretary of corrections, wants to see the

United States do more on the front end to save children before they commit crimes.

"How about fixing the freaking schools?" Wetzel asked. "Forty percent of people in Pennsylvania state prisons don't have a high school diploma. The average reading level is eighth grade. In Philadelphia, the average is third grade. We looked at what school district the inmates in our population came from and most inmates came from the twenty lowest performing school districts.

"Mass incarceration is how disparities in education show up," he said. "Whatever reform we make must include creating better schools and economic opportunities for people in inner-city communities. We can and should build healthier community. There is research that shows blocks with more green grass have less violence."

Where life is precious, life is precious.

Both Qadree Jacobs and Steve Blackburn spoke of being children who were overwhelmed by hopelessness before turning to crime. Inner-city children are abandoned by society to navigate violent streets, to live in dense poverty, searching for beauty in places without green parks. They arrive already traumatized at poor performing schools that are not well equipped because their neighbors cannot sustain them with significant taxes.

A child should not have to find hope in prison. Wetzel hears plenty of stories of hopelessness from the grown men and incarcerated children in the prisons he oversees.

"I tour SCI Pine Grove, and the story I hear there from young people is the same every time," Wetzel said. "In Pennsylvania you can be incarcerated in a prison at age thirteen. You talk to these kids and they say, 'I have no hope. I'll be dead by twenty, so why should I care about living.' It's an explanation, not an excuse."

Allowing children to grow up unprotected in unsafe neighborhoods of poverty assures they will become hopeless, said New York justice advocate Pryor.

"The hopelessness is passed down through generations," he said. "The children witness their parents being involved in the drug culture, which comes with domestic violence. If money is going to drugs, kids aren't eating or wearing clothes they want to have. If there are no role models for them to see, they are ensnared by crime in that way.

"Then I have metal detectors and police officers at the school," continued Pryor. "I want to prepare you for when you assume the position for me when I process you into the criminal punishment system. There are schools in white communities where there have been mass murders and still, there are not metal detectors. They get therapy and bring in psychiatrists; they want to reduce the impact trauma has on the children. They don't bring in therapists to our communities. They bring in metal detectors and more police."

Wetzel thinks a new constitutional amendment may be needed to address mass incarceration in this country. (Justice advocates frequently cite the Thirteenth Amendment to the United States Constitution, which says slavery and involuntary servitude are allowed as punishment for people who have been convicted.)

"In Germany, they actually have in the constitution this principle of normality," he said. "They recognize that the punishment is incarceration itself, that a person is not incarcerated for further punishment. I think you can make an argument for a constitutional amendment that requires that incarceration does not impede upon any other civil rights."

Wetzel believes the long-term fix is to give people, especially families headed by single parents, education, resources, and economic opportunities to "fix themselves on the front end."

While people deny that the prison system constructed today was built by structural racism, Wetzel said, "The result looks like what a policy built on racism would look like: No educational opportunities or economic opportunities in inner-city Black communities and the disproportionate incarceration of Black people."

On the other hand, author and civil rights advocate Michelle Alexander has said we must ask ourselves what a just system would look like. "Would we criminalize the simple possession of drugs for personal use? Would we do that? Or would we treat drug use and drug addiction as a public health problem rather than a crime?"

Alexander suggests, "We need to end the war on drugs and the war mentality that we have, which means ending zero-tolerance policies. It means transforming our criminal justice system from one that is purely punitive to one that is based on principles of restorative and transformative justice, you know, systems that take seriously the interests of the victim, the offender, and the community as a whole. We need to abolish all of the laws that authorize legal discrimination against people who have criminal records, legal discrimination that denies them basic human rights—to work, to shelter, to education, to food."

Now is the time we must have honest conversations about the real intentions behind and the true impact of the criminal justice system, as well as the magnitude of the task of dismantling it.

A prison sentence should not be a perpetual punishment.

Laws are not colorblind.

Alexander reminds us: "Colorblind rhetoric has been used to justify the most deleterious laws and programs; it has allowed us to ignore subtler forms of racism and claim we live in a country freed from the legacy of its racist past."

Dealing honestly with our past, we can ask new questions: Should life sentences exist? Are prisons the violent manifestation of a society that has always responded to violence with violence? Do we need prisons to have justice?

"I believe that what people choose when they have only one option is no predicator of what they will choose when they have others," said Danielle Sered, a renowned justice advocate who created a New York–based program called Common Justice.

"At the heart of our work is a restorative justice–based alternative to prison for serious and violent felonies like assault, robbery, and attempted murder," Sered said. "We know part of our role in our movement is to prove it is possible to address violence without prison—that it is possible for people to make things right, and for people to produce the safety that prison never can and never will."

Sered said she has found that when survivors are given the chance to choose whether they want the person who harmed them incarcerated or in a restorative justice process, 90 percent of the survivors choose the restorative process. This is in direct opposition to what the public has been told for years: that victims want the people who hurt them to be caged and treated harshly. With restorative justice, people are empowered because, unlike in the traditional punitive corrections process, it offers those directly impacted by acts of violence an opportunity to design what repair will look like.

"One thing we learn from survivors is that options are transformative, that we cannot predict in the absence of options what people will do in the presence of options," Sered said. "As we expand the options, more and more people will see in what we do a thing worth their life force to fight for. As a country, we have failed to provide victims of violence with real options other than incarceration to hold the person who harmed them accountable."

Our current way of responding to violence is with violence, she said. "For that reason and countless others, we believe deeply that people who cause harm do not belong in cages. But we also believe pain requires repair. And so, we do accountability—which is different from punishment. Punishment is passive. Accountability is active."

Sered, who is white, believes that to have real change, in these historic days following massive protests, "white people will have to become ready to lay down the current, old world that is made of death but, for us, also made of privilege and power and can at times feel like protection. We have to own all the parts of it that destroy and

211

all the parts that benefit us and be ready to move to something new, something not yet fully known."

She believes the process to address harm should be the same for this country as it is for individuals who have caused violence: "Acknowledge our actions, acknowledge their impact. Express genuine remorse, repair the harm to the degree possible—ideally in ways defined by those harmed, and become a nation who will never do it again."

The criminal justice system in this country labels people as criminals and felons to devalue their worth; sends them away so they are invisible. But parents, sons, daughters, spouses, and loved ones know without Ruth Wilson Gilmore telling them: Where life is precious, life is precious.

There are a growing number of justice advocates who, like Marc Mauer, for years did not consider abolition as a possibility, but now find the word on their lips.

"I'm evolving toward the idea of abolitionist," said Mauer, senior advisor and former executive director of the Sentencing Project. "I see abolition as a goal that should be right up there with ending racism. It may not happen in my lifetime, but why would we not want to live in a society that thinks it does not have to put people in cages to maintain order.

"We have the possibility—between Black Lives Matter and the COVID-19 crisis—a moment when we could see significant change in how we structure our lives in our communities," Mauer said. "I don't know how optimistic I am that it'll happen. But it's clear we can't go back to doing things as we did before. The question is: How much of a shift are we willing to engage in?"

The videotape of George Floyd's killing and the callous disregard of the fellow officers who did nothing to stop it exemplified the disrespect U.S. law enforcement has for Black lives. Mixed in among the protesters were people who had already experienced the brutality of the arm of law enforcement known as the criminal justice system.

In the crowd were formerly incarcerated people, as well as grieving relatives with children in cages in faraway towns. They demonstrated while worrying about loved ones who were locked up in a space that made it difficult to social distance during the pandemic.

At the current rate of incarceration, it will be difficult in the near future to be Black in America and not know another Black person who has been caged or whose life is controlled by the government's probation policy. Black people do not have to read the research data or statistics on collateral damage. They have lived it, witnessed it.

And the protests that rocked America in 2020 didn't give an exasperated Qadree Jacobs any new sense of hope.

"The marching, the rioting, the protesting is not new," he said on his way to work at the Philadelphia water company. "It is not going to change anything anytime soon."

His frustration was drawn from an ancient well. Author James Baldwin, who died in 1987, expressed it this way near the end of his life: "What is it you want me to reconcile myself to?...You always told me it takes time. It has taken my father's time, my mother's time, my uncle's time, my brothers' and my sisters' time, my nieces', and my nephews' time. How much time do you want for your 'progress'?"

CHURCH IN THE AGE OF THE BLM MOVEMENT

BY NICK CHARLES

IN THE BEGINNING, THERE was the church, and while their masters' God promised enslaved Africans a measure of salvation even as they endured the whip and the lash, the Black church, as it evolved, vowed it could also deliver African Americans comfort beyond religion, including liberation and freedom.

The mission expanded over time as the Black church went from sole institution of refuge and power for African Americans to a vessel and vehicle for aspirations beyond slavery, beyond the epidemic of lynching, beyond the destruction of communities such as Tulsa, Oklahoma's Black Wall Street in 1921, beyond Jim and Jane Crow and *de jure* segregation.

But now, almost 400 years later, the church faces another challenge as less mature, yet even more feverish and blunt secular mass movements are at the societal helm, directing and demanding racial and social justice change, gender equality, defunding of or abolition of police forces, reform of the carceral state, and promoting LGBTQ rights. The question is, has the church overpromised and underdelivered?

"Well, I think seriously, if you look at Black movements in the United States, they've never been led by the church," the Reverend Traci Blackmon said.

For decades, some observers have commented there has always been this "creation myth" around the civil rights movement: that the Black church was the first responder and was ever-present among frontline workers during the struggle for Black dignity and Black legal and political rights. The soaring rhetoric of the Reverend Dr. Martin Luther King Jr. was always the call to the faithful, the commanding voice in the ears and heads of people; the "I Have a Dream" speech, when they recall the battles fought to gain basic rights, such as the 1964 Civil Rights Act, which ended segregation in public spaces, and the 1965 Voting Rights Act, which prohibited racial discrimination in voting.

But was the African American church really that white knight?

"It's a fallacy of how we present a story after the fact. Certainly, there was involvement, but the church has never been the leading actor of Black movements for liberation," Blackmon said. "They've been a partner...But just because Martin Luther King Jr. was a preacher doesn't mean that the church was leading the movement."

That might sound like blasphemy to many in the Black community, which has been weaned on a history that the church was always closely aligned with the push for civil rights. But even though Dr. King's first church, Dexter Avenue Baptist Church (the name changed in 1978, to Dexter Avenue King Memorial Baptist Church, to honor Dr. King) in Montgomery, Alabama, was where he incubated his civil rights leadership, he moved on when his activism was deemed a distraction from his ministry.

He was once admonished that they, the church leadership, had hired a preacher, not an activist. Dr. King co-founded the Southern Christian Leadership Conference (SCLC) in 1957, which ultimately freed him to do social justice and Black liberation work with the practice of nonviolent protest. While led by ministers, the SCLC is a quasi-religious organization, more concerned with civil and political rights than with prayer and worship. Other Black religious groups, such as the separatist Nation of Islam, were not interested in actively soliciting the United States for human or civil rights. It wanted to be separate: an autonomous state within a nation. Malcolm X, before and after an epiphany around race on a trip to several African countries, was adamant that the United States was venal and corrupt, and wondered aloud, why would Black people want to be a part of that? Dr. King himself once said, in exasperation, to the entertainer and activist Harry Belafonte Jr.: "I fear I am integrating my people into a burning house."

During the late fifties and early sixties, in Birmingham, more than "90 percent of the Black ministers shunned the activities of the Southern Christian Leadership Conference," according to Paul Harvey, professor of history at the University of Colorado, Colorado Springs, and author of *Civil Rights Movements and Religion in America* and *The Color of Christ: The Son of God and the Saga of Race in America*. "Only a minority of churches and clergymen were involved in the movement."

Some were comfortable with their standing in the Black community and fearful of the backlash from white society and their own parishioners. They too were apt to see marchers and protesters, Northern or otherwise, as troublemakers and agitators. Dr. King's SCLC cofounders included the Reverend Joseph Lowery, the Reverend Ralph Abernathy, and the Reverend Fred Shuttlesworth. Even with those stalwarts on board, it's not insulting to question the role of the church, even as we still mourn the 2020 losses of other church-based, civil rights titans, Congressman John Lewis and the Reverend C. T. Vivian.

In the encomiums and sweeping hagiography offered for the duo, the civil rights movement, once again, was offered up as a church-led, male-centered effort, when it was actually far more complicated.

"It was never led by the Black church. That's a myth. It was a coalition between Black men and Black women," said Ruby Sales, legendary social justice and civil rights activist and executive director of the Spirit House Project, a nonprofit organization that uses the arts and education to help bring about racial and social justice change and spiritual maturity. "Ordinary share crop farmers, maids, janitors, and teachers were the backbone of the Civil Rights Movement. And it's only in the hands of people who bring to the telling of the movement, their own prejudices, their own aspects that they have reduced it to an either/or dynamic, when in fact it was simultaneous."

In *Upon This Rock: The Black Church, Nonviolence, and the Civil Rights Movement,* author Allison Calhoun-Brown, who teaches at Georgia State University, wrote: "Churches have traditionally been viewed as places of stability and strength in the African American community. In church, one could find politics, arts, music, education, economic development, social services, civic associations, leadership opportunities and business enterprises. Black churches have been aggregated into the singular institution called 'the Black church' to the extent that they are united by their cultural, historic, social and spiritual mission of fighting the ravages of racism."

Over the decades, the church has become less of a focus for Black life, and congregations are shrinking and aging. That said, when motivated, when it feels that it is singularly under attack, it can be energized and transformed into a potent force. Reverend Raphael Warnock's victory in Georgia's Senate runoff election was fueled in part by an unholy campaign waged by his opponent, Senator Kelly Loeffler, which characterized Reverend Warnock as "radical" and sought to demonize Black liberation theology. The fact that Reverend Warnock, a Democrat, commands the pulpit in Atlanta, at the church, Ebenezer Baptist Church, Dr. King once occupied, made it seem to some that the attacks were on the late, great man's legacy.

"Don't come for the Black church" became a rallying cry, which helped Reverend Warnock ride a tsunami of urban and rural Black voter turnout to make history as the first-ever Black senator from the state.

But as many churches face financial challenges, some in church leadership have foregone their mission and mandate to simply survive, even though it might mean leasing their souls to political actors who don't have the interests of African Americans at heart. Some have accepted government funding through numerous federal programs to stay afloat. During President Donald J. Trump's one term, it was not uncommon to see groups of Black, mostly male, ministers (to be fair, leaders of some Historically Black Colleges and Universities, HBCUs, gave sop to Trump, too) who would appear for photo opportunities as the then-president signed some executive order benefiting religious institutions.

In May 2020, in honor of the National Day of Prayer, Trump, with his Evangelical Advisory Board alongside, held a ceremony in the Rose Garden and signed an executive order on the establishment of a White House Faith and Opportunity Initiative.

"Under the guise of religious freedom, this executive order further entrenches the Administration's policies to allow religion to discriminate," warned Americans United for Separation of Church and State, a nonprofit lobbying organization. "At the same time, it strips the limited religious liberty protections that exist for individuals who use the government-funded social services. First, the order creates 'Faith and Opportunity' offices or liaisons in every federal agency and department and tasks them with enforcing the U.S. Department of Justice's 25-page 'guidance on religious liberty.'

"This guidance contains extreme interpretations of the law in an effort to give a green light to religious exemptions, regardless of how an exemption would affect other people or the public interest. For example, the guidance explicitly states that faith-based organizations may accept taxpayer dollars to perform social services and use those funds to discriminate in hiring. And we know some government contractors want to cite religion to refuse to provide vital services required under their contract, like reproductive health care to victims of sexual assault."

The church, white and Black, has been the beneficiary of federal largesse, particularly, though not exclusively, during Republican administrations. In turn, especially in the white evangelical and some other mainline denominations, they delivered at the ballot box for conservative candidates and the Republican Party. In exchange for legislation and proximity to power, some have been willing to turn a blind eye to governmental policies, such as sequestering children in cages at the southwestern border, which are antithetical to Christ's example.

Some Black churches and ministers were unabashedly complicit. They were muted about the atrocities at the border. And some still claimed that President Trump was not a racist, even as he rolled back policies aimed at diversity, equality, and equity. At the funeral in Houston for George Floyd, the Reverend Al Sharpton delivered a eulogy that emphatically called out his fellow clergy: "There are too many cowards in the pulpit!"

One minister with a national profile who would not be called a coward is Reverend William Barber. Firmly in the tradition of Dr. King, Reverend Barber's crusade, virtual and in person, centers on support of racial, economic, and environmental justice for everyone, specifically the poor and "low wealth" American, who he is convinced remain but an afterthought. "I do believe, and I'll be honest with you, I'm conservative in this way, that our sins can find us out. I do believe that there can be retribution," said Reverend Barber in a Q & A with *The New York Times Magazine*. "What you sow, you can reap."

BLM AND THE BLACK CHURCH

In the aftermath of the killing of Floyd, the Black Lives Matter movement had arguably become the largest, most effective, and most far-ranging social justice and human rights movement...ever.

Black Lives Matter certainly has overshadowed some of the roles that always defaulted to the Black church, and some wondered if it hadn't totally eclipsed the church. By marshaling the burgeoning power of social media, BLM did not depend on institutions or bureaucracies that might exclude marginalized communities, specifically LGBTQ ones, or go through the regular community and church-based channels to reach an attentive audience and activate it.

It was an adhocracy made powerful by technology. Simple hashtags such as #JusticeforTrayvon, #Blacklivesmatter, #Sandrabland, about the death of a young Black woman while in police custody in a small Texas town, and #SamuelDubose, who died at the hands of a Cincinnati police officer, became the jumping-off points for sharing information, stimulating conversation, and mobilizing groups to initiate corporeal protests.

"Black Twitter was instrumental in marshaling people and energy around issues like police shootings of unarmed African Americans in Ferguson and beyond," says Karen Grigsby Bates, a veteran journalist and correspondent for National Public Radio. "It brought attention to aggressive policing before op-ed writers started to weigh in on the cause."

Reverend Blackmon, the senior pastor of Christ the King United Church of Christ in Florissant, Missouri, won't definitively say that the church has been sidelined. "There have always been preachers and Black leaders who have been deeply engaged in public square ministry and who show up in new and continuing ways with young people," she said. "And that's historical. And that's current."

Some agree with Reverend Blackmon, who was intimately involved in the protests in Ferguson after the 2014 shooting of Michael Brown by Officer Darren Wilson. "When they came to Ferguson, by the bus-loads, kind of Freedom Ride–style, I don't think I was in town when they initially showed," recalled Blackmon. "But they slept in and met in the basement of a church, Saint John United Church of Christ, and began to strategize and organize in new ways. They weren't there because they wanted to go to church. They were there because the church provided resources in terms of spaces to sleep and a place to eat. But they did end up going to worship there on that Sunday, out of deep gratitude."

The support the BLM movement received in Ferguson was not a one-off, as more clergy got involved, not in the organizing, but in the lending of tangible brick-and-mortar support and spiritual sustenance.

In her book *Ferguson & Faith: Sparking Leadership & Awakening Community*, Leah Gunning Francis, who teaches at Eden Theological Seminary in St. Louis, recalled the memorable turn of events that took place on the night of September 29, 2014:

Young activists were present and chanting fervently, and the police were posted in front of them, fully dressed in riot gear. However, on this day, more clergy were present than usual, because word had spread that young protesters were often being arrested during these evening protests. In the midst of the stand-off, a few clergy took a decidedly different public action: they knelt on the sidewalk outside the police station and prayed. They symbolically laid down their collars on the altar of justice and made clear that their resistance was an action of their faith.

One can point to high-profile performative incidents such as that to bolster the view that while the church may not always be fully on board with the BLM movement, faith and spirituality are.

"The fight for Black liberation has always been a faith movement," Hebah Farrag, assistant director of research at the University of California Center for Religion and Civic Culture, explained. "It is just a different, newer faith." In some ways the BLM movement has embraced West African religions, such as Yoruba Itan and Ifa; their spirituality and practices and ceremonies before meetings may include pouring of sacrificial libation and the invoking of ancestors.

"Reporting focused on the dissent and the protest and clouded the movement in a sense of aggression," Farrag added. "I was seeing people carrying sage dressed in white. I was seeing ceremony and ritual...and I didn't see any of that being picked up in the media."

Reverend Dr. Valerie Toney Parker, a young adult minister on Chicago's South Side, said, "It's a fair critique" to ask if the Black church has been AWOL at this critical groundswell moment in the fight for universal social and racial justice.

"In fact, my work was centered [on] the assertion by Professor Eddie Glaude Jr., of Princeton, that the Black church is dead," Parker said. "The Black church is not the center of Black life as it once was forty or fifty years ago. And because it's not the center of Black life, a lot of social ills go unchecked. The church continues to operate more in a space and place of piety. The Black church is still alive with its vibrant worship. But as we've known it as the center of Black life and as we've known it as a pillar of our community for addressing civil rights and social justice matters, that part is dead. But like Lazarus, the question is: Can it be called back to life? That really is the question."

Whether it's comatose and on life support, or going through the motions, while the traditional Black church has never been at odds with the goals of racial justice and racial equality, there is a disconnect between what can be referred to as the traditional church and the BLM movement, given the provenance of the latter.

"So, the church sees itself as the moral compass of Black people, really. And yet does maintain this patriarchal and homophobic position, putting both as biblically supported and projecting that," said the Reverend Nana Carmen Ashurst, who serves on the ministerial staff of the Greater Centennial African Methodist Episcopal (AME) Zion Church in Mount Vernon, New York.

Reverend Ashurst, who was once the president of Def Jam Recordings and Rush Communications and is presently the chair of the board of the Universal Hip Hop Museum, added that the composition of congregations should make them more inclusive. "The Black Church thinks of itself as having a long history in the leadership in the Black community, the fight for social justice, even though as an organizational structure in itself, it's oppressive against women. It's a funny thing, I'm an AME Zion and we call ourselves 'the freedom church,' and Harriet Tubman was a member of the AME Zion Church and left her home to the Zion Church, and Frederick Douglass was an AME Zion preacher. So, a long history in the freedom movement and then of course, the civil rights movement.

"And of course, the majority of members of the churches, of all Black churches, are women. But they nonetheless maintain the patriarchal hierarchy, and the churches are extremely hierarchical; the pastor is the center of everything."

It's not gone unnoticed to many that in Reverend Warnock's senatorial victory the paradigm of the traditional Black church plays out: The pastor ascends, even as the foundational, hard work is done by Black women. In this case, the persistent efforts of Stacey Yvonne Abrams, founder of the voting rights group Fair Fight Action and leadership of the state's Democratic apparatus that includes Representative Lucy McBath and the chair of the Democratic Party of Georgia, state senator Nikema Williams, who represents the late congressman John Lewis's district.

That has always been a salient tension between the church, Black and white, and the BLM movement. When Alicia Garza, Patrisse Cullors, and Opal Tometi formed BLM in 2013, in response to the acquittal of George Zimmerman, who a year earlier had followed and shot to death seventeen-year-old Trayvon Martin, it was neither male-dominated nor male-centered. It was much more inclusive than previous groups, organizations, or movements.

"By virtue of who we are," Tometi, the daughter of Nigerian immigrants, who built the Black Lives Matter website, told the *Guardian*, "me being the daughter of immigrants, Alicia and Patrisse being queer...naturally our own identities inform the work."

They took inspiration from activists such as Bayard Rustin, a co-founder of the SCLC and an architect of many of the civil rights strategies in the late 1950s and 1960s, who also led the organizing of the March on Washington for Jobs and Freedom on August 28, 1963. It was there, from that open-air pulpit, that Dr. King delivered the historic "I Have a Dream" speech/sermon. Rustin was gay, and many in Dr. King's inner circle were openly hostile to him. He was not allowed to speak on that hot, late-summer day.

"That's the nature of the times and that's the nature of what it's always been," added Tometi. "I think about Bayard Rustin and James Baldwin and Audre Lorde, and just so many people who've come before us, who didn't necessarily get their shine, maybe because of their queerness. Now we're saying: 'Yeah, let's bring our full selves to the table, and all of that matters.'"

One's full self can be too much for some, whether you are an organizer, writer, or poet. "Within the Black community, or more so, within the Black church, many Black churches do not condone or necessarily support homosexuality or transgender people," said the Reverend Dr. Keisha Agard, assistant pastor at Vanderveer Park United Methodist Church in Brooklyn, New York. "And it's my belief and understanding that many of the people that do not go to church in this day and age are people that have been wounded or hurt by the church at some point, and not only just being hurt but being checked or challenged by the church."

One can point to the Black church's initial slow and ambivalent response to the HIV/AIDs crisis when it was decimating the gay community and the prevailing line was: "Love the sinner, not the sin." HIV/AIDS is still bedeviling African American communities, though not to the extent it once was. It is no longer a death sentence, given effective therapies, drug cocktails, and preventive measures. The church is more responsive, if not more tolerant, and does its part around raising awareness and providing some support for families afflicted with and affected by the disease, for which there is still no cure.

"If we have a common goal, I don't care where you come from, what you're dealing with, because the reality is all of us come with stuff," said the Reverend Agard. "We sometimes lose focus and we major in the minors and minor in the majors. And so we get to the point where we're dealing with people that had AIDS, that pandemic, and instead of dealing with that reality, we were more concerned with homosexuality."

In the age of COVID-19, many are suffering physically, emotionally, and psychologically. But among the groups most hard hit are LGBTQ youth, who don't always have the most supportive environments in the best of times. A report released in summer 2020 by the Trevor Project found that 68 percent had reported symptoms of anxiety disorder and 40 percent had contemplated suicide. Social distancing connected to the pandemic engendered limited access to mental health services, and if traditional organizations such as the Black church were unwilling to step up, young people, particularly African American LGBTQ youth, were the most at risk.

"If an African American church, not *the* African American church, I don't want to broad stroke this, but if an African American church is still struggling around sexuality and LGBTQ," the Reverend Jacqueline Lewis said, "which by the way gets to biblical authority, gets to hermeneutics, gets to interpretation, if they're struggling with gay, if they're struggling with queer, if they're still struggling about whether women can preach, come on, that is a huge handicap, a huge disability for Black churches to lead a movement that's led by women and queer people. So that's a theological problem. And it's not the Black church, but many Black churches."

The Reverend Parker emphasized that the church is aging and "still stuck on who people love. They can't understand that whether you're LGBTQ, whether you're trans, which is part of the LGBTQ [community], that there is still hatred in the form of policy and hatred in the form of brutality that still afflicts and affects the Black community. So, rather than seeing all people as God's creation, the piety in them picks and chooses who is important, and in doing so, it has an impact on the broader community of people writ large called humanity. They can't get out of their own way. So now what you're left with is eighty-year-old and ninety-year-old Miss Johnson...sitting in the pews, not able to get out and do the footwork that's important for social change...And I know this to be true in many churches, including mine: Where are the young people? They're not here, and they're not coming back. You dismissed who they loved. You dismissed how they lived. You dismissed everything except for the extension of your hand for their offering."

As an African American pastor of a sizable church—1,500 members, mixed congregation of about 45 percent Black and 40 percent white and Asian—the Reverend Lewis recognizes the "hugely odd animal that I'm in. Most of the multiracial churches in the country are led by white evangelicals." The Reverend Lewis also acknowledges that too many churches, at the very least the large and mega churches, now focus on the gospel of prosperity and the attainment of personal wealth, which are not seen as part of Christ's teachings and can turn people off. She mentioned the continuing work of the Reverend Barber, who has pastored Greenleaf Christian Church in Goldsboro, North Carolina, since 1993, and is co-chair of the Poor People's Campaign: A National Call for Moral Revival.

"Some of the things he talks about are what the church promotes on the grassroots level: the church that feeds people; tries to house folks," said the Reverend Lewis. "But he talks a lot about the fact that lots of folks don't talk about poverty anymore. A lot of folks are not connected to that kind of reality; sacrificial, collective uplift. We have gotten disconnected from social innovation, justice, right, and Black churches cannot be divorced from those realities, given who they are and what they are."

Many young people have moved on from traditional denominations to more progressive churches, or are eschewing church altogether for more tolerant, intimate communities of faith. Farrag emphasized, "There is a deep sense of hurt you can often feel from BLM activists. Relics of spiritual pain and abuse. Many of them were raised in traditional faiths and kicked out because some aspect of their identity didn't fit."

But it's not only homophobia, it's sexism as well. As a female preacher, the Reverend Agard said she has had to come up against the "stained glass window" that limits the opportunities for women to lead and, by extension, maybe transform congregations.

"When I was in seminary [at Howard University School of Divinity and the Alliance Theological Seminary in Nyack, New York], there were more females in my classes than there were males. I know in corporate America they talk about the 'glass ceiling.' But in the church community, which to many inside has become a corporation or business venture, many females often have to deal with the same thing. And let me say, it's not only the men that question female leadership. Let's be clear, it's not just the brothers. I know that my biggest challenge has been from the females. It's sad, women don't necessarily always support women."

BELIEVER

If anyone ever exhibited the impassioned dedication to faith and the church, while embodying the things that the traditional church has been hostile to, it's the Reverend Jasolyn Harris. Born and raised in San Diego, California, the bubbly and effusive millennial, whose speech is peppered with "like" and "kinda," grew up in the church and is the kind of ride-or-die Christian the church yearns for. Her father had been a minister and pastor all of her life in the Black Missionary Baptist Church denomination, which she describes as being very conservative.

"So, women can't preach, women can't pastor, women-can't-even-stand-in-the-pulpit kinda conservative. Kinda, if-you're-gay-you're-going-to-hell conservative," Harris said. "Just kinda your standard, what people think how right-wing Christianity is. However, I didn't always know or understand that that was a bad thing growing up, so I really enjoyed church. I loved my dad and my mom, who were just like really good examples. And by good examples, I mean we saw them the same at church and at home. We never saw them being like different people. Although they had these really conservative views, they were still really like, they really believed in God, and there was some genuineness there that certainly came off to us as kids. It was truly an enjoyable experience for us growing up in the church."

When she was eight, her father got an opportunity to pastor a church in Stockton, California, and he relocated the family. In the beginning it was a struggle since the congregation was small, around thirty people, recalled Harris. But within five years the congregation had swelled to several hundred, and it became one of the bigger churches in the small central valley city.

"It was kinda a big deal," she said. Then in an instant, one Sunday, her world imploded. As the family sat in church, a bomb-shell was detonated. "One day he [her father] got up in front of the congregation and was just like, yo, 'I'm divorcing my wife' and it was this whole announcement and everybody was devastated. It was really dramatic. I have three brothers, that I'm really, really close to. I'm the third born and the only girl. And so, I just really was impacted by the way he went about letting us know."

It was not just that one revelation that rocked her world, it was subsequent decisions made by her father that completely unmoored her family. Without warning, soon after the divorce, her father moved to Portland, Oregon. One day he was in the house, then the divorce, and then he was living in another state. "We were all like, 'What the hell is going on?' Three months into it, my mom finds out he cheated with a lady in the church and he had moved to Portland with her and her kids."

It was a challenging time for the family, and her mother was alone, trying to raise four children with no financial support. Her mother plunged into extreme depression once she became a single parent. What sustained them all was their faith, and even though it was the site of the family's most severe traumas, they continued to attend the same church. "For a while we were still going to the same church that my dad left, but that was traumatizing for my mom, so we tried different churches. But it still didn't work."

Her father's actions shook her foundation and haunted her for years through her teens, and that nightmare accompanied her when she left for college, at Fresno State, where she found herself questioning why she was even still attending church.

"Why am I going? What is this about? I was lost, but also, I kept going because it was something that I did," Harris said. "And then I was introduced to another group of people who were Christians, who were talking about, 'There's more to the Bible than going to church on Sundays. Church is about justice work and looking out for the poor.' That really resonated with me. I had never heard that before. I got involved in that ministry."

Then, at nineteen, she had what she termed a "surreal" experience. She was walking from a classroom to her dormitory and got this sense that "I was called to ministry. Again, I'm nineteen. I'm like, huh? Nothing like this has ever happened. I didn't know what it was and basically, I just kept walking. I kept living my life, but remembering that moment and not knowing what it meant. Again, this is in the context that I grew up in a Black Baptist church where women weren't able to be ministers. But I continue to be involved in this urban ministry."

The call to preach the gospel is not to be taken lightly. It is not simply a desire or aspiration to do something, like, say, become a doctor. The famed Welsh minister Martyn Lloyd-Jones admonished that it is an obsession that grips one's soul. It's not a fly-by-night experience or a passing fancy. "You do your utmost to push back and to rid yourself of this disturbance in your spirit which comes in these various ways," said Lloyd-Jones. "But you reach the point when you cannot do so any longer. It almost becomes an obsession, and so overwhelming that in the end you say, 'I can do nothing else, I cannot resist any longer.'"

When she graduated from college, Reverend Harris found herself at one of many crossroads that we all encounter. What to do next? Which path to take? How do I know that the choice I make will be the right one? She did have options: go to graduate school and study social work or stay at her job serving underprivileged children. Still living in Fresno, she ran a tutoring program and would take the mostly inner-city and underprivileged children on trips to Yosemite National Park.

"These kids had never been to Yosemite, and it was forty minutes from where they lived. I said, 'We got to get them here.' I got a bus and we ended up there. I was really happy, but something inside me said, 'At least apply for graduate school.'"

She did not get into Fresno State or San Francisco State, so she thought that was a sign from God to continue working with kids.

Then one day she received a letter in the mail from San Francisco State stating that she was still in the running. Two weeks later, she got an acceptance letter, and with it the realization that she would have to move north to the Bay area.

It took her over a year to find her spiritual footing and a welcoming church community. Her younger brother, Moses, sixteen months her junior, moved to Oakland a year after she did, and within a week, he called her and said, "'Jas, I found us a church!' We went to The Way and that was that; we've never left. The Way just felt like home."

The Way Christian Center, a West Berkeley holistic ministry founded by Pastor Michael McBride, known as Pastor Mike, has been a huge influence on Harris. "Pastor Mike was just such a gem from the moment I met him...super empowering and looking over my life, and always saying, 'Let me know when you're ready to get into leadership' and really encouraging me. I was like, 'What is this guy talking about?'"

What McBride pushed is activism and fostering leadership of young people. His mantra is "My pulpit is wherever the people gather, and my parish is the neighborhood." His greatest area of concern is gun violence that plagues so many cities and specifically communities of color, and he co-founded the National Black and Brown Gun Violence Prevention Consortium.

"At both the leadership and participation level, many of the young people that I know didn't find their 'people,' whether they were Christian or Muslim," said the Reverend McBride, who had spent time pastoring in Ferguson, Missouri. "Now, they just find a home or primarily identify being with a movement, work, not necessarily re-ligious work. So, I do think that the particular take around leadership models is the necessary draw-out."

The more he guided Harris, the more that "calling" at nineteen weighed on her. It became more intense the more she got involved with The Way. As much as she resisted, it was clear to her that her destiny lay in ministry, and she finally decided to attend seminary after completing her graduate degree from San Francisco State University in social work.

"I had a lot of barriers around me being a woman in leadership, given the way I was raised and what theologically I was exposed to," Harris explained. "But if I was going to do this, I wanted to be responsible and ethical. And my two mentors both went to Duke [University's Divinity School]. So, I applied, and I was like, 'Oh my God.' I actually got in. Then I freaked out! 'I can't do this; I can't move to North Carolina!'"

She deferred her enrollment for a year and taught sociology at Diablo Valley College while also studying for her LSCW exam to be a licensed therapist in California, which she would go on to pass. In 2016, she finally matriculated at Duke. Yet, throughout her entire journey, she dealt with the familial breach orchestrated by her father and a lifelong struggle with her weight.

"I'm a plus-sized person, but a little while after graduate school I ended up losing about a hundred twenty-three pounds. I became this thing I never thought I would be. And all my life I was kind of obsessed around if I'm small, that's going to be the answer to all of my problems. Once I'm small, then this. Once I'm small, then that. I finally got small, like a size four, and life still sucked. Wait, this really sucks!

"I was always trying to be small and not confident in who I was. I thought everything was going to be different, but it wasn't, and in a year's time, I gained all the weight back before starting seminary school the next month," she added. Each month she gained twelve to fourteen pounds back, she said, and each month she fell deeper and deeper into depression.

"In my mind, I got to the point of 'If I gain all the weight back, if I get fat again, there's no point in living.' That's how much I despised being fat. I thought it was the end of the world."

Compounding all of this, Harris questioned her sexuality. "I identified as straight most of my life, but since I was twelve there was something there, some sort of attraction to women. But it was not a viable thing for the community I grew up in, my family and my church community. Also, my eldest brother is queer; he's a gay man, and I saw what his life was like and how he was treated, and subconsciously I was like, 'No. I'm going to keep doing this thing over here because it works for me.'

"I repressed and denied for as long as I could, but as I got older, this was more and more on my mind, and [I] felt really ashamed about it and didn't want to talk to anyone about it. Mind you, at this point, I was also like an affirming person. I wanted to become a minister. I wanted to marry queer people. But when it came to me, I was just like, 'I cannot be this as well as a Black, fat, queer woman.' I'm like, 'Jesus! Please don't let that be my story. That sounds so heavy and so difficult.' My life is already so difficult as a big, Black woman living in the world. I didn't want to add another thing."

Everything descended on her: weight gain, wrestling with sexuality, starting seminary, being away from her beloved family on the West Coast, a pause on her career. But the time was also transformational in so many ways as she addressed some of those core theological beliefs that confronted her.

"I was able to address them and be freed from them," she said. "I was able to understand all the complexities of how this particular faith was so colonized, so shaped by white, Western Christianity, like learning about queer theology, liberation theology, womynism, which is Black woman theology, all these other ways that people were thinking about God in an academic and scholarly way. It was really transformational."

In the end, Harris continued attending therapy to process her feelings and manage her anxieties, and Harris came out as queer.

"I started dating, and got a better understanding of who and where

I was. It was somewhat of a safe place to come out. Duke Divinity School most certainly wasn't a safe space, but Durham surprisingly has a strong Black, queer community," she explained. "And I ended up working with this great nutritionist who was way more body positive."

Even after navigating all of that and graduating from seminary, Harris was still not certain the ministry was for her. The seeds planted by her childhood experiences, brought up in a conservative church, were deeply rooted.

"Again, my dad is a pastor and my dad is someone, current day, I don't have a good relationship with. I don't talk to him. He's not affirming. He didn't come to my graduation. It's not a good relationship. Especially now that we're in the same field and I don't have that experience with him, there's a lot of hurt and sadness around that. In many respects it will always be sad, based on the decisions my dad is making not to be part of my life, although the door is open, of course."

Harris pressed on and finally began having the conversation with McBride about where she might begin her ministry. Long story short, together they concluded that she was going to be a pastor, and it then became a matter of where. Since her siblings all lived in Los Angeles and it had been difficult for her to be away from them, when the chance came to return, she jumped at it. She moved to Los Angeles in July 2019 and got ordained as a pastor that month at the Lake Christian Center and also started her own private practice as a mental health therapist. The transition was hectic and not without challenges. For the first six months she had to adjust to the cost of living.

"It's super expensive! But things kinda turned around at the top of [2020] and I was able to come out of the fog of…leaving seminary," she said. "Someone in my church community offered to help me find affordable therapy and I was able to get back on track and feel better about things. In March, we were getting ready for Easter. We were planning a sunrise service at the top of a mountain. And then, COVID happened."

THE PANDEMIC AND THE CHURCH

The pandemic exposed the long-standing racial inequities in the United States that permeate all strata of society and throughout every index, including labor, economic, educational, and especially health. At its onset some church leadership, Black and white, balked at restrictive measures and protocols that would keep houses of worship shut to help prevent the spread of the virus. Some openly defied the edicts, and others went to court to have them overturned. Many services and choir practices became super-spreader events and led to infection and death. The toll on African American communities was so apparent that houses of worship had little choice but to restrict in-person worship. As the pandemic dragged on, many churches, which are after all businesses, pivoted to online services and discovered PayPal and Venmo to keep tithes coming.

According to a study published by the British medical journal *The Lancet*, Black people were twice as likely to become infected with COVID-19 as white people, and people of Asian descent are one and a half times as likely.

The pandemic also revealed just who was an "essential" worker, and therefore more apt to be exposed to the virus, and who could afford to remain relatively safe working from home, facilitated by technology, Zoom, and Google Hangouts. Remote learning became a necessity at all levels of education, but it was made easier in school districts where students had easy access to Internet connections, high-speed broadband, and hardware.

Those in elder care and medical fields—health care workers in nursing homes, nurses, orderlies, nurses' aides—were disproportionately people of color, as were civil servants, such as bus drivers and rail employees. Not to mention those who work in the retail and service industry: mom and pop stores, bodegas, kitchen and back-of-the-house restaurant support staff. They were the ones who bore the brunt of the pandemic, specifically when it was pummeling New York City in March, April, and May of 2020. In the rollout of vaccines to stem the rising tide of infections and deaths, structural racism, the silent, working arm of white supremacy, is afoot as African Americans and people of color are getting vaccinated at rates two to three times lower than whites.

But COVID-19 also had another effect: It was instrumental in the swell of global demonstrations as people decided to brave getting infected and began protesting police use of deadly force. This is what George Floyd's daughter meant when she said: "Daddy changed the world." Floyd, by all accounts, was a person of faith, especially in his original hometown of Houston. "He was like the OG of the neighborhood and made sure we were welcomed in," Pastor Patrick "PT" Ngwolo of the church Resurrection Houston, told Religion Unplugged. "In the Bible we call it a person of peace."

One pandemic exposed and highlighted another. People sat in their homes and in a three-month period learned about the white vigilante killing of a Georgia man, Ahmaud Marquez Arbery, and a Louisville, Kentucky, EMT, Breonna Taylor, who was shot and killed by police officers as they forced entry into her home. And then there was Floyd's killing.

The comedian Dave Chappelle joked, "Thank God for COVID," because of the paucity of mass shootings, school or otherwise, since the onset of the virus. But the epidemic of Black people being shot by police seemed to continue unabated. In the United States, according to the Brookings Institution, one Black person is killed by police about every forty hours. Black teenagers are twenty-one times more likely than white teenagers to be shot by police. And one out of every

1,000 Black men can expect to be killed by police. It's against this backdrop that the video, literally a snuff film, of Floyd went viral.

"Yeah, of course, I watched it," Reverend Lewis said. She sighed heavily. "I will never get the picture of the officer's knee on his neck out of my mind. Those hands in his pocket...if you really pay attention you could see that he is squirming his knee against cartilage and bone. All of those people kneeling on him...that I will never forget. And I'm of a certain age, I'm sixty-one, so I can vividly remember the picture of Emmett Till on the cover of *Jet* magazine and how his mother let us see that, so we would not forget. So, what came to mind was that it was a lynching."

The Reverend Lewis, who recalls as a child how she hid below her bed as "bullets flew" in her Chicago neighborhood in the aftermath of the assassination of Dr. King, is the senior minister for public theology and transformation at Middle Church in Manhattan, New York. She also connects what was done to Floyd to the most sickening images from the 1960s civil rights era.

"If we really watch again, the [Edmund] Pettus Bridge beatings, the hoses being sprayed strong enough on our children to send them flying down a street, you know, streams of water that are strong enough to strip bark off trees, the violence against Black people, the violence against brown people in cages, this is horrific blight, blessed by the church: blessed by the white church. So, when I watch it, I'm motivated. I am outraged. And I know just because we saw it on camera, there's so many more that we haven't seen on camera."

WHITE CHRISTIAN NATIONALISM

There can be no discussion of the Black church without an examination of the white church. In many ways the Black church was and is set up in opposition to the white church, since for most of the nation's history, and like the rest of society, worship was not integrated.

"It is appalling that the most segregated hour of Christian America is eleven o'clock on Sunday morning," Dr. King said in 1963.

While that has changed some, the Pew Research Center has found that at least eight out of ten parishioners still attend service where the congregation is exclusively of one race. But even separated, much of what the Black and Latinx churches have absorbed around religion and theology is an aping of the white church.

Dana Milbank, a columnist at the *Washington Post*, delved into how important white evangelical Christians were to President Trump's failed 2020 reelection efforts.

"White evangelicals are only 15 percent of the population, but their share of the electorate was 28 percent, according to Edison Research exit polling, and 23 percent, according to the Associated Press version," Milbank wrote. "Though exit polls are imprecise, it seems clear that white evangelicals maintained the roughly 26 percent proportion of the electorate they've occupied since 2008, even though their proportion of the population has steadily shrunk from 21 percent in 2008.

"The white evangelicals' overperformance also shows, unfortunately, why the racist appeal Trump made in this campaign was effective," Milbank wrote. "White evangelicals were fired up like no other group by Trump's encouragement of white supremacy."

The use of the word "unfortunately" in Milbank's prose betrays the can't-believe-this-is-true attitude that much of the corporate media and social and political commentators adopt when the topic rears its ugly head. "This can't *really* be us" is the clutch-your-pearls posture some assume. They would like that to be true, but it isn't. This *is* them! Most everything in American society benefits white comfort and discounts and/or dismisses Black pain.

Robert P. Jones, who runs the Public Religion Research Institute, told Milbank, "Trump inspired white Christians, 'not despite, but through appeals to white supremacy,' attracting them not because of economics or morality, 'but rather that he evoked powerful fears about the loss of white Christian dominance.'"

The Reverend Miguel A. De La Torre, professor of social ethics and Latinx studies at Iliff School of Theology in Denver, Colorado, said, "A lot of it probably has to do with these churches who were oppressed, copying the theology of the white churches. So, when white churches sent missionaries to Puerto Rico and Latin America, they were mostly fundamentalist churches back in the early 1900s.

"Black churches that found their own spaces many times copied the theology of the masters and of the overseers, and Paulo Freire (most notably in his groundbreaking 1968 text, *Pedagogy of the Oppressed*) talks about this: 'What happens when the oppressed copy the structures of the oppressors?' And I think that legacy continues to be manifested today."

Author of more than two dozen books, De La Torre is an unflagging and relentless critic of the white church and its minions, which he said is "killing Christianity." In one of his most incendiary books, *Burying White Privilege: Resurrecting a Badass Christianity*, De La Torre mercilessly flogs the white church:

The gospel is slowly dying in the hands of so-called Christians, with evangelicals supplying the morphine drip. Christ's message of love, peace, and liberation, has been distorted and disfigured by Trumpish flim flammers who made a Faustian bargain for the sake of expediency, whose licentious desire for ultra conservative Supreme Court justices trumped God's call to judge justly. These Euro-American Christians have made a preferential option for the golden calf over and against the Golden Rule as they revel in an unadulterated power grab, deeming white privilege to be more attractive than waiting for the inheritance promised to the meek. White Christianity has more than a simple PR problem; it is inherently problematic.

De La Torre references President Trump and the unwavering support he had, and continued to receive, from white evangelicals, who in the 2016 presidential election voted 81 percent for Trump. Other denominations also went for Trump in 2016 in great numbers: 58 percent of Protestants; 60 percent of white Catholics; and 61 percent of Mormons. In his lost 2020 reelection bid, according to the AP VoteCast survey, 81 percent of white evangelicals again voted for Trump, though there were slight shifts in some crucial states. In 2016, 92 percent of white evangelicals in Georgia voted for Trump. But in 2020 that number dipped to 85 percent. Former vice president Biden won the state by less than 14,000 votes. And in Georgia, Biden, a practicing Catholic, out-balloted Trump among Catholics by a competitive 52 percent to 47 percent.

"These individuals—Protestants, Catholics, Mormons, and evangelicals—share more than an ethnic identity," De La Torre wrote. "They share a cultural identity: white Christian. They voted for a person who promised them power and standing even though his entire life repudiates everything Christ modeled and taught. What kind of religion tolerates separating crying children from nursing mothers?"

De La Torre is not a singular voice on this subject.

Jemar Tisby, a church historian and the author of *The Color of Compromise*, said, "What Black Lives Matter did was highlight the racism and white supremacy that still has a stranglehold on much of white Christianity. You have this phrase and this movement that is forcing people, essentially, to take sides."

The dean of Black religious scholarship and Black liberation theology, James H. Cone, who died in 2018, once wrote: "Black theologians and preachers have rejected the white church's attempt to separate love from justice and religion from politics because we are proud descendants of a Black religious tradition that has always interpreted its confession of faith according to the people's commitment to the struggle for earthly freedom."

In the essay, Cone explained that the Black church was faced with a choice: "The cry of Black Power by Willie Ricks (a field secretary alongside John Lewis in SNCC who later changed his name to Mukasa Dada), its political and intellectual development by Stokely Carmichael (later, Kwame Ture) and others challenged the Black church to move beyond the models of love defined in the context of white religion and theology. The Black church was thus faced with a theological dilemma: either reject Black Power as a contradiction of Christian love (and thereby join the white church in its condemnation of Black Power advocates as un-American and unchristian), or accept Black Power as a socio-political expression of the truth of the gospel. These two possibilities were the only genuine alternatives before us, and we had to decide on whose side we would take our stand."

That struggle endures. It's not that the Black church ignores the racism that is part of the DNA of the white church, but it's a devil it knows. The BLM movement is one they haven't gotten a handle on as yet. On one side you have Black Christians, some of whom are wrestling with what they have been taught, what they have lived, and what they think the BLM movement represents.

"BLM grew initially out of the death of Trayvon Martin," John Edmerson, senior minister of Church of Christ at the Vineyard in Phoenix, Arizona, told the *Christian Chronicle*, "but has now expanded to include Black people represented in any societal setting with special emphasis supporting the LGBTQ plus platform and the doing away with male-orientated leadership in the family."

Many white Christians who express contempt for the BLM movement don't mince words.

"Their own writing shows that they are on the opposite side of

the spectrum from those of us who try to follow Christ's teachings,"
Merijo Alter, a member of the High Ridge Church of Christ in
Missouri and whose husband is a former Republican state senator,
said to the *Christian Chronicle*. "We should be at the forefront of
being politically incorrect by affirming that 'All Lives Matter,' yet this
is construed as a racist remark. I was taught as a child (to sing), 'Red
and yellow, Black and white, we are precious in his sight.' We have
been hijacked by this disgusting organization."

Ruby Sales is adamant that the reasons—destroying the traditional
family and subverting a tacit, religious-based racial harmony—
white evangelicals and others proffer for their disdain of the BLM
movement are smoke screens. "They think the Black Lives Matter
movement is a movement to destroy them," Sales said. "Because,
somehow, they believe that Black people have savage anxieties, that
we pose a threat to their security and that we are savages. And I'm
saying savages are mostly those who cannot be civilized and who
must be destroyed. It is not about the 'family.' That's a bunch of
crap, because you can't say you care for the family and then turn
around and not pass gun control legislation when *your* children are
being shot up in schools."

In demonizing and seeking to diminish the BLM movement,
congregants of all stripes resist facing the patriarchy or homophobia
that exists in the church. For white believers, the mention of white
supremacy is ofttimes a bridge too far. The Reverend Dr. Paul Ramsey,
the senior minister at the progressive Mayflower Congregational
Church in Denver, Colorado, explained that for many the church is
one of the last bastions in society that harkens to a fading reality.

"One of the parts of the church that happens in the white church
and in the Black church, especially in the male-dominated piece of
what I would consider kind of mainline Black church and evangelical
white church, is that the patriarchy that has the power, their power is
only in the church. They have very little power outside of that, unless

they are in a small evangelical community, unless they have some sort of a traditional place where they're the head of the rotary.

"But because of that, they try to channel everything back into the church so that there's more say. So, the outside world to them, or in that kind of construct, is scary and represents a wilderness or a wildness that they can't contain and that they no longer have control of."

Ramsey's measured sermons admonish his small flock to step outside their comfort zone and have the difficult conversations around racism, sexism, and homophobia with their relatives and those within their communities. Because, he said, we are in a changing world, where the norms that gave white Christians a sense of power and even dominion have been radically altered, most recently by the BLM movement. He notes that too many white Christians, in an effort to retain and maintain what they see as their ordained place atop the caste system that is the United States, ignore or lash out and cling even more to their interpretations of scripture.

"It's really just the Bible translated as their idea of a kind of idyllic America, you know, the *Andy Griffith Show* kind of America, and they have no way to navigate a world where there's equity," added the Reverend Ramsey. "So, they don't; they don't say much at all because they're painting this completely dysmorphic picture of what the world is supposed to be like.

"That's how Trump gets a stronghold because there's a nonsensical world at work, so then why wouldn't an immoral person be able to lead the charge of morality? The world is just so abstract that they are able to develop a plan with all these evil characters with all these kinds of weird conspiracies that see Trump as the Messiah figure, because they are so far away from an ideal of an equitable world that's loving and non-bigoted. And, so it really is this kind of fairy tale, but more like a Brothers Grimm–style fairy tale that they have to paint these monsters and the wolves in the Hansel and Gretel–style craziness, and it seems that we're back to that kind of weird reality that I say has nothing to do with the redemptive power of Christ."

In the aftermath of the rioting and looting by domestic terrorists at the Capitol building on January 6, which resulted in the deaths of five people including a police officer, Reverend Ramsey chucked his prepared sermon for January 10. "I'm not going to give the sermon I started to write on Monday. I'm not going to talk to you about the power that comes from knowing God loves you. That he, she loves just because you are. I'm not going to give that sermon because I can't. There are more pressing things that have to be discussed, right. The elephant in the room cannot be ignored; faith has to inform the context of our lives."

What Reverend Ramsey, like most of us glued to cable news, saw was a mob of Americans, domestic terrorists, amassed in the name of the outgoing president and God—some waved flags, "Jesus Saves" and "GOD, GUNS & GUTS MADE AMERICA, LET'S KEEP ALL THREE!"—perpetrate an assault on American democracy. It was based on a big lie, that President Trump lost the 2020 election because of massive voter fraud, specifically in cities with large numbers of African American voters.

"Think of January sixth, which happened to be the Day of Epiphany on the Christian calendar," Reverend Ramsey added. "And the events at the Capitol, and no reasonable person can ever argue about inequity again, no reasonable, faithful person can ever doubt the existence of white privilege again. I say all of this not to be political, I say all this to be faithful, to be human, to help us take on the role of healers, to take on the role of people of promise, people of hope."

De La Torre said he consistently asked his students: "Why do you want to become a minister? Because you can make a living off of this and you can have some security? How are you doing this? Because it's a *calling!* You risk everything, even your life, for the gospel message. You know, we have domesticated the calling. We're more concerned with the pension plans once the minister retires, as opposed to the official part of doing the work of the gospel."

Even though he lost reelection, Trump's influence remains. Avowed white nationalist groups have been emboldened by his rhetoric and recall his admonition to one fringe group, the Proud Boys, during a presidential debate. Asked to rebuff them, Trump said, "Stand back and stand by."

There is an even more virulent strain of white evangelicalism now manifesting as Patriot Churches. It's a small patchwork of non-denominational congregations that view the Democratic Party and the political left as godless and giving succor to socialists, the LGBTQ community, and those who favor a woman's right to choose. It's no accident that Trump threatened to form his very own "Patriot" party to challenge what is left of the traditional Republican one.

"The Patriot Churches belong to what religion experts describe as a loosely organized Christian nationalist movement that has flourished under President Trump," wrote Sarah Pulliam Bailey of the *Washington Post*. "In just four years he has helped reshape the landscape of American Christianity by elevating Christians once considered fringe, including Messianic Jews, preachers of the prosperity gospel and self-styled prophets."

But Trump didn't invent any of this. Republicans, traditional, moderate, and conservative, for decades have been supplying just enough oxygen to white fear of a Black planet. In Trump, they found the ideal avatar. One of the myths promoted by the media and politicians, when it serves their purposes, is that the United States is divided, and divisiveness is the order of the day. But the results of the 2020 presidential election, where Black voters in major cities such as Milwaukee, Detroit, Philadelphia, and Atlanta repudiated Trump and Vice President Mike Pence and put President Joe Biden and Vice President Kamala Harris over the top, is evidence that *America* is not divided. Rather, it's *white people* who are divided over whether to support equality, equity, diversity, and representation, or to reinforce white supremacy. And though there are many who would consider themselves allies and be considered allies by African Americans and BIPOC communities, how many are disrupters? Those willing to literally cast their lot in with movements dedicated to making a more perfect union.

CAN I GET A WITNESS?

Ruby Sales grew up in the Baptist tradition in Jemison, Alabama, and her father was a minister. As a young woman, she felt compelled to get involved in the upheaval happening in the streets across the United States, as mostly Black people demonstrated for human and civil rights. She joined the Student Nonviolent Coordinating Committee (SNCC), a civil rights group formed to give young people more of a voice during the civil rights movement.

"I was done and through with religion when I joined the movement," Sales said. "And it took me years to understand that movements are where people connect their internalized, inner consciousness with the world we live in outside. That movements are about the very breath that we take in and the very breath that we put out."

Sales debunks the binary assertions that the Black church was either arm in arm with Black liberation movements or hostile to them.

"There's a difference between the Black church that has been defined by the prosperity gospel that says that the verification of who we are is what we have and what we have comes from the empire rather than God," she said. "Up until the Southern freedom movement and during the Southern freedom movement, the Black churches themselves had to create a theological discourse about the significance of Black lives in a society that enslaved us, in a society that reduced us to property. And so, I think the Black church, like any other institution, is dynamic, not static. What it is today does not necessarily mean what it was prior to integration."

What the civil rights movement did was invert and reposition roles in the Black community, Sales said, since it was the congregants, ordinary Black Christians, who were members of the Black church that used it as a place to have mass meetings. What made it a freedom movement was that leadership "rearranged class relationships. And it changed who could have access to the public microphone and who was considered to be legitimate articulators of the Black condition and the Black agenda."

It had not happened since Black reconstruction, so this was the second time that ordinary Black people, such as Fannie Lou Hamer, who could barely read and write and only went to the fourth grade, were the setters of the Black agenda. It was not only unsettling to white supremacy; it was unsettling to class in the Black community.

"And also," added Sales, "what people missed was that in those Black churches, it also rearranged white, patriarchal power, because Black women were standing up in pulpits, not only articulating the movement goals but exegeting the meaning of biblical scripture as they talked about movement. And the problem with the retelling of the story is that people have not understood the deep redemptive, restorative meaning of what was not simply a civil rights movement. We sang freedom songs; we lived in freedom houses; we had freedom summer; so civil rights were part of a larger struggle, which was freedom."

In Sales's recounting of her firsthand experience in the movement, there was homophobia, but it played out differently for gay men and lesbians. Black gays could find a place in the church and, though seemingly stereotypical, they were the choir directors and they were the heads of youth organizations.

"They were welcome. They were very visible," Sales said. "The problem in the Black church was never with Black gay men more so than it was with Black women. Because, as Toni Morrison pointed out in *Beloved*, there was some tension between Black men and Black women...that Black men were fighting for their manhood, any threat to what they perceived what is meant to be a man was treated differently, included how they treated Black men who were gay. It's not true to paint the Black church as being the same with Black gay men as it was with Black gay women."

Comparing the movements of the 1960s with the Black Lives Matter movement of today is difficult for Sales, given how disparate the eras are. One still existed in the industrial age, while today's is swaddled in and fueled by technology.

"In the sixties communities were still intact, we were moving towards a technocracy," she said. "But our feet are now firmly planted in a technocracy that decimates intimacy, that decimates community. And so the question [of] whether Black folk are interested in [a] movement, or even if white folk are interested in [a] movement, is how is it that you build a movement that requires intimacy in a capitalist technocracy where intimacy is virtual and lived history doesn't matter?"

The faux racial reconciliation offered by the white church is hypocritical and impotent, said De La Torre. All this reaching across the pew or across the political aisle does nothing to improve the lot of people of color and only serves the interests of white supremacy.

"No, I will not hold hands and sing 'Kumbaya' with white oppressors," he wrote at the end of his book. "Instead I will ask all who seek justice, especially whites willing to repent of their complicity with white privilege, to join me in solidarity as I choose to sing a different badass song. Let us finally sing: 'Basta! (Enough)!'"

A RECKONING

So we now know where some in the white church are headed, but where does the Black church go from here? The nation itself seems comfortable normalizing everything—genocide against indigenous peoples; slavery; domestic abuse; violence against Black and brown bodies; penning children in cages; war; poverty; white hegemony and white supremacy. Citizens clamored for a return to "normal" amid a pandemic that claimed hundreds of thousands of lives. The virus ruptured routines and diminished patience to where people were willing to risk infection and even death to belly up to the bar, dine indoors at restaurants, travel for the holidays—all against the advice of medical and health experts.

There were calls from many, who sought to downplay the insurrection of January 6, for healing, for unity. But healing and unity are also languages of white supremacy, because they seek to ignore and diminish white violence as they seek to bind a wound with gauze and bandages that needs radical surgery. John the Baptist speaks of reconciliation, but admonishes that there can be none without repentance.

Too many want to avoid accountability; the let's-just-put-this-all-behind-us attitude that avoids rigorous review and clinical autopsy. Americans always want the quick fix—in the case of COVID-19, the vaccine. Even then there will be no return to normal. The change has been profound and lasting. As of the end of 2020, more than 8 million people had slipped into poverty, 1.2 million of them African American. The racial wealth gap is now a yawning chasm, income inequality is at an all-time high and rising, and the promise of a more egalitarian social and political union is threatened. And that threat comes from a political party that once touted personal responsibility, but now traffics in grievance and promotes white identity politics.

Across the aisle is a party that resists fully embracing a mandate of change demanded by the groups of voters, African Americans, people of color, young people, and progressives that continue to show up for it. It's still too concerned with white comfort; how to placate the "forgotten Americans"—code for white people, who are intent on maintaining their caste dominance.

Despite that stark and foreboding reality, Ruby Sales is optimistic. "This is not the first time that Black, brown, and white young folks have stood together. I mean, the anti-war movement (of the sixties and seventies); college takeovers. That's reflected now in the movement that is saying that Black lives finally matter as much as white lives. Remember 'Occupy Wall Street'? That was part of it as well. Movements don't happen without a buildup."

What positive change that does exist may now be reflected in church practice, which has been forced by the pandemic and police brutality to innovate and evolve.

The Reverend Blackmon said, "You know, this moment in time has created a need and opportunity for the institutional church to have to figure out who we are and how we are going to be and what we're going to accomplish outside of our buildings.

"The playing field has been leveled in a lot of ways. What do you have to offer when your only way of communicating is virtual?" she said. "And when the people whose attention you have held captive for at least once a week and sometimes more are not just given the opportunity to listen to you, but can listen to any number of people over virtual space. What is it about what you offer in church, not you as a person, but you as collected bodies?"

The church, many believe, has to either lead, follow, or get out of the way. "Many of us are trying to figure out how we navigate between generations," Reverend McBride said, "between an older generation that doesn't recognize the world they live in and an emergent generation, which is creating a whole new world. And they need the same kind of pastoral care and spiritual support."

"Boom!" Reverend Lewis said. "And shut it down! Woe unto the church that can't be the sanctuary, right, for the immigrant; for the queer Black woman meeting, with a baby suckling; for the poor; for the disenfranchised. Woe to the church that doesn't understand that our mentor is an outsider, who was outside of the power structure of the empire, who pushed every barrier for the sick; for the poor; for the outcasts; for the lepers; for the women; for the children; every barrier smashed to say the kingdom of God, the reign of God, is this kind of place where everyone belongs, where everyone has enough. If we don't get that, that part of the church needs to die, so something else can rise again."

BLACK POLITICAL LINEAGE: FROM ADAM CLAYTON POWELL TO BARACK OBAMA

BY MICHAEL H. COTTMAN AND CURTIS BUNN

BLACK PEOPLE OFTEN POSED these profound questions:

Who will stand up for us?
Who will champion *our* causes?
Who will have *our* backs?
Who will have the courage to speak *our* names?

While well-intentioned whites have sometimes thought they were the answer to these questions, the brunt of the civil rights changes in this country are the result of the hard work of Black politicians.

The lineage is long and winding, and it captures the essence of Black people's survival in a country that has morally, socially, and legislatively oppressed them at every turn. As Black Lives Matter forges ahead to raise awareness of police brutality, mass incarceration, and the shame of public health (among other indecencies), enacting lasting change is still largely the domain of the political arena.

The contemporary civil rights battle is an old-school truth. Black men and women, in a far more racially explosive terrain, navigated the land mines with dexterity and skill, but mostly with commitment and bravery. Some were eloquent and unassuming. Many were audacious and loud. Still more were a mixture of all that. While this country has had Black politicians since before the end of slavery, the most significant Black politicians, whose actions led, most notably, to the election of President Barack Obama and, later, the election of Vice President Kamala Harris, began in the 1940s—and each decade produced more and more politicians who made an impact.

THE 1940S

Reverend Adam Clayton Powell was arguably the first Black politician, who worked at a federal level, who saw it as a sacred obligation to improve the lot of Black people in this country.

Reverend Powell pastored the historic Abyssinian Baptist Church in Harlem, the same church that Reverend Raphael Warnock would someday lead, and his congregants, as well as his title, undoubtedly influenced his agenda and his belief in his ability to overcome the obstacles he was to face.

In 1945, the Baptist minister became the first congressman from Harlem and served in that position for twenty-six years. Legislatively he argued for laws that would elevate Black people, while also doing the personal-touch work that made him a beloved figure uptown.

Powell helped to organize clothing drives and fed poor Black residents. He organized rent strikes and staged boycotts against companies that were discriminating against Black workers—both of which are hard to imagine a sitting congressperson doing now.

Powell was a community organizer, the way Obama would later be before he embarked on his own political journey. Powell helped build a Black political powerhouse that was unparalleled during his time. As the respected pastor of that time's version of a mega church, Powell leveraged his congregation as a built-in voting bloc to effect change.

Black voters packed the wooden pews every Sunday and listened to Powell's message, registered to vote, and headed to the polls in large numbers for elections.

The history of Powell's church underscored Powell's quest for social justice activism and his staunch advocacy for civil rights: It was built in 1809, by seamen from the Ethiopian Empire, known as Abyssinia. The Abyssinian Baptist Church leadership believed worshippers should not be segregated by race inside the church, and led protests for open seating.

Powell embraced this history and infused the church with his fire-and-brimstone rhetoric. His strategic approach thus marked a new and successful branding of Black politics that in many ways led to the more well-known civil rights changes that were to come in the following decades.

"The black masses must demand and refuse to accept nothing less than that proportionate percentage of the political spoils such as jobs, elective offices, and appointments," Powell said. "They must reject the shameful racial tokenism that characterizes the political life of America today."

Historian Charles V. Hamilton, in his 1992 political biography about Powell, wrote: "Here was a person who [in the 1940s] would at least speak out...That would be different...Many Negroes were angry that no Northern liberals would get up on the floor of Congress and challenge the segregationists...Powell certainly promised to do that.

"[In] the 1940s and 1950s, he was, indeed, virtually alone...And precisely because of that, he was exceptionally crucial. In many instances during those earlier times, if *he* did not speak out, the issue would not have been raised."

Powell, in a bold calculation, challenged Mississippi congressman John Elliott Rankin on the house floor for using the word "nigger." It was call-out culture before there was call-out culture. And it marked a historic shift in how Black politicians managed the racism of their colleagues.

"He certainly did not change Rankin's mind or behavior," Hamilton wrote, "but he gave solace to millions who longed for a little retaliatory defiance." And hope.

THE 1950S

In the 1950s, Dr. Martin Luther King Jr. took over the political and social world order. He elevated Black causes to a higher plateau. But King was not a political figure, and while his behavior influenced political decisions, he had no hand in them.

As Dr. King changed the course of history—and Malcolm X emerged as an indomitable force in his own right—Black politicians made their own marks in various ways, many of which echoed the starkest differences between Dr. King and Malcolm.

When Charles C. Diggs Jr. was just thirty-one, he was elected to the House of Representatives, making him the first Black congressman from Michigan. Like Powell before him, Diggs was vocal in his support of civil rights. He was among the first Black politicians to fight for Congress to issue government aid to various parts of Africa, a continent that had been all but dismissed due in no small part to racist attitudes and beliefs.

But whereas Powell had been fueled by the benevolence that comes from enacting God's will, Diggs was less conciliatory. Whereas Powell pushed the envelope with what a Black politician could do, Diggs set that envelope on fire.

After the death of Emmett Till, Diggs called for white racists to be killed. "That picture [of Till in a casket] stimulated a lot of interest and anger on the part of Blacks all over the country," Diggs said.

U.S. Representative John Conyers Jr. of Detroit said Diggs paved the way for an entire generation of Black political leaders.

THE 1960S

In the 1960s, James Brown's "Say It Loud, I'm Black and I'm Proud" served as the anthem to an acceptance of Black beauty and a belief in Black power. Just as before with Dr. King and Malcolm, political machinations ran parallel to social justice initiatives, such as the marches and sit-ins, that dominated the news media at that time.

In 1965, John Conyers of Michigan was elected to the House of Representatives. He took the political power that was individuated by Black members of Congress and he collectivized it, uniting Black politicians.

In addition to being a leader for his Black colleagues, he also got in the ring with the powerful whites. Conyers was the sole African American member of the House Judiciary Committee, one of the most powerful committees in Congress.

After Dr. King's assassination on April 4, 1968, Conyers spent the next fifteen years fighting alongside powerhouse representative Shirley Chisholm of New York to make King's birthday a federal holiday. That year was also a historic year for another reason: It saw the election of Chisholm.

Chisholm was the first Black woman elected to the United States Congress, at a time when Black women held virtually no positions of power within government.

As with Powell before her, Chisholm was a staunch advocate for the poor and sponsored food and nutrition programs for residents in her district. Like Diggs, she was not bashful about what she saw as her place in the world—or her legacy.

"My greatest political asset, which professional politicians fear, is my mouth, out of which come all kinds of things one shouldn't always discuss for reasons of political expediency," Chisholm said.

In 1972, Chisholm became the first Black woman to seek the presidency, even though she knew the country was far from ready. "I want history to remember me, not as the first Black woman to have made a bid for the presidency of the United States," she said, "but as a Black woman who lived in the twentieth century and who dared to be herself. I want to be remembered as a catalyst for change in America."

Indeed where Powell, Diggs, and Conyers before her had their eyes on what was wrong with this country, Chisholm had her eyes on the future.

Inspired by how far Chisholm had gone, Barbara Jordan ran for the state senate and later became the first Black Texas state senator after Reconstruction and the first Black woman to sit in the Texas State Senate. But for Jordan, it wasn't enough that she succeed. She made it her mission to get more Black women elected: "Life is too large to hang out a sign: 'For Men Only,'" she said. And life was definitely too short to hang a "For Whites Only" sign.

In Austin, Jordan worked to pass a state minimum wage law that covered struggling farmworkers—a crowning achievement in such a red state. She sponsored bills helping elders, children, and the homeless. She considered supporting teachers critical. She said education is critical to achieving economic and political empowerment.

THE 1970S

As Jordan fought for the rights of Black Texans, Charles Rangel was fighting for Black rights at a federal level. In 1971, he replaced Adam Clayton Powell as congressman in New York, winning the election by just 150 votes. Rangel's arrival in D.C. grew the number of Black congressmen to thirteen, and that February, he built off the work Conyers had done to collectivize Black voices in Congress and made the motion that declared them to be the Congressional Black Caucus (CBC).

The CBC puts forth policy and legislation that ensure equal rights, opportunity, and access to Black Americans and other marginalized communities. Over the years, the group has only grown in influence.

In addition to co-founding the CBC (with Conyers), Rangel became the first Black to chair the powerful House Ways and Means Committee, a post that represented a monumental step in Black politics. It signaled there were few limits to where Black politicians could rise.

While Powell's work lived at the intersection of religion and politics, Rangel's incorporated business. A lawyer, he centered much of his platform on empowering Black New Yorkers through entrepreneurship. In 1995, he helped establish the Upper Manhattan Empowerment Zone Development Corporation, which significantly boosted Harlem's economic status for African Americans and helped create Black businesses. Rangel marks a shift in Black politicians who saw their role as not only being about securing the welfare of Black individuals but also about helping to increase their economic prosperity. In doing so, he aligned himself with members of the Black church who would later do the same thing.

THE 1980S

Chicago was becoming a focal point for an emerging Black political crusade. As Black people in Chicago became more disillusioned in a political system that continued to ignore them, a Baptist preacher who had marched with Dr. King and served as a disciple in King's inner circle emerged as Chicago's next Black leader with an eye on politics: Jesse Jackson.

Calls for "RUN, JESSE, RUN!" echoed through Black communities across the nation, and in 1984, Jackson became the second African American to make a national bid for the U.S. presidency. The historic campaign garnered 3.5 million votes, which was about 3 million more votes than Chisholm had received.

"That explosion of hope—despite voter suppression and systemic racist policies—was shocking to many people," said Dorothy Butler Gilliam, the first Black female reporter for the *Washington Post*. "I remember Jesse Jackson's shout to his audiences when he ran for president in 1984: 'Keep Hope Alive! Keep Hope Alive!'"

Whereas other politicians had worked to mobilize their base, Jackson formed a coalition based on a multicultural alliance and a campaign to address voter intimidation and harassment, as well as stricter voter ID and ballot requirements. Jackson's campaign also featured an extensive voter registration drive, which increased Black turnout.

"The Jackson '88 campaign theme was 'The Empowerment of All People.' The reverend sought to empower individuals to provide for themselves and challenged the political narrative by using words such as 'hope' and presenting policies that expanded people's sense of the possible," said Craig Kirby, a seasoned Democratic operative who served as Jackson's political aide in 1988.

The 1980s also brought the emergence of another influential Black politician: David Dinkins. In 1989, Dinkins became the first African American to serve as mayor of New York City. He defeated Republican Rudy Giuliani, who years later would become a Trump minion.

While Dinkins sought to make New York City a more just place, he also navigated the blatant racism of a city that was then known as "Up South." In one example, in 1992, an estimated 10,000 off-duty, nearly all-white NYPD officers stormed City Hall to protest Dinkins's policies. Many of the officers carried guns, drank beer, cursed, and some screamed racial epithets.

Some reporters and bystanders were assaulted by the mob, which vandalized property and carried signs that read "Dump the Washroom Attendant."

"Beer cans and broken beer bottles littered the streets as Mr. Giuliani led the crowd in chants," the *New York Times* reported. "It was his second appearance at a police gathering in several weeks. Earlier, Mr. Giuliani attended a Patrolmen's Benevolent Association convention in the Catskills. At the City Hall demonstration, at least one Giuliani supporter circulated through the crowd handing out voter registration cards, and many protesters wore paraphernalia with a decidedly political slant: new white T-shirts bearing the words 'Dinkins must go' and buttons printed: 'Fight Crime. Dump Dinkins.'"

Unlike many of the firebrands who had come before Dinkins on the political stage, Dinkins's reaction to the protests, as well as his approach more generally, was calm and measured, in a way that would later be echoed by President Obama.

"Dave Dinkins was the road that ultimately led to the election of Barack Obama," Reverend Al Sharpton said. "There was David Dinkins talking about the gorgeous mosaic that made many of us understand when Obama said, 'Yes we can' because we had done it in New York under David Dinkins. He mentored many that went on to state and city legislatures. He mentored me as an activist."

But unlike Obama, Dinkins would lose reelection. In 1993, Dinkins's historic term would end and Giuliani's would begin, in what would presage Trump's ascent at the end of Obama's historic presidency.

THE 1990S

The decade opened with a bang: Douglas Wilder was sworn in as the first Black governor elected in U.S. history. Five months into his tenure in Virginia, Wilder ordered state agencies and universities to divest themselves of investments in South Africa because of its policy of apartheid, making his the first Southern state to take such action.

A product of historically Black Virginia Union University in Richmond, Wilder said during his inauguration speech: "As complexities of human relationships increase, the power to govern them also increases. The proper use of that power must always be subordinated to the public good and that shall be uppermost in the hearts and minds of those to whom those powers are justly delegated by the people.

"We shall not pause; we shall not rest upon laurels. For we have not fulfilled our destinies."

Wilder's political destinies were many. He also was the state's first African American senator when he won a runoff election in 1969. After his term as governor, he became the mayor of Richmond.

Lawyer Carol Moseley Braun was another force. She watched Chisholm and Jordan gain political power, and she followed their path, becoming the first Black woman in the U.S. Senate and the first woman to defeat an incumbent U.S. senator in an election.

Moseley Braun took up the mantle of those who had come before her in refusing to keep silent about the unseen barriers preventing Black people and women from holding more political power. She said, "The reason that minorities and women don't have a better shot at getting elected to the Senate or to statewide office is because the campaign finance rules are so skewed as to make it very difficult for non-traditional candidates to raise the money necessary to get elected."

Whereas Powell had called his colleagues out for their racist behavior, Moseley Braun subverted it. In 1993, Moseley Braun persuaded the Senate Judiciary Committee not to renew a design patent for the United Daughters of the Confederacy because it contained the Confederate flag, which conjures images of slavery for many African Americans. It was a historic move.

Like Chisholm before her, Moseley Braun visualized a Black woman in the White House. And if not herself, then she understood that her actions paved the way for someone else. "Frankly, for me the big challenge is to have people believe that I can be the president of the United States," she said.

For Moseley Braun, women in politics is crucial.

"Because the whole idea of democracy is that you tap the population for ideas about how government should work," she said. "And if you start off with a narrow band of people whose ideas are being heard and paid attention to, then what you're going to do is wind up with lopsided policies.

"Women are everywhere on the spectrum in terms of [ideology]. But they do bring a different set of life experiences to bear on the policy question. They can reach a conclusion that doesn't require, if you will, winners and losers...And that serves everybody's interests, because what you wind up with are policies that serve the interests of the entire population."

The 1990s was also when Representative Maxine Waters of California, who has knocked on the door for justice for fifteen terms, was elected to Congress, making her the most senior Black female voice in D.C.

Like Powell before her, Waters did not believe in sitting idle during times of civil unrest. During the traumatic aftermath of the Rodney King verdict in 1992, which acquitted officers who were caught on film beating King with batons as he struggled on the ground, Waters led the powerful chant, "No justice, no peace" during marches.

Waters helped deliver relief supplies in Watts and demanded the resumption of vital services. "If you call it a riot, it sounds like it was just a bunch of crazy people who went out and did bad things for no reason," Waters said. "I maintain it was somewhat understandable, if not acceptable."

The dramatic response to the verdict, she said, "was a spontaneous reaction to a lot of injustice. There were mothers who took this as an opportunity to take some milk, to take some bread, to take some shoes. They are not crooks."

During fourteen years in the California State Assembly, Waters rose to the powerful position of Democratic caucus chair. She was responsible for some of the boldest legislation California has ever seen: the largest divestment of state pension funds from South Africa; landmark affirmative action legislation; the nation's first statewide child abuse prevention training program; the prohibition of police strip searches for nonviolent misdemeanors; and the introduction of the nation's first plant closure law.

She also helped shape public policy that delivered $10 billion in Section 108 loan guarantees to cities for economic and infrastructure development, housing, and small business expansion; appropriated $50 million for the "Youth Fair Chance" program, which established a job and life skills training program for unskilled, unemployed youth; expanded the U.S. debt relief for Africa and other developing nations; and created a Center for Women Veterans, among others.

"I've been in this struggle for many years now," Waters said. "I understand racism. I understand that there are a lot of people in this country who don't care about the problems of the inner city. We have to fight every day that we get up for every little thing that we get. And so I keep struggling."

THE 2000S

Barack Obama's election in 2008 to the highest office in the country was a change that was only possible because of the work the Black politicians before him had done to pave the way.

Obama's presence in the White House served as the manifestation of the often-used proclamation by Black parents that, "You can be whatever you want to be." They had never seen a Black president and were not optimistic they ever would. But there was Obama, and that proverbial proclamation became an infusion of real promise.

In an interview with a Black reporter in 2008, Obama said: "The decline of wages and incomes for African American families during the Bush era has been significant." He added, "So I think nobody has more of a stake in the reversal in these policies than the African American community does. And they can be the difference makers in a lot of these states."

For Obama, his historic election was a complex proposition that required a delicate equilibrium: He tried to balance being the president for all Americans while also embracing his African heritage and speaking out about racism. Obama couldn't be too Black for his white constituents; and he couldn't be too white for Black supporters.

"There's no doubt that there's some folks who just really dislike me because they don't like the idea of a Black president," Obama said in 2012. "Now, the flip side of it is there are some Black folks and maybe some white folks who really like me and give me the benefit of the doubt precisely because I'm a Black president." Obama's political persona, which was more Dinkins than it was Diggs, made him particularly vulnerable to this type of attack.

Valerie Jarrett, Obama's senior advisor, put it this way: "Children today are growing up thinking it's perfectly normal to have a president who is African American. We're not afraid to say this is going to help Black people."

But it couldn't last forever.

In 2016, Obama ended his last speech as president at the Democratic National Convention the way he started his journey: with hope, fire, and a charge to do more that symbolized Black political clout.

"The America I know is full of courage and optimism and ingenuity. The America I know is decent and generous," Obama said in the months leading up to the end of his terms. "We've still got more work to do. More work to do for every American still in need of a good job or a raise, paid leave or a decent retirement; for every child who needs a sturdier ladder out of poverty or a world-class education; for everyone who hasn't yet felt the progress of these past seven and a half years."

Even though Obama had left the office, his election was a watershed moment for Black Americans. Powell showed a Black person could be an agent of change within the federal government. Shirley Chisholm showed a Black person could run for president. Jesse Jackson showed a Black candidate could garner significant support. David Dinkins showed us how far this nation still had to go. Douglas Wilder showed no job is too big.

Obama's victories were a cumulative effort of that lineage that spanned decades.

After his presidency, though, the push and pull of American politics came into play, much like it did after Dinkins was mayor of New York.

"What I did for New York," Giuliani said, "Donald Trump will do for America."

He was dishearteningly right.

THE 2010S

While the 2010s were undoubtedly a dark period in American politics, where Donald Trump was elected despite his incompetence and his inflamed racist rhetoric, there were some incandescent spots during this period, in particular with the rise of Kamala Harris.

In 2011, Kamala Harris became the thirty-second attorney general of California, having previously served as the district attorney of San Francisco. Harris was the first woman district attorney in San Francisco, as well as the first African American woman to serve as attorney general of California. As attorney general, Harris pioneered the "Back on Track" initiative, which had participants fill out a personal responsibility plan regarding their goals, rather than serve jail time. It wasn't perfect, but it was a step in the right direction.

Harris received sometimes harsh criticism for what was called a "failure to police the police" when there were officer-involved shootings. As a prosecutor in San Francisco, her record on jailing Black defendants drew the ire of many who believed she issued lengthy sentences that did not fit the crimes.

For her part, Harris vehemently defends her record. "There have been those who have questioned my motivations, my beliefs and what I've done. But my mother used to say, 'You don't let people tell them who you are. You tell them who you are.' Self-appointed political commentators do not get to define who we are and what we believe.

"I knew prosecutors have not always done the work of justice," Harris said, to approving murmurs in the audience. "There have been prosecutors that refused to seat Black jurors, refused to prosecute lynchings, disproportionately condemned young Black men to death row, and looked the other way in the face of police brutality.

"It matters who is in those rooms," she added. "I knew I had to be in those rooms. We always have to be in those rooms, especially and even when there aren't many like us there."

In 2017, Kamala Harris would be elected to the U.S. Senate. Not long after, she would announce her candidacy for president of the United States.

One of Harris's allies in the Senate was Cory Booker of New Jersey, who was elected in 2013 after serving as mayor of Newark, New Jersey. Booker, who would later run against Harris in the presidential primaries, was the first African American to be elected to the Senate since Barack Obama. As a U.S. senator, Booker wrote, sponsored, and helped pass legislation on affirmative action, advancing women's rights, same-sex marriage, and single-payer health care.

Like Rangel, Booker considered the racial wealth gap to be a critical issue and has pushed for economic reforms. Reforming the criminal justice system was another area he took to heart. As mayor of Newark, Booker made a name for himself in fighting crime—literally—when he chased down an armed robber in front of city hall. He also saved a woman's life by rescuing her from a burning building. He also lived for eight years in a high-rise apartment where many low-income tenants relied on federal housing assistance. That was his power: He connected to his constituents.

Substantively, Newark saw restaurants and hotels rise, companies moved their headquarters downtown, and the city earned $1 billion in real estate sales in 2012 and 2013. And after sixty years of decreased population, Newark's population grew under Booker.

2020

Before Harris left the Senate for the vice presidency, she and Booker teamed to write an article in 2020 for *Rolling Stone*: "To Save Black Lives, Congress Must Act Boldly." In it, they wrote a piece that served as a clarion call to their colleagues.

"Across our nation, protesters are again forcing America to confront the ways our country has failed, and continues to fail, Black Americans and fall short of our foundational aspirations, that we are a nation of liberty and justice for all.

"And, critically, these activists are calling on all of us to make this time in our history more than a passing moment, but a movement. To do that, we have to act boldly.

"We cannot settle on an inadequate middle ground that will simply nibble around the edges instead of making real change. If someone's knee is on your neck, you cannot take it halfway off and call it progress.

"There is no halfway when people's lives are at stake. We save them or we do not.

"The choice is still up to Congress."

The responsibility they wrote about was to be assumed, in particular, by Black women politicians, who made history and galvanized a key voting bloc that changed the power structure in Congress.

BLACK WOMEN STAND TALL

BY CURTIS BUNN

IF THERE WAS ANY doubt about the power and influence of the Black woman or questions about her galvanizing force and burgeoning strength, such notions were eviscerated in 2020.

In a year of so much upheaval, when the nation was desperate for change—socially and politically—Black women seized the opportunity to save America from itself. And they delivered.

So much was on the line: justice, civility, public health, national security—and all of it depended on flipping the White House from an administration that had botched the deadly coronavirus pandemic response, intensified the racial divide, fabricated a culture of contemptible behavior, and weakened the country's ability to protect itself from foreign adversaries.

Once that was done, the next challenge was the two up-for-grabs Senate seats that Democrats needed to control lawmaking ability in Washington, D.C.

None of it was too daunting for Black women—especially Stacey Abrams, the former Georgia state representative who ascended from a gut-wrenching loss in a gubernatorial race to become perhaps the most celebrated and galvanizing force around the vote.

In 2018, Stacey Abrams lost her bid to become the state's first

Black governor to Brian Kemp by 55,000 votes in a contentious race. She said she spent ten days in mourning, or sitting "shiva. And then I started plotting."

Abrams was devastated by the voter suppression that became a major rallying cry for Black Lives Matter and others who wanted to protect the right of Black people to vote.

The thing about voter suppression is that the efforts are usually designed to impact Black people. Of all the tactics used over the years to squash the Black vote—gerrymandering, questionable voter identification laws, voter registration restrictions, voter purges, felony disenfranchisement—Trump's claims may have been the most blatant.

As he continually spewed the unfounded idea that an election he lost by 7 million votes was rigged against him, he essentially wanted to cast aside millions of Black votes that he knew were likely for Biden.

Interesting that Trump's issues were not only in the states he lost that he needed and expected to win—Georgia, Pennsylvania, Wisconsin, and Arizona—but that the votes he wanted to contest—throw out— were in the cities with high Black population: Atlanta, Philadelphia, Milwaukee, and Phoenix, respectively. That was not a coincidence. And because America is America, he believed his attempt to negate the Black vote would be accepted universally. It was not.

But there was damage done by Trump's tricks. It riled his venomous supporters. And surely in the future, GOP candidates will find his way viable. "Even after Trump's presidency ends, that message will pave the way for GOP politicians and judges to further one of their party's and the conservative movement's most important ongoing projects: restricting voting rights," attorney Jay Willis affirmed. "Trump lost this election, but he can still help Republicans win in the future."

And Black voters will lose—but not if Abrams has a say in it. She created Fair Fight, an organization that worked to fight voter suppression and assure fair elections. Abrams and her group covering

Georgia worked with an edge, ferocity, and commitment. They registered an astonishing 800,000 new voters in advance of the 2020 general election. Stop right there when looking for reasons Biden took out Trump.

Abrams's achievement is heightened by the circumstances under which she operated. Many have declared that the governorship was swiped from her. Her opponent, Kemp, was secretary of state and in charge of the election—a red flag. Weeks before voting day, an investigation found the state had improperly purged 340,000 people from voter registration rolls without warning. Additionally, Kemp blocked 53,000 people—80 percent of whom were Black—from being able to register to vote because of minor discrepancies. Probable voter suppression. Clearly, forces were at work to prevent her from making history.

Abrams—another product of a historically Black college, specifically Spelman College—acquiesced to the verdict, but she did not concede defeat.

In what was a nonconcession speech, Abrams made it clear her discontent with not just the outcome, but how it came to be. There was "deliberate and intentional" voter suppression by Kemp, she said.

"Pundits and hyperpartisans will hear my words as a rejection of the normal order," Abrams said. "You see, I'm supposed to say nice things and accept my fate. They will complain that I should not use this moment to recap what was done wrong or to demand a remedy. You see, as a leader I should be stoic in my outrage and silent in my rebuke.

"But stoicism is a luxury and silence is a weapon for those who would quiet the voices of the people. And I will not concede because the erosion of our democracy is not right."

The depths of Abrams's resolve, though, came to the fore in the run-up to the 2020 presidential election. Not many would have blamed her if she had receded from public view to mend from the pain of her defeat. But Abrams would not allow the erosion of democracy to erode her spirit.

"I learned long ago that winning doesn't always mean you get the prize. Sometimes you get progress, and that counts," she said.

Abrams achieved progress that hardly anyone believed was possible in Georgia. Fair Fight Action—and other ground-game organizations—galvanized the Black vote. The Biden-Harris ticket won, a stunning accomplishment.

More than 1.2 million Blacks voted in Georgia, more than double the number in the 2016 election, according to the Georgia Legislative Black Caucus. Of those registered to vote after November 2018, half were people of color and 45 percent were under thirty, demographics that customarily lean Democrat. Biden won by 11,000 votes, making it clear that the Abrams-led voter push took him over the top.

As gracious as she was determined, Abrams often demurred when praised for her work. She refused several interviews and at one point in November sent out an all-encompassing Tweet: "My heart is full. Georgia, let's shout out those who've been in the trenches and deserve the plaudits for change."

For sure, there was a contingent of other Black women who were instrumental in turning Georgia from red to blue, including Tamieka Atkins, Helen Butler, Nsé Ufot, and Deborah Scott, all from other organizations that were committed to catapulting Biden over Trump. There also was LaTosha Brown's Black Votes Matter organization, which tapped into counties small and large around Georgia to register voters.

But Abrams's efforts were particularly noteworthy because of what it took for her to rebound from the loss. "It's one of those few moments where we have this power to shape the future for ourselves, to insist upon at least attention to our plight, and to demand behavior that meets this notion that we have as a nation that there should be justice for all," she said.

Abrams's efforts created a sort of cult following or admiration society among Black women from all walks. Inside and outside of politics, they were inspired by her bounce back from the loss to Kemp and the commitment she showed in galvanizing the vote. Bonita Potter-Brown, principal of Lenna W. Conrow Early Childhood Learning Center in Long Branch, New Jersey, was one of the many Black women Abrams touched. She said Abrams's efforts inspire her as a leader of young students.

"Stacey Abrams didn't lose [in 2018]," Potter-Brown said. "She won. The power she brought to the 2020 election was enormous. Many people, no matter who the president is, will be okay. We may not like them, but it may be not so crushing that we couldn't live. But we care because it's about the community at large, people who look like me and who need leadership that cares about them.

"That's why Stacey Abrams is such a big deal. She didn't let that [2018] election stop her. She worked for a bigger purpose. And think about it: If she had won the Georgia governor position, would she have had the opportunity to raise all that money and get out eight hundred thousand people to vote, flipping Georgia? As an insider, her hands may have been tied.

"And from a spiritual standpoint, you may feel defeated, but God always has something better planned for you on the other side. That's a lesson for all of us in her. God allowed her to keep her faith and keep her purpose in mind. And it's working for the better good for all citizens."

La Detra White, a business owner in Atlanta who is engrossed in politics and women's causes, was another Black Abrams inspired. "Stacey, they tore her to kibbles and bits," White said. "And she got stronger. She knew everyone coming after her was emboldened by Trump. Southerners like being racists but they don't want to be called a racist.

"What Trump did, is he showed people's slips. He shed a light on the worse of the worse of the worse. And Stacey did her thing in the face of all that."

Abrams faced defeat, devastating defeat, in the past, but did not let it block her from her path. She was in contention for the prestigious Rhodes Scholarship, an honor that was unthinkable to her mother raising her daughter in Gulfport, Mississippi. Abrams wanted it badly—but did not get it. And yet, she carried on, not accepting it as a loss, but as an inspiration.

In her impassioned book *Lead from the Outside*—a title that was prophetic—she wrote:

Concession accepts an act as right or proper. And society's existence necessitates the act of compromise—of bending our wants to the needs of others. Leadership is a constant search for the distinction between when compromise is an act of power and when concession masks submission—or when the fight is on.

I don't simply speak for myself. I had the hopes, dreams, and demands of 1.9 million Georgians standing with me. And thousands more who had been unfairly, unlawfully silenced. And whether speaking up is about an unfair election or a flawed system of workplace promotion, the obligation remains the same: once we recognize that wrong exists, we must fight to change it every day.

But this passage by Abrams offers high-definition insight into who she is and why she has done what she has done:

When we win, we achieve beyond ourselves. We become models for others, known or unknown, who see our victories as proof they can win, too. Even by simply embracing ambition, talking about it, trying and failing, we mentor others to see their potential. And by going beyond our own limits, we change the places we inhabit. We bring a fresh perspective to a company or a cause, a minority lens that expands and shifts how the work gets done. This is not news.

When I work with young people and others seeking leadership positions, they are primed to jump to the third question, to the how of it, without understanding the what or the why. Some pick a place they want to land or a title they like and then expect teleportation. It may sound corny, but so many of us forget that finding and fulfilling ambition is truly a journey, and one that does not come with a map or GPS, especially for those of us on the outside looking to get in. The effort can be sweaty, teary, and messy as much as it can be rewarding and empowering. I call it the hard work of becoming more.

She has personified that ideal. And so did Kamala Harris, the former California senator who was elevated to become the first Black and South Asian woman vice president, alongside Biden.

Her nomination was a watershed moment in American history. Her presence on Biden's ticket was, in the end, a stroke of political acumen by Biden, although it was questioned in many circles when he locked himself in by committing to a Black woman running mate.

Was America ready for a Black woman as second in command behind a seventy-eight-year-old president? Barack Obama was one thing, but in a vastly chauvinistic and racist society, could the U.S. embrace the fact that a Black woman would be one step away from commander in chief?

The Biden-Harris ticket prevailed because Black women saw to it for more than the fact that Harris, in many ways, represented them—although that surely mattered. She was relatable in that she embraced her Blackness, was a graduate from historically Black Howard University and a member of the oldest Black women's sorority, Alpha Kappa Alpha. She connected with HBCUers, overall, and the Divine

Nine—the collection of Black sororities and fraternities, historically rife with competitive instincts—joined forces in supporting "one of their own" in the groundbreaking bid.

More importantly, Harris was a viable VP candidate, a former attorney general in California and a fiery senator who handled herself with aplomb in her ill-fated run for president. Harris's nomination and subsequent election were so prodigious San Francisco artist Bria Goeller created a 2020 version of Norman Rockwell's famous 1964 painting of six-year-old Ruby Bridges, with law enforcement by her side, as she integrated schools in New Orleans. This updated adaptation included Harris strutting along a wall with a photoshopped image of Bridges's shadow.

Bridges said about the image: "It made me feel a sense of pride to be a part of that journey. But I also felt a responsibility to all of those who came before me. Because I'm also standing on the shoulders and in the shadows of people who made huge sacrifices for all of us."

Harris is standing on the shoulders of Bridges and Shirley Chisholm, Barbara Jordan, and Ida B. Wells, Sojourner Truth and Harriet Tubman...and the countless other Black women who have served as pioneers.

In the book *Vanguard: How Black Women Broke Barriers, Won the Vote, and Insisted on Equality for All*, the author Martha S. Jones wrote on the power of Black women this way:

Terming Black women the "Vanguard" has a double meaning. Despite the burdens of racism, they blazed trails across the whole of two centuries. In public speaking, journalism, banking, and education, Black women led American women, showing the way forward. Some "first" Black women leapt out front because nothing less would get them where they aimed to go.

Black women emerged from brutal encounters with enslavement, sexual violence, economic exploitation, and cultural denigration as visionaries prepared to remedy their own circumstances and, by doing so, cure the world.

As the vanguard, Black women also pointed the nation toward its best ideals. They were the first to reject arbitrary distinctions, including racism and sexism, as rooted in outdated and disproved fictions. They were the nation's original feminists and antiracists, and they built a movement on these core principles. The women of Vanguard continued to reach for political power that was redemptive, transformative, and a means toward realizing the equality and dignity of all.

Jones said in a *Time* magazine article that the Black women's movement from championing voting rights to being on the ballot is a natural progression that started in the 1800s—and protecting themselves from being prey was a major factor in their commitment.

"I place the origins of that in the stories told by enslaved women who aren't speaking expressly about politics but put their own experiences of sexual violence into the public sphere," she said. "Then we come to the modern era and the stories of Rosa Parks and Fannie Lou Hamer, women in the modern civil rights era whose politics are affected by and influenced by sexual violence. We can tie it all the way to the #MeToo movement in Tarana Burke, who continues to center those concerns for us.

"The story of racism is often told from the perspective of men; Black women experience racism in ways that are distinct and defining for them, and sexual violence is a good example of that."

Harris rode the wave of Black women's support. In one of her first moves as vice president–elect in late November 2020, Harris appointed Symone Sanders, a Black woman who was a former press secretary for the 2016 presidential campaign of Senator Bernie Sanders, as her chief spokesperson.

Parts of Harris's acceptance speech when they clinched the election magnified the significance of Black women in the political process:

Congressman John Lewis, before his passing, wrote: "Democracy is not a state. It is an act."

And what he meant was that America's democracy is not guaranteed.

It is only as strong as our willingness to fight for it, to guard it and never take it for granted... Because "We the People" have the power to build a better future.

So, I'm thinking about... the generations of women—Black women... Asian, White, Latina, and Native American women throughout our nation's history who have paved the way for this moment tonight.

Women who fought and sacrificed so much for equality, liberty, and justice for all, including the Black women, who are too often overlooked, but so often prove that they are the backbone of our democracy.

All the women who worked to secure and protect the right to vote for over a century: a hundred years ago with the Nineteenth Amendment, fifty-five years ago with the Voting Rights Act, and now, in 2020, with a new generation of women in our country who cast their ballots and continued the fight for their fundamental right to vote and be heard.

But while I may be the first woman in this office, I won't be the last. Because every little girl watching tonight sees that this is a country of possibilities.

La Detra White, the entrepreneur in Atlanta, has applauded Harris for quite some time. She attended Howard University with the vice president and was part of the Alpha Kappa Alpha Sorority, Inc., chapter that initiated Harris into the organization.

"The most respectful thing I could say is, 'Hallelujah, hallelujah, hallelujah.' The world makes a way for everybody," White said. "You have to be ready to step into frame.

"I feel like I grew up with Kamala. Her number's in my cell phone. She's phenomenal. She was ready. But was the world ready? There was nothing in the world that told me it was ready for her. *Nothing*.

"I believe Kamala will provide another level of connection to the masses because she went to Howard," White added. "This isn't cheerleading. This isn't bias. We're taught to see the world as ours, not mine. We're conditioned to accept someone daring us to not be able to do something. Everything she's done, she's earned—and none of it was easy."

Indeed, Harris has been a groundbreaking force her entire career. She never lost a campaign before running for president. She has been the first person like her to hold every office she has ever won: the first Black woman and person of color to serve as San Francisco district attorney; the first Black and woman to be attorney general of California; the first Black senator in California.

With Harris's and Howard's prolific reputation for creating leaders, White's teenage daughter, Hannah, enrolled at Howard in 2017.

"Hannah went to Howard in a bubble—well-traveled, but under-exposed," White said. "It has been wonderful to see how our conversations have evolved over her time at Howard. She went from listening, to engaging, to leading the discussions on things that impact Black women.

"She went from being a friend in the group to becoming president of her class of the School of Business. She has come into that because she's been witnessing all of the wonderful but difficult progress that has transpired in our communities. And because she's at Howard, she has a front seat on how her peer group has responded to and benefited from the progress and the struggle. She's having the same experience the vice president had. That's pretty powerful."

During a roundtable discussion in 2019, Harris said to Harry L. Williams, Thurgood Marshall College Fund CEO and president: "There are [three] things that shaped who I am today: my mother and my family, and Howard University."

It was in that atmosphere on the HBCU campus that Kamala Harris was raised—and that experience informs who she is as a politician. She wrote in her memoir, *The Truths We Hold*:

"As was the case for most Howard students, my favorite place to hang out was an area we called the Yard, a grass-covered place, the size of a city block, right smack in the heart of campus," the vice president wrote. "On any given day you can stand in the middle of the Yard, and see, on your right, young dancers practicing their steps or musicians playing instruments.

"Look to your left and there were brief-case toting students strolling out of the business school, and medical students in their white coats, heading back to the lab.

"That was the beauty of Howard. Every signal told students that we could be anything—that we were young, gifted, and Black, and we shouldn't let anything get in the way of our success. The campus was a place where you didn't have to be confined to the box of another person's choosing. At Howard, you could come as you were and leave as the person you aspired to be."

Howard University president Wayne A. I. Frederick called Harris's selection in a statement: "An extraordinary moment in the history of America and of Howard University. It's a milestone opportunity for our democracy to acknowledge the leadership Black women have always exhibited, but has too often been ignored. Let's pause and take a collective breath that has been denied to so many."

Three years before she became the vice president, Harris implored the 2017 Howard graduating class to accept no boundaries in what they could do or become. "You can march for Black lives on the street, and you can ensure law enforcement accountability by serving as a prosecutor or on a police commission," she said. "The reality is, on most matters, somebody is going to make the decision—so why not let it be you? Because, if we're going to make progress anywhere, we need you everywhere."

THE BLACK WOMAN VOTE

Black women changed the course of the country in the 2020 election, and stand to be formidable in the future, too.

The election, many thought, would be a referendum against Trump and his unseemly antics. But America did not repudiate Trump; Black women did.

Trump's wild and unsophisticated posture and inflammatory racist remarks did not prevent as much as 20 percent of Black men from voting for him, an increase from 2016 and a stunning number considering the former president's support of white supremacists.

On the other hand, Biden received 94 percent of Black women's votes, according to an Associated Press survey.

"I want to speak directly to the Black women in our country. Thank you," Harris said. "You are too often overlooked, and yet are asked time and again to step up and be the backbone of our democracy. We could not have done this without you."

"Once again, Black women were the gold standard for American voter participation," Ben Jealous, former president and CEO of the NAACP, added. "The holy grail for us as a community must be getting Black men to vote at the same rate as Black women."

The Black vote presented Black people with perhaps its best chance to garner significant change in Washington, D.C. President Obama had a malicious Republican side of the aisle working against him every step of the way over his eight years, which did not prevent him from accomplishing much, but it did hinder him at most every turn.

The Biden administration has the House and the Senate, thanks to the massive Black vote across the country. Harris's position as the number two and Black women's voices from the outside promise to apply pressure on Biden and others to make good on criminal justice and police reform, fairness issues around wages, education, and public health—concerns that shape the Black Lives Matter movement.

In that spirit, Patrisse Cullors, a BLM co-founder, sent a letter to Biden and Harris the day the presidential race was called to congratulate them and call for the construction of a "fully resourced" agenda that addresses the challenges Black people face and make it a "top priority."

That kind of pressure, if Black women had anything to do with it—and they did—would be unrelenting. It was critical to get rid of Trump.

As the Biden-Harris administration goes about its business, Black women, empowered by Harris and Abrams in particular, go about their work with a renewed passion and awareness of their influence.

Atlanta mayor Keisha Lance Bottoms, for instance, emerged as a politician with a future that could extend beyond her influential city in Georgia. She was rumored to be a vice president candidate along with Florida representative Val Demings and Susan Rice, former National Security advisor and U.S. ambassador to the United Nations. All remain on the front lines, working and presenting examples for young Black girls and displaying the Black women efficiency that has turned heads.

Bottoms, who turned down a Biden offer to be the U.S. ambassador to the Bahamas, exemplified the progressive nature of Black women leaders. She created the first LGBTQ Affairs Coordinator position within her administration just before Thanksgiving 2020, appointing Malik Brown to the historic position.

"My hope is that we create institutional and equitable change for LGBTQ Atlantans," Brown said to NBC News. "One day Mayor Bottoms and I won't be at Atlanta City Hall anymore, but our hope is that the LGBTQ-supportive infrastructure that we've created will still be here."

Black women mayors were at the forefront of leading their cities during the concurrent crises of the pandemic and social justice demonstrations—a display of leadership and strength that has only gained in momentum.

Bottoms became a national factor when she made an impassioned plea on television for the looting to end in Atlanta in the aftermath of the George Floyd killing. And her remarks that a meddling Trump "should be quiet" elevated her to another plateau as a leader with gumption.

Chicago mayor Lori Lightfoot was unabashed in her pain after Floyd's death. "It's impossible for me, as a Black woman who has been the target of blatant racism over the course of my life, not to take the killing of George Floyd personally," she said. "Being Black in America should not be a death sentence." She has worked hard to reform law enforcement in her embattled city.

LaToya Cantrell was the first Black woman mayor of New Orleans, and she related to Floyd's killing as "an African American woman who has felt the sting of oppression," she said. "I am very much tired of this happening over and over and over again in the Black community, to Black people, in particular Black men."

Like Cantrell, London Breed was the first Black woman to serve as mayor of her city, San Francisco. But she made it clear where her heart lies. "Yes, I'm a mayor, but I'm a Black woman first," she said. And the fact that she lost a relative to police violence gave her an emotional proximity to the horror that many do not have. Along with protesters, Breed said she was intent on not sitting "quietly by and letting it happen again."

Mayor Muriel Bowser, of Washington, D.C., was a strong voice against Trump and was the first in America to have "Black Lives Matter" painted in the city streets. The huge black-and-gold mural rests on what is now Black Lives Matter Plaza and leads menacingly up to the front of the White House. Bowser was intentional in choosing that location.

She was "shocked and outraged" when federal law enforcement used force on peaceful protesters outside the White House to make way for Trump to walk across the street to pose for photos holding a Bible. And Bowser took a lead role in assuring a second insurrection of Trump supporters would not succeed in storming the Capitol a second time.

Vi Lyles made history as Charlotte's first Black woman mayor. She's established herself as a "deliberate listener," a leader whose position has been to hear the grievances and concerns of the protesters that had so much frustration about law enforcement's violence against Black people.

Mayor Sharon Weston Broome of Baton Rouge, Louisiana, like Lyles, met with protesters to let them know their concerns were heard. Black man Alton Sterling had been killed in 2016 in her city, and she used that gut-wrenching incident to build a coalition between local police officers and citizens to bridge the divide.

And the stories went on and on. The refrain "strong Black woman" fits these leaders—and many more. It is far beyond a societal trope. They wear multiple hats, manage myriad responsibilities—and do it all with aplomb and grace. They are wives and mothers and family members. They lead a team of people working to bring America from a position of unjust to just, and sometimes at a cost.

The "superwoman" syndrome is a real thing with real consequences.

A 2019 study called "Racial Discrimination, The Superwoman Schema, and Allostatic Load: Exploring an Integrative Stress-Coping Model among African American Women" in the *Annals of New York*

Academy of Sciences revealed that "racial discrimination has been linked to allostatic load (i.e., cumulative biological stress) among African American women."

Stress comes with the mission, which is not good for the body. The study added, though: "In the face of high levels of racial discrimination, some aspects of the superwoman persona, including feeling an obligation to present an image of strength and to suppress one's emotions, seemed to be protective of health, diminishing the negative health effects of chronic racial discrimination."

The superwoman schema includes five elements: feeling an obligation to present an image of strength, feeling an obligation to suppress emotions, resistance to being vulnerable, a drive to succeed despite limited resources, and feeling an obligation to help others.

As forces in the political landscape, the Black women who have forged ahead will continue to endure the added racism and pressure that comes with their positions.

Dr. Amani M. Allen, associate professor of community health sciences and epidemiology at the University of California, Berkeley, the lead author of the study, said: "The problem is racial discrimination itself and the need for interventions intended to address racial discrimination as experienced in the workplace, by police, and in society at large."

La Detra White said she has felt workplace discrimination in corporate America, which sparked her to become an entrepreneur. Politics became important to her as an empowering tool. So she looks at Black women political leaders and she sees inspiration to forge ahead in business, using their strength as fuel.

"When you see Keisha [Lance Bottoms] go up against Kemp [about whether to shut down Atlanta during the coronavirus], she's not going up just against him," White said. "That was Trump pulling those strings. And that's added pressure. And Kamala, did you see the meme that called her 'Joe's hoe' made by white Christian men?

She will always be tested. And you can bet there will be death threats. Stacey [Abrams] caught a lot of grief. There are more behind-the-scenes stories than we'd ever want to know. But we never see their cracks. They show the likes of my daughter that you can take control of that center stage. It's all incredible, yet difficult.

"It's a magnificent time to be a Black woman."

THE RISE OF GEORGIA BLACK VOTERS

BY CURTIS BUNN

IN GEORGIA, THE BLACK vote did not always matter—at least to the Black voter in Georgia. African Americans in the state overwhelmingly cast their ballots for Barack Obama in 2008 and 2012, and Obama made history by becoming the first Black president of the United States.

For Black Georgians, the exhilaration of his victories surmounted the reality: Obama did not win Georgia, and in the archaic Electoral College—which counts state votes and not the popular vote—their ballot did not help Obama achieve history. Hence, the feeling that their vote did not matter.

"Psychologically, that messed with me a little bit," Jackie Joseph Brown, a Columbus, Georgia, native, said. "My friends in New York and Chicago and California were all saying, 'We did it. We did it.' And here I was in Georgia, and…with the way the system is set up, we didn't do it. It was a weird feeling to be so excited and proud about President Obama, but, technically, my vote didn't help put him in office. And I think a lot of Black people struggled with that over the years."

The emotions were far different in 2020 than they were in 2016, when Trump won the state. Black people were decisive in Biden turning the traditional Republican red state Democratic blue. It was the first time a Democrat won Georgia since President Bill Clinton in 1992.

"Biden winning here in Georgia was definitely a sigh of relief," Atlanta native Amber Holmes said. "I felt like I helped make a difference. I voted for him, and I persuaded two of my friends, who never voted in the past, to participate in the election. I also, unfortunately, had to stop being friends with someone who tried to convince me that Trump was the best candidate for the Black community. So, that election was very emotional for me, and a lot of other people in Georgia. With Biden's win, I felt a small sense of satisfaction and accomplishment, which I didn't get when President Obama won because we didn't win Georgia."

That feeling of satisfaction subsided quickly, however, and turned into pressure. Two Georgia Senate seats were set for a runoff two months later, seats that would sway the balance of lawmaking power. The Democrats needed the Reverend Raphael Warnock to become the first Black senator of Georgia and Jon Ossoff to become the first Jewish senator from the state to avoid a Republican Senate majority and obstructionism toward Biden's agenda. They were pitted against Kelly Loeffler, a billionaire Trump loyalist who had been appointed senator to replace Johnny Isakson, who stepped down because of illness, and David Perdue, a conservative also closely linked to Trump.

For Black voters, there was another call to action, and with it a burden.

"I received so many calls from people around the country who told me they wished they could vote in the Georgia Senate runoff," Brown said. "Everyone was so excited. But that was also another way of telling me how important it was for us to get out there and do it again. They were counting on us. Some friends weren't subtle. They'd say, 'Y'all gotta take Georgia.' 'We need both those Senate seats.' 'Y'all need to get it done.' At first it was cool that we were in the middle of an election that the whole country was watching. But as it got closer, the pressure mounted."

"That pressure was real, even though I was just one vote," Holmes said. "Racial tensions were high. Black people had turned Georgia blue and we had to turn around and do it again. This was an election where your vote could make the difference. We literally had to save democracy, as they called it. I knew I needed to vote early; I was concerned that the runoff election would fall prey to more voter suppression. But as the pressure turned up, I could feel that we took pride in being a political force. We came out. Our votes mattered in Georgia. And we turned two elections in two months."

How galvanized were Georgia voters for the Senate races? There were more than 100,000 people in the state who cast a ballot in the Senate runoff but did not vote in the November presidential election.

Warnock, the eloquent preacher from Savannah, understood the magnitude of the occasion. "I'm really proud of Georgia in this moment," he said, "because we built a multiracial, multiethnic, multigenerational coalition, which ushered into office at this defining moment in America a young, Jewish man who is the son of an immigrant and interned for John Lewis, and an African American man, the pastor of Ebenezer Baptist Church, where Dr. King served.

"This is a representation of the best in America. That old [Southern] strategy, where politicians came to office by dividing people, [is over]. Jon and I are coming into office by bringing people together."

Warnock's ascension marked an exciting new era of Georgia politics, a significant cultural and demographic transition. Black voters sought and achieved an alternative political vision from its conservative past through a statewide power base with roots in local governance.

Warnock went from a powerful voice in the pulpit to a power player in the Senate. He took over as lead pastor of famed Ebenezer Baptist Church in 2005, seemingly always with an eye on a political career. From the lectern, he shared his strong views on social issues and community concerns in earnest, and the notion was floated back then that he had designs on D.C. He acted on his impulses in 2020, anchored in his faith.

"I preached in my campaign the same message I have been preaching for years," Warnock said. "I've been trying to point us toward the highest ideals in our humanity and in the covenant we have with one another as American people—that all of us deserve an opportunity to create a prosperous life for us and our families."

John Lewis inspired Warnock, who often spoke of his intention to work hard to have the John Lewis Voting Rights Act passed in the Senate. In 2017, Warnock was arrested in the U.S. Capitol as he protested the GOP health care proposal.

"I've always tried to leverage the moral truth to create moral good," Warnock said. "My whole life has been about service. And that doesn't end at the church door; it starts there. My ideals are driven by my faith and what has caused me to fight for access to affordable health care, the dignity of work, and voting rights. I think your vote is your voice, and your voice is human dignity. And we've got to make sure everyone has a voice in our democracy."

Black voters' voice resounded in 2020. Receiving less fanfare than Warnock's triumph but indicative of the Georgia Black voter influence were changes in other local positions in and around Atlanta, the ubiquitous capital of the New South.

In November 2020, Black voters helped supplant five incumbent Republican district attorneys and elected Black candidates in four of those races. In Cobb County, an Atlanta suburb where Black voters turned out in large numbers, Democrat Flynn Broady defeated incumbent district attorney Republican Joyette Holmes, a Black woman who was assigned by Kemp to prosecute three white men charged in the killing of Ahmaud Arbery. Her unsteady handling of the tragic incident dissatisfied many Black voters.

Also, in Brunswick, incumbent district attorney Republican Jackie Johnson, who many thought initially mishandled the Arbery case, was voted out of office, too.

Black voters made important changes in Fulton County, the largest voting bloc in the state, made up of mostly African Americans. Paul Howard, first-elected Black prosecutor in the state, in 1997, was voted out after allegations of financial misconduct (which he denied), replaced by Fani Willis, a Black woman and first of her kind in Fulton County. It was that way around much of the state—Black voters voting their interests and making a difference.

"As a native of Atlanta, of Georgia, it's inspiring to see Black people using their vote to make change," Holmes said. "It hasn't always been this way. There was a time when we didn't necessarily feel like our vote mattered. But it's a new day."

THE NEED FOR FAIR LEGISLATION

BY CURTIS BUNN AND MICHAEL H. COTTMAN

A MISSOURI STATE SENATOR proposed a bill in January 2021 that crystallized how Black people in general and the Black Lives Matter movement, in particular, were demonized by the white political construct.

Republican Rick Brattin sponsored a law that called for the use of deadly force by law enforcement against protesters on private property to be legal, and to grant immunity to people who run over with a vehicle demonstrators who are blocking traffic.

The paradox was astounding: *Deadly force* by law enforcement could be officially sanctioned on people peacefully demonstrating against deadly force by law enforcement.

The irony was also deeply troubling and emblematic of legislation throughout history that has placed Black people in harm's way or at a sizable disadvantage. Brattin's proposed bill did not have a strong chance at becoming law. The Missouri ACLU decried it, as did many Democrats. But that was less the point than the notion that he would present something so blatantly violent, a direct response to the BLM protests, making it a racially charged initiative.

Remarkably, Florida passed a law similar to Brattin's proposal, potentially making Black protesters roadkill.

One consequence of such a law would be that the white man convicted of murdering Heather Heyer, who was killed at a protest when a white supremacist drove his car through a crowd in Charlottesville four years earlier, would not have been charged or prosecuted. Heyer was a white woman—the message being not only Black people who fought against systemic racism were in the line of fire, but also white people who supported them.

Remarkably, Iowa and Oklahoma also were among the states that actually made running over protesters with cars legal—a direct assault on BLM marchers. Under the new provisions, a driver would not be liable for striking—or even killing—a person if the driver is "fleeing from a riot…under a reasonable belief that fleeing was necessary to protect the motor vehicle operator from serious injury or death."

Additionally, the violent measure created new penalties for protesters who obstruct streets or vehicle traffic, including fines of up to $5,000 and as much as a year in jail.

The insidious laws were Republican–pushed and supported, despite the fact that the *Washington Post* reported that 98 percent of the largest protests in U.S. history resulted in no injuries to "participants, bystanders or police."

Translation: In 2021, edicts reminiscent of Jim Crow laws that abused Black people were in play.

"Totally preposterous," U.S. District judge Susan Davis Wigenton said of the proposed bill. Wigenton's dismay with the bill was matched by the urgency she feels about the need for legislation overhaul if Black people are to experience any measurable change—and fairness—in America.

Wigenton, a product of historically Black Norfolk State University, said Black America's civil liberties had been most recently under assault during the Trump administration, and adhering to the 1964 Civil Rights Act would be a start to leveling democracy.

"When we talk about civil rights, most of the time, we're talking about people of color," said Wigenton, who is from New Jersey and was appointed by President George W. Bush in 2006. "Legislation is lovely. Let's be clear. If you want to prosecute someone, there are already laws in existence to do it."

And many of those laws, too many, are to the detriment of Black people, especially as they relate to law enforcement. The Obama administration worked to counter bad laws. After the fatal shooting of Michael Brown in Ferguson and subsequent racial justice demonstrations, Obama established a task force to examine better policing practices. His administration also investigated patterns or practices of misconduct in police departments, entered into court-binding agreements that require departments to correct misconduct, conducted reviews of various police departments, and put monitors in place to ban racial profiling by federal law enforcement agencies.

"The Obama administration did more with respect to police reform and misconduct than any administration in the modern era, and it was a personal commitment for the president and for Attorney General Eric Holder," said David Kennedy, director of the National Network for Safe Communities at John Jay College of Criminal Justice.

But Obama's work essentially was abandoned and aborted during the Trump administration, which eliminated the practices.

"We have to go back," Wigenton said. "It's the focus of the Department of Justice that has to change. People have to understand after what happened in the summer of 2020, the focus on civil rights, equality, and justice for all has to start at the top. Not one of those officers [who harmed Black people] has been charged with a civil rights violation. It has to start at the top."

The Justice Department, which is responsible for defining how the law forbids discrimination, submitted for White House approval before Trump's departure a change to how it enforced Title VI of the 1964 Civil Rights Act, which prohibits recipients of federal funding from discriminating based on race, color, or national origin. The regulation covered housing programs, employers, schools, hospitals, and other organizations and programs—another attempt to remove protections for Black people.

The Trump administration also sought to eliminate protections for groups at risk of suffering civil rights violations by law enforcement, claiming that the Civil Rights Act as passed by Congress only safeguarded against intentional acts of discrimination.

All of this could be considered a dirty pool, a muddied pit in which Black people have waded forever. The Biden-Harris administration rolled back those changes, but hardly did that make life equitable for Black people.

There was the issue of oversentencing legislation that Black people have had to endure as well.

"People of color get charged with much more serious criminal offenses and the amount of time they face is different than [non-Black people]," Wigenton said.

The inequities in legislation inspired Brittany K. Barnett, a corporate attorney in east Texas, to work to gain the freedom of oversentenced Black people. Pro bono work introduced her to cases where Blacks were serving significant federal prison time for nonviolent drug charges.

"These cases tugged on my soul," she said.

She learned of the case of Sharanda Jones, a Black woman who went to trial as a first-time offender. The trial lasted a week. Prosecutors did not produce any evidence that she had possessed, bought, or sold drugs. Rather, they relied on the testimony of admitted drug abusers and dealers who were given lighter sentences for their testimony against Jones.

In August 1999, she was convicted of one count of conspiracy to distribute cocaine base (crack cocaine). She was sentenced to life without the possibility of parole.

A first-time offender was sentenced to life without the possibility of parole for conspiracy to distribute crack.

"She is a woman who is a Black daughter of the rural South like me," Barnett said. "I saw so much of myself in her that I decided I would fight for her life as if it were my own—because it was."

It was 2009 when Barnett read about Jones's case. She showed up as an unexpected visitor at prison and told Jones she would battle for her freedom.

"I bring a different dynamic, a different lens," Barnett said. "I grew up in rural East Texas. My mom had a drug addiction. My mom went to prison. I dated a drug dealer. My early years of college, some involvement in drugs was the norm. You either knew somebody selling drugs, using drugs…and at the time it was something we didn't really think that much about.

"Having that proximity to it gave me a unique perspective."

And the length of time Jones received struck her. Jones had run out of appeals. Barnett did not care. She told her new client she would take her case to the White House, and she did.

It took six years, but Barnett was true to her word—and talent. President Obama granted Jones clemency, setting her free in 2016 after sixteen years in prison.

Barnett had the honor of placing the call to Jones. "You're going home," she screamed into the phone. Jones cried. (President Obama pardoned 231 individuals in December 2016, most whose cases were similar to Jones's.)

She is among nine formerly imprisoned clients Barnett has achieved clemency for in five years—all of which were laden with extreme sentencing. "This is about poor legislation," Barnett said. "It is critical that we look out for our own, the wrongly accused or those who receive outrageous lengths for crimes that do not call for it."

Barnett was part of the team that helped grant the freedom of Alice Johnson, a sixty-five-year-old grandmother who served twenty-one years in prison as a nonviolent first offender. She had been sentenced to life without possibility of parole. Trump, with urging from Kim Kardashian, granted Johnson clemency.

"Clients are serving life sentences under outdated drug laws," she said. "So my clients are set to die in prison, set to never breathe air with free people again. So, to be a part of the journey to help save their lives…"

In 2020, Barnett wrote her best-selling memoir, *A Knock at Midnight: A Story of Hope, Justice, and Freedom.* "I wanted to tell the truth about the racial injustice that bleeds through the system," she said. But that was not the only reason she penned her book. "For young Black girls from the South like me and hope that they will see themselves in me and see that they can do anything they set their minds to."

She had no idea she would be attacking legislation that contributes to the ill of mass incarceration and destroys Black families and communities and squashes potential leaders.

"The untapped genius," she said. "We're locking away brilliant minds and ingenuity for decades that our nation needs to thrive. My clients are some of the most brilliant people I've ever met. We're not trying to get around that selling drugs is a crime or glorify it in any way. The argument is that the punishment for the crime is entirely too severe.

"We have to completely reimagine what justice looks like. And I think that is attainable."

Her optimism comes from criminal justice reform rising to a hot-button political issue in recent years. The Biden administration listed it as a priority. "Where people who are impacted can help is by voting," Barnett said. "We have to get into Congress and the Senate progressive thinkers who are open to change. It's necessary for us to build a better nation."

Wigenton points to voting—more specifically, voter suppression as legislation that has to be addressed. States have various laws for the same election.

"Why is that and how is that acceptable?" she asked. "We need to have uniformity that would make it clearer and a lot easier for people to vote. We need consistency in our laws."

Republicans did not appear to agree. The most sacred liberty of an American, the ability to vote, remains under attack, especially for Black people. Democrats are seeking to pass H.R. 4, the Voting Rights Advancement Act—renamed the "John Lewis Voting Rights Act of 2020" after the civil rights icon who passed in July 2020.

Broken down, the bill would thwart an individual state's plans to make changes to the original 1965 Voting Rights Act—changes that would make it more difficult to vote—without preclearance from the Justice Department. The Supreme Court in 2013 struck down the preclearance requirement, saying it singled out states with a history of racialized voter suppression at the time the act was passed, which is strange because they were the states that exercised voter suppression.

In any case, Democrats control Congress after Georgia delivered Senators Raphael Warnock and Jon Ossoff in runoff elections, giving them a possible path forward for the legislation.

There was also a bill that would create a commission to address a controversial subject: reparations for the African American descendants of slavery.

Formerly enslaved people and their descendants have long sought compensation for their immense suffering under slavery, segregation, and systemic racism that clouds every institution in America. These efforts have been stalled at every turn.

U.S. representative Sheila Jackson Lee, a Texas Democrat, wants to try again and reintroduced the bill, known as H.R. 40.

"The call for reparations represents a commitment to entering a constructive dialogue on the role of slavery and racism in shaping present-day conditions in our community and American society," Lee said in a statement. "It is a holistic bill in the sense that it seeks to establish a commission to also examine the moral and social implications of slavery."

The issue of reparations has been discussed by some Black Americans ever since United States Union Army general William Tecumseh Sherman promised forty acres and a mule to 4 million freed slaves in 1865.

But many Black Americans think that while reparations is an important issue to be considered, it is an unwieldy topic that is hard to quantify and manage. Some say reparations could cost the federal government trillions of dollars. The question that confounds many Black Americans is who would receive the money? And how would the cash be dispersed? And how much would people get?

"The reparations movement would be an amusing sideshow were it not for its damaging distractions," Walter Williams, a professor of economics at George Mason University, wrote in a 2019 essay. "It grossly misallocates resources that could be better spent elsewhere."

Author Ta-Nehisi Coates disagreed, saying: "The case I make for reparations is, virtually every institution with some degree of history in America, be it public, be it private, has a history of extracting wealth and resources out of the African-American community. I think what has often been missing…behind all of that oppression was actually theft. In other words, this is not just mean. This is not just maltreatment. This is the theft of resources out of that community."

And that theft needs to be paid back, Coates argued. And the thieves need to make restitution.

Talk of reparations diminished some, as the focus by many Black Americans centered on shootings of unarmed Black men and women by police and enacting federal policies to support health care and combat the coronavirus pandemic. And the overpolicing of Black people. And fair housing and…

Indeed, the legislative concerns were plentiful, and the ratification— or failure—of bills would determine the opportunity for substantive change—or facilitate much of the same.

THE MATTER OF THE WEALTH GAP

BY CURTIS BUNN

THE PROTESTS AROUND THE country were about far more than the disturbing pattern of the killing of Black people at the hands of law enforcement. Like the uprisings in the 1960s, those horrific encounters served to elevate myriad points that crystallized the glaring disparities that stunt fairness and progress in the United States.

America's wealth gap was a significant point of contention. Financial experts agree that home ownership is the most effective way to close that blatant chasm with the Federal Reserve indicating that the average homeowner's wealth in 2016 was $231,400, while the average renter's wealth was $5,200.

The Census Bureau reported that Black homeownership fell to a record low of 40.6 percent in the second half of 2019, affirming Black people's ranking as the lowest in homeownership among all ethnic groups in America. Whites had a 2020 homeownership rate of 76 percent; Asians, Native Hawaiians, and Pacific Islanders 61.4 percent; and Hispanics 51.4 percent.

The Urban Institute—a Washington, D.C.–based think tank that executes economic and social policy research to "open minds, shape decisions, and offer solutions"—looked at one hundred American cities with the largest population of Black households, and did not find a single city that had a Black and white homeownership gap that is near to being close.

Minneapolis, for example, had an astounding 50 percent homeownership gap between white and Black residents. Measuring larger, more progressive cities such as Los Angeles and Washington, D.C., the gaps were still 25 percent and 20 percent, respectively.

It's telling that the almost 30 percent gap across the country in white and Black homeownership of 2020 is larger than the 27 percent gap from 1960, when housing discrimination was legal.

How has this occurred? One reason is, according to the Home Mortgage Disclosure Act of 2020, Black people were denied mortgages an astounding 80 percent more often than white applicants.

That outrage lines up with the gentrification phenomenon that has been seen across the United States. Washington, D.C., once proudly hailed as "Chocolate City" because of its predominant number of Black citizens, is vanilla now, with just 47.1 percent of its population Black. African Americans in Harlem, New York, which was 70 percent Black in the 1930s, are no longer in the majority.

In Chicago and Detroit, once famously Black cities, the numbers have dwindled each year. Indeed, in areas where Black residents were once dominant, research shows that homeownership levels have shifted in dramatic fashion because of gentrification and the increased housing costs that come with it. Atlanta maintains a predominantly Black population, but there are growing concerns that many people of color will be pushed to the suburbs as real estate prices continue to rise.

"If we look at where people end up if they move, poor residents moving from historically Black gentrifying neighborhoods tend to move to poorer non-gentrifying neighborhoods within the city," the Home Mortgage Disclosure Act said, "while residents moving from other gentrifying neighborhoods tend to move to wealthier neighborhoods in the city and in the suburbs."

An area was considered to be gentrifying if it experienced a significant increase, compared to other areas of the same city, either in median gross rent or median home value coupled with an increase in college-educated residents.

"Gentrification is reconfiguring the urban landscape by shrinking residential options within cities for disadvantaged residents and expanding them for more advantaged residents," the study said.

A paradoxical problem with gentrification: Once white people move into communities where Black people were the majority, investment in businesses and services come that had been previously absent. Which begs a question: Why was there not a quality grocery store, restaurants, banks, and other service-related enterprises when whites did not live there in abundance?

The answer is obvious—and offensive to Black people.

Advocates for gentrification have said it can work fairly with more housing construction in gentrifying areas to absorb newcomers, reducing displacement and curbing rents. At the same time, others have emphasized that adding apartments in high-income areas would allow others to enjoy their advantages and ease gentrification elsewhere.

But there are other social and cultural aspects of gentrification that cause resentment within Black communities. New white residents in the area of Howard University in Washington, D.C., have walked their dogs on the campus and allowed their pets to leave waste on the grounds. Instead of affording one of the most prestigious historically Black colleges—an institution that produced the first Black woman vice president in Kamala Harris and the first Black Supreme Court justice in Thurgood Marshall, among other notable alums—the respect and deference it deserved, one white man interviewed on local news said that if the students and administration had a problem with them walking their dogs on campus, "Then maybe they should move the campus."

Filmmaker Spike Lee vehemently complained in 2014 about the attitude of the influx of wealthy white neighbors in his Brooklyn community who issued demands and disregarded the established culture. During a Black History Month appearance at the Pratt Institute, he laid out his concerns and ire in no uncertain terms, a controlled, profanity-laced tirade that summed up many people's feelings.

"Why does it take an influx of white New Yorkers in the south Bronx, in Harlem, in Bed Stuy, in Crown Heights for the facilities to get better?" Lee said. "The garbage wasn't picked up every motherfuckin' day when I was living in 165 Washington Park. P.S. 20 was not good. P.S. 11. Rothschild 294. The police weren't around. When you see white mothers pushing their babies in strollers, three o'clock in the morning on 125th Street, that must tell you something."

The disdain or attempt to eliminate long-established cultural traditions also drew Lee's indignation.

"Then comes the motherfuckin' Christopher Columbus Syndrome," the Oscar-winning writer and director said. "You can't discover this! We been here. You just can't come and bogart. There were brothers playing motherfuckin' African drums in Mount Morris Park for forty years and now they can't do it anymore because the new inhabitants said the drums are loud. My father's a great jazz musician. He bought a house in nineteen-motherfuckin'-sixty-eight, and the motherfuckin' people moved in last year and called the cops on my father. He doesn't even play electric bass! It's acoustic! We bought the motherfuckin' house in nineteen-sixty-motherfuckin'-eight and now you call the cops? In 2013? Get the fuck outta here!

"Nah. You can't do that. You can't just come in the neighborhood and start bogarting and...like you're motherfuckin' Columbus and kill off the Native Americans. Or what they do in Brazil, what they did to the indigenous people. You have to come with respect. There's a code. There's people."

Lee's fury was in keeping with frustrations from countless Black people across the country. The issue, they and Lee contend, is not so much that white people move into historically Black neighborhoods, but that they seem hell bent on altering the landscape and without regard for those who had made those neighborhoods their home.

With gentrification, community names have been changed—like Stuyvesant Heights replacing Bedford-Stuyvesant in Brooklyn and SpaHa for Spanish Harlem in Harlem—an alarming trend that speaks to the issue of invisibility and communities effectively being erased, displaced, and separated from their culture, reminiscent of slavery.

"I'm for democracy and letting everybody live, but you gotta have some respect," Lee said. "You can't just come in when people have a culture that's been laid down for generations and you come in and now shit gotta change because you're here? Get the fuck outta here. Can't do that!"

As profane, pointed, and on point as Lee's seven-minute soliloquy may have been, the gentrification train plows on, with seemingly no way to slow it down. And, per usual in America, Black people will be impacted negatively the most.

Karen Garcia, a Bed-Stuy resident, was so disenchanted with the vast changes in her neighborhood that she founded makenewyork-grimeyagain.com, an anti-gentrification organization that illuminates how this phenomenon impacts Black people and families.

"People were already facing homelessness due to the lack of re-sources," she said, "but gentrification even heightens it because these landlords are tailoring their rents to people who are leaving the places they're from and want to come to the hip and urban neighborhoods."

The National Community Reinvestment Coalition reports that in the first thirteen years since the turn of the twenty-first century, more than 135,000 residents were displaced from their homes in 230 neighborhoods across the country. Blacks and Hispanics were the majority of these residents, NCRC said.

These concerns have resonated for some time with Thomas W.

Mitchell, a Black property law scholar who in October 2020 received the prestigious MacArthur "Genius Grant"—one of the most celebrated honors in America. Mitchell, a law professor at Texas A&M University, has spent his career helping disadvantaged people maintain ownership of their real estate wealth.

The Howard Law School graduate was the principal author of the heralded model state statute designed to shift the paradigm of heirs' property owners, especially Black land and homeowners. It is known as the Uniform Partition of Heirs Property Act and is in effect in eighteen states, eight of them in the South, where doubters insisted it would never fly. Mitchell's work has fortified the ability of thousands of heirs and Black property owners to retain their land, which historically had not been the case.

Mitchell took an indirect path to his influential work. Born in San Francisco's Fillmore District, he was inspired by family photos shared with him after the funeral of his grandfather in Newark, New Jersey, during his junior year of college. Many of the images were from southwest Georgia, sparking a thought: to link the displacement of Black people in major cities like San Francisco to the taking of Black-owned land in the South.

"I stumbled on some articles from the 1900s that talked about how African Americans lost a fair amount of land at the end of the Civil War," Mitchell said. "I decided to study some of the laws that could explain that loss of property.

"I learned there were a variety of factors responsible for the involuntary loss of property. There's a constellation of state laws that took advantage of African American property owners. And I learned there had been little effort to address these kinds of state and federal laws that were systemic discrimination."

What Mitchell learned was startling, but not surprising, considering the history of backlash against Black people who built their wealth and communities. One hundred years ago in Tulsa, Oklahoma, a seventeen-year-old white girl accused a Black teenager of assaulting her in the city's downtown area. As was the case repeatedly, white people went on a terrorist killing spree.

More than 300 Black people were slain and their thriving community that included Black-owned banks, grocery stores, and other businesses were burned to the ground in one of the worst and most infamous cases of destroying Black wealth.

Two years after Tulsa, a Black community was set ablaze after a white woman named Fannie Taylor claimed she was assaulted by a Black man on January 1, 1923, in Rosewood, Florida. Sam Carter, a local blacksmith, was tortured, and his mutilated body was hung from a tree.

By the time white people were done, as many as 150 Black people were killed, and their city was ashes. After Rosewood was destroyed, a grand jury and special prosecutor decided there was not enough evidence to prosecute the white men who had killed innocent Black people—mirroring much of what so often happens today and gives the Black Lives Matter movement fuel.

Twenty-three years before Tulsa's destruction, jealous and angry white men similarly destroyed a successful Black community in Wilmington, North Carolina. Because the town's political power structure was split between Black and white, white people feared the "threat of Negro rule."

The local white-owned newspaper wrote with no evidence that white women were in danger because of Black men. It read, in part: "If it requires lynching to protect woman's dearest possession from ravening, drunken human beasts, then I say lynch a thousand negroes a week...if it is necessary."

In the 1898 election, Black men were prevented from voting. But they had already accumulated wealth in their communities. Threatened still, whites announced the "white declaration of independence," overthrew the Wilmington government, and a gang of white men attacked Black citizens who had done nothing wrong, except thrive. As many as 300 Black people were massacred. Wilmington officials spent the next one hundred years trying to eliminate the carnage from its history.

Among the most coldhearted tragedies was that of the Colored Orphan Asylum in New York in 1863. The orphanage was the first of its kind in America for Black children. Before the orphanage, Black youths were placed in jails or worked as chimney sweeps and beggars on the street.

White men grew angry that federal laws drafted them into the Union Army and went on a rampage. They stormed federal buildings. And for reasons no one could fathom, they ravaged Black neighborhoods and sought to kill Black children by burning down the four-story orphanage that housed 400 African American youths a year.

More than one hundred lives were lost, and the asylum, a beautiful Greek Revival building off Fifth Avenue between West 43rd and West 44th Streets, was destroyed by the mob.

"Some 500 of them entered the house," the asylum managers reported on July 25, 1863, in a record book housed at the New-York Historical Society. "After despoiling it of furniture, bedding, clothing, etc., they deliberately set fire to it, in different parts—simply because it was the home of unoffending colored Orphan Children." The building was destroyed, and after a period of confusion and disappointment, the children were displaced to a facility on what is now Roosevelt Island.

"The destruction of this asylum, supported, as it was, solely by charity, is certainly one of the worst and wickedest of crimes that were perpetrated during this memorable day," the *New York Times* wrote in a story two days later, "and clearly shows that resistance to the draft is but a cry raised to cover the most atrocious crimes that human nature is capable of committing."

New York in the mid-1800s was also home to Seneca Village, a community of about 225 residents, 75 percent of them Black. It was a haven in a city that was already growing into the bustling New York it is today. Most importantly, it was separated from the fierce racism that was rampant, although New York State had abolished slavery in 1827. Discrimination reigned and hampered African American life.

In 1853, the New York state legislature reserved 775 acres of land in Manhattan to create America's first major landscaped public park. To do so, the city used eminent domain to procure the land where Seneca Village sat, meaning as a government agency it was able to take private land for public use, with compensation to the landowners.

That payment for Black people was less than its value, of course. By 1857, Seneca Village was no more, and another self-built wealth-building Black community was abolished to make way for what is now Central Park.

Today, the destruction of Black wealth is more sophisticated and less violent, but devastating nonetheless, Mitchell points out. For decades, Black farmers owned the land where they grew their crops and raised their cattle, but against racism that eventually doomed them.

The United States Department of Agriculture *admittedly* "systemically discriminated" against Black farmers for countless years. Further, after decades of denying it had discriminated, the USDA, in a 1999 class action lawsuit called *Pigford v. Glickman*, confessed that it had denied Black farmers the ability to apply for federal loans and other resources to sustain themselves, while welcoming and financing white farmers.

The suit ended up being the largest government settlement in U.S. history, with nearly $1 billion paid or credited to more than 13,300 farmers under the settlement's consent decree. Some Black farmers received only $62,500 each—barely enough to balance the years of debt built up from being denied loans or having loans with high interest rates. And that doesn't include the Black farmers who were unaware of the suit and therefore received nothing.

Even after the settlement, the USDA did not stop its racist practices, through Republican and Democratic administrations, Mitchell,
the property law attorney, said. According to a USDA report, there
were nearly 1 million Black farmers in 1920, but only 50,000 in 2017.
Additionally, the think tank the Center for American Progress wrote
in a report that "structural racism has robbed Black farmers of the
opportunity to build wealth" and contributed to "the loss of more than
36 million acres of farmland between 1920 and 1978."

"The USDA's Office of Civil Rights crafted a report that said, 'Yes,
we have discriminated after years of lying.' Essentially," Mitchell said,
"the Black farmers were continued to be denied the ability to apply
for loan programs and other programs that rendered their ownership
vulnerable because they weren't generating any income and it drove
them into foreclosure.

"Often losing their land resulted in a decline of status. So, there's
a loss of status, a loss of income, and when there were these forced
sales, they usually yielded a price far below market value. In many
cases, they would sell for 10 percent of the market value. So not
only did they lose their property, if you look at their asset portfolio,
they were far less diversified than whites. So, you have this utter
devastation of economic impact."

In 2010, President Barack Obama signed into law a bill authorizing
$1.25 billion to the late claimants—known as Pigford II. This influx
of funds helped—18,000 Black farmers received $62,500 each, taxes
paid on the award and debt relief and the settlement—but not before
many Black farmers had lost their businesses and land.

"I was offended when I began my studies," Mitchell said, "because
there were people who were justifying these forced sales by saying
they were trying to make it a public good. 'Our society needs to have
reserved property so it can develop economically, and this growth
will increase the GDP and be the benefit of everyone.' My point
was when we talk about access to land—the land that was viewed

as being 'appropriately available'—it was disproportionately owned by Black and brown people. So, it wasn't like they decided to take land from people irrespective of their racial, ethnic, or social economic standing.

"This notion was that it was a normal position for African Americans to have very insecure property rights, property rights that at any time could be undermined for what they considered better and higher economic use of the property...[It] was offensive. Underlining that notion that we had to accept that Black people's lives are just not that important. Their property ownership, their communities are not as important. They should be at the ready to have their rights sacrificed for the greater good."

At the same time, the destruction of Black people's way of living comes with a bonus indiscretion: a destruction of history and culture. Mitchell visited his hometown of San Francisco years after he left to see how his old neighborhood and city had changed. He saw a deficit that he could not quantify. The city that was 13 percent African American when he'd grown up there had diminished to 3 percent. "And most of those left were homeless," Mitchell said.

"The loss of these residents of color and businesses in the Fillmore District was enormous. And it was insulting that the justification the city used was there were all kinds of crime and prostitution. So, anything they had to say about my old neighborhood was negative to justify that redevelopment.

"My mother still lives in San Francisco. There's hardly any middle-class African Americans left in the city of San Francisco.

"I'm like, 'Wow. No Black people. Gone.' The banners on the streets label it the Historic Jazz District. In the 1960s, San Francisco was known as the Harlem of the West. There were more jazz clubs there than any place west of the Mississippi River. Now, after driving out the Black people, they are using that reference of the jazz district to drive tourists in, which I find ironic because when African Americans were there, we never heard about this positive history. But now that the African American community is gone, the city is capitalizing on this rich, important history that is essentially erased.

"Whether you're talking about Harlem or southwest Georgia, there's often an erasure of important culture and history."

All of this illuminates the importance of Mitchell's Uniform Partition of Heirs Property Act of 2016. It gives Black property owners power to protect their land, which protects their wealth and their culture and history.

In writing the law, Mitchell said he "looked at legal ways that [wealthy] people structured their acquisition of property with the most sophisticated real estate lawyers and attorneys who specialized in wills and estates. I looked at the nature of those types of agreements, and I borrowed from those so disadvantaged property owners can have some of the same advantages that wealthier people have.

"It's been important because it preserves family wealth that comes with the opportunity to pass on property to your children. It preserves that family history. It matters that everyone has a fair chance at protecting what's theirs."

MOVING ON

BY CURTIS BUNN

SO VOLATILE AND EMOTIONALLY charged were Donald Trump's four years in the White House that Black people who had been conditioned to doubt America roundly applauded his downfall in the 2020 presidential election and framed his demise as a symbol of a better future.

But "better" was a relative term. Better than the Trump term of racial vitriol, either spewed, alluded to, suggested, supported, applauded, or condoned? Yes, it would be markedly "better," a desperately needed departure from the exhaustive rhetoric and policies that galvanized and emboldened many individuals and factions that espoused racist ideals, probably incited violence, and generally contributed to the morose feeling that hovered over the nation.

All this was amplified during the coronavirus pandemic that virtually shut down the economy and disproportionately fulminated African American communities...and Trump did virtually nothing to decelerate the spread.

But Joe Biden's landslide victory—uselessly challenged by Trump and his band of insalubrious lawyers—did not foreshadow a "better" America; it promised a return to normalcy of the pre-Trump United States, which was not especially kind to Black people, either.

A message on social media after the election was called on November 7, 2020, was noteworthy: "Now maybe we can get back to normal racism. This ultra racism of the last four years was too much."

Those two sentences, while glib, resounded with truth. If Trump and his sycophants performed a phlebotomy on the African American community, draining it of its peace, a Biden administration would serve as a transfusion of sunlight, restoring the status quo. The status quo was, indeed, more acceptable than Trumpism. But the existential yearning was that the making of a better America could come out of the carnage.

And *that* was the rub: Ousting the anomalous Trump did not make America better. It gave America the *chance* to be better.

First, though, America in general and Black people in particular had to heal. The stress of the racial division ignited by Trump and fostered by his minions dumped stress on the population that had historically been stressed out by structural and systemic racism for nearly 400 years. The four years of Trump were a figurative pandemic in and of itself.

Sonja Sackor lived a mile from one of Trump's Texas stronghold areas, Rockwall County, just outside of Dallas. It had been a comfortable place to reside for Sackor before Trump stunned many by winning the 2016 election over Hillary Clinton. Throughout his presidency, his inflammatory rhetoric increased by the year, empowering his supporters to exercise their previously pent-up maliciousness on anyone who did not view the world through Trump's narrow, jaded prism.

When the election neared, the contempt was so forceful that she said she had to mentally "put on my armor" just to leave the house to execute a routine errand.

"I knew something could be done or said," Sackor said. "I had a Biden-Harris sign removed from my yard. Trump-Pence signs popped up everywhere. It was unsettling."

Sackor's discomfort was magnified by a succession of rallies for Trump in the nearby county that usually presented a hostile environment for a Black woman who did not look like the typical Trump radical bootlicker.

"People yelled things as they drove by, blew their horns. It [was] so exhausting for four years, filled with anger, depression, fatigue and insomnia," Sackor said. "Self-medicating to just get through the day...I faced...bigotry, racism, bullying, 'unpeaceful' protesters publicly protesting with open-carry weapons, yelling profanities and derogatory comments regarding the election. Very unnerving and intimidating."

Sackor's case was similar to countless Black Americans who felt like Trump's bluster suffocated them.

The ex-president's public demeanor more than offended Black people; it injured them, emotionally and physically, according to Dr. Jessica Isom, an African American psychiatrist who works at the Codman Square Health Center in Boston. Through his words or Tweets, tension from Trump's defending of white nationalists and militia, his calling African nations "shithole countries," vice president Kamala Harris a "monster," and countless other indignations on Black people, anger developed in the Black body, which transformed into stress, which manifested itself in tangible ways.

"For a lot of people there has been release of a long-held breath," Isom said. "For one, there has been lots of anti-Blackness in how [Trump] talks about Black people. And two, his policy decisions had an overall detrimental impact on our ability to feel like the highest leader in the land cares about our well-being. The [coronavirus] pandemic, Lord knows, you can call that anti-Black and anti-indigenous—the people who are most vulnerable suffered the most because he did not make moves that would take care of them."

And so myriad impacts occurred: unexplained body aches, especially in the back and neck, lack of sleep or too much sleep, moodiness, stomach pain, over- or undereating, and anxiety. "Those are ways stress comes out," Isom said.

Yale University psychiatrist Terrell Holloway said anxiety in the body created the potential for future health issues. "You experience [this stress] and due to the physiology response, it leaves you more vulnerable to heart issues and diabetes because it modulates your digestive system through secreting cortisol, which impacts how you release your digestive enzymes.

"It all co-relates with the health disparities that are unique to Black people because of structural racism. When you have a president who triggers these stressors, particularly over an extended period of time, issues can occur."

It was also a psychological blow that, while Biden eventually won in a blowout, more than 75 million people voted for Trump in the largest voter turnout in U.S. history.

"That's a clear message that the country is divided," Sheila Miller, a Washington, D.C., native said. "It takes away from the joy you had knowing Trump was gone. We still have to deal with almost half of the voting population who support this man's racist ideology. That's scary."

The chance to be a better America came out of Trump's failure, which was as much as anyone could hope for at that point.

HOPE FOR THE FUTURE

BY CURTIS BUNN AND MICHAEL H. COTTMAN

THE IRONY OF TRUMP'S madness is that in a real but un-quantifiable way, his apparent attempts to further marginalize the already-marginalized Black community galvanized the next wave of racial dissidents.

From high school students on up, Black youth and young adults stepped to the front, leading in various ways to fight the injustices that seemed to be illuminated under Trump.

Jordan Sims did not plan to create the organization Teenagers Looking for Change when he entered his junior year at Westlake High School in Atlanta. But George Floyd's killing—on top of the other slayings of Black people by law enforcement—inspired him to take a lead in bringing together his peers to effect change.

For his troubles, Sims was sprayed in his eyes with mace by cops during a Floyd protest in downtown Atlanta. "I was on the front line," Sims explained. "The police officers got agitated and started pushing us back. And it turned into chaos, and someone pulled out the pepper spray and got me.

"The pepper spray is terrible; it hurts," he continued. "But I was glad I was there. I wouldn't take any part of it back. I wanted to show I care and send the message that we're sick and tired of being treated as we are. We want to be treated better. We *should* be treated better."

Sims described himself and his political disposition as "Malcolm X more than I am Martin Luther King," he said. "It's time for action. It's time for change. And, as teenagers, the next generation, we have to step up."

Dorothy Butler Gilliam, the first Black female journalist at the *Washington Post*, has been writing about building a better nation for five decades as she chronicled American life. The four years of the Trump presidency disturbed her and made her wonder about what the future would look like.

But the country that elected Trump in 2016 voted him out in 2020, which infused Gilliam with optimism that better days are ahead, especially for Black people.

"America saw an explosion of Black hope in the 2020 elections," she said. "The Black communities in Wisconsin, Michigan, Georgia, and Pennsylvania were needed to end the white supremacist, narcissistic rule in the White House and open the door for Joe Biden and Kamala Harris, the first black woman vice president of the United States ... and they did it.

"This is a time for celebration, but also a time to invest in Black leaders to take the lead in campaigns and committees. We are headed into the 117th Congress with a larger caucus that will fight for Black America, which, in turn, fights for all Americans. We have worked hard this cycle to support candidates who will embrace the values we know will move the country in the right direction."

Gilliam's optimism was shared by many—and questioned by just as many, who have witnessed the country go through change before, but not enough change.

"Donald Trump blasted a serious hole in the American ship of state," award-winning veteran journalist Clem Richardson said. "Four years of his addled leadership has shaken American allies and divided her citizenry, clearly for election cycles to come.

"The contentious issues arising from his inept presidential steward-ship are almost too innumerable to list," Richardson said. "In his wake Trump leaves America facing more existential issues than our nation has had to confront almost since the Civil War."

The path forward, Richardson said, requires the public to bone up on the responsibilities of government and how it impacts every-day life.

"The first steps in our nation's way forward are clear: a return to and an expansion of civics education in our nation's schools and colleges, and a reinstitution of the Fairness Doctrine governing American media entities," Richardson said. "The 2020 presidential election made clear that many Americans, including President Trump, who, in too frequent public statements, made clear that he saw presidential power as almost dictatorial, have no idea how the government works.

"One in four Americans could not name the three branches of government. Trump supporters' chants of 'stop the count' outside Philadelphia election centers as the votes were being tabulated—and not in his favor—provide bitter testimony to a lack of knowledge of how America goes about the business of democracy, as does the millions of Americans who chose not to vote in probably the most important and contentious election of their lifetimes."

Richardson called for mandatory teaching of civics as a start to developing an informed electorate.

"How civics has almost vanished from school curriculums doesn't matter as much as it be returned posthaste and is made mandatory for every pupil, from elementary through college," he said. "We expect people who want driver's licenses to learn the rules of the road, and test their knowledge before legally being allowed to drive. Surely we can demand as much from people we entrust to help choose, with their vote, the course of a nation."

Neil Foote, the president of Foote Communications public relations and marketing group, said Kamala Harris becoming the first Black woman vice president inspired hope that cannot be calculated.

"The added bonus is the historic election of Harris, who fueled hope for all of us, but particularly for Black Americans and South Asians who see that America, despite its imperfections, offers the opportunity to live up to the promise of equal justice for all," Foote said. "As a team, Biden and Harris serve as beacons of what America is becoming: a vibrant, diverse, multicultural community where race, culture, ethnicity is the norm, not the exception; where the politics of hate can be drowned out by the politics of hope."

"But hope demands action," Gilliam said. "It is not static. It demands forward movement. We saw hope in the election in part because of the leadership of Stacey Abrams and great hope in the election of Kamala Harris. But it happened because of the work of Black Lives Matter and protesters who were in the streets, day and night.

"One urgent step African Americans must take is to take back our power and stop yielding it to whites who will use it to create a reign of fear and terror. When we focus on what we have in our ancestors—not what we don't have—we will see God's power within us in a way that white people don't possess."

Craig Kirby, the civil rights activist and nonprofit CEO, said the energy around the 2020 election and the future evoked memories of his grandfather, who told him, "Sonny Boy—keep on living, you will come to appreciate life's second acts."

He said the 2020 election was a second act for the country after Trump—and a good setup for the future.

"I developed an appreciation for this axiom after spending nearly four decades in national politics and civil rights," Kirby said. "I also recognize that the racial reckoning of 2020 and the socio-political implications for Black Americans embodies the principles that my grandfather spoke of that day to an eleven-year-old boy as we stood on our family farm in Rocky Mount, Virginia.

"The social environment in 2020 which compelled more than 161 million Americans to the polls was eerily reminiscent of the 1988 election when nearly 91 million Americans cast votes. The climate then was led by Reverend Jesse Jackson Sr.'s chants of hope and keeping it alive. Today's call-and-response touches on everything from Black Lives Matter to defunding the police. But the common thread, which seems to rear its head every few decades, is the unfettered will of the people to be heard, to claim their sovereignty above tainted political whimsy and capricious external influences."

Former president Barack Obama's historical election in 2008 spawned hope over his two terms in office. But Trump was a different commander in chief, changing the course of Black people's outlook, Kirby said. Indeed, the inspiration Obama provided was quelled almost instantly by Trump's undisciplined, anti-unity, and bombastic approach.

"We all celebrated President Obama's message of change, but the nation changed after his eight-year rule and in response to the harbinger of a turn from liberal democratic traditions, increasing tolerance, and an intolerant regressive era," he said. "Which leads us to now a divided nation, a disgruntled nation, and a nation both disturbed and in despair. We are evolving from a four-year period in which power was pursued based upon the perceptions of the five senses—an external power which has metamorphosed in the pursuit of authentic power—a power that is based upon the perceptions and values of the unseen and unheard."

Richardson said the country has not been helped by media outlets that do not abide by the principle of fair and balanced reporting, and instead push a singular, jaded agenda, which contributes to the divide and the idea that the future can be bright for one side, not all.

"The Fairness Doctrine held that, because the airways were publicly owned and televisions stations public trustees, they would best serve the nation by presenting all sides of controversial issues," Richardson explained. "In practice it meant news programs tended to balance their presentations.

"[But] in 1987, in the declining days of Ronald Reagan's presidency, the FCC announced it would no longer enforce the Fairness Doctrine," Richardson said. "Partisanship rapidly ensued, devolving to the current debacle, where not only do entities like Fox News and her subsidiary newspaper, the *New York Post*, not present opposing arguments, they present lies as fact—Fox personalities Sean Hannity and Laura Ingraham have made outrageous lies part of their brand."

So, Richardson said, there is only one recourse: reinstitute the Fairness Doctrine, the idea being that impartial reporting on the issues, political candidates, and the like will diminish some of the vitriol that is so prominent.

"It would make sure people are at least exposed to all sides of an argument. There was a time, in recognizing the tremendous influence news organizations had on the nation, that few newspapers, radio, or television news organizations offered opinions not clearly labeled as such," he said. "Even then these groups were compelled to present the opposing argument to whatever point they were making."

In its time of American healing, Foote was reminded of the words Shirley Chisholm, the first Black woman elected to Congress, spoke about infamous ex-president Richard M. Nixon, who was a divisive presence in the White House that Trump seemed to emulate, times ten.

Foote quoted the words of Chisholm in 1972, when she announced her run for president: "We have looked in vain to the Nixon administration for the courage, the spirit, the character, and the words to lift us, to bring out the best in us, to rekindle in each of us the faith of the American dream.

"Yet all that we have received in return is just another smooth exercise in political manipulation, deceit and deception, callousness and indifference to our individual problems, and the disgusting playing of divisive politics, pitting the young against the old, labor against management, North against South, blacks against whites."

Foote recalled those words because he found them meaningful in America nearly fifty years later.

"Fast forward to the election of President Barack Obama and Vice President Joseph Biden," he said. "They, too, got elected by people who sought out healing from global warfare and economic turmoil. As President Trump ripped away at Obama and Biden's legacy, he dug a hole deeper for himself, piercing the soul of America so deeply that his failures blew up in his face.

"Enter Biden and Senator Kamala Harris. *Finally, there was a prospect of hope.*

"Finally, there was the belief that the president and his vice president would honor their roles to protect and serve the interests of the American people. Finally, there was a sense that world order would be restored, particularly as the world battled against the horrific COVID-19 pandemic. Finally, there was the belief that the hateful, shameful, embarrassing disdain spewing from the White House would be silenced."

So the counterpoints of caution and optimism pushed back on a presidential term that exposed the worst in people, in America. Black people being Black people—a population that has been conditioned to seek the best in a situation because it always exists in the worst situation—the future promises something upbeat, particularly with the faith entrusted to the Black vice president.

Gilliam, who has written brilliantly about the ills of the country, burst with optimism for Black people based on more than 2020 election results.

"That explosion of hope—despite voter suppression and systemic racist policies—was shocking to many people," Gilliam said. "But the fact is hope—a spiritual principle—has been threaded into the fabric of the lives of Black Americans since 1619...I believe the key to Black hope is our ancestors. As he lay dying, George Floyd called on his ancestors. There was hope in his cry for his mother. The country and the world turned a new page after his death."

BIBLIOGRAPHY

WHY BLACK LIVES MATTER MATTERS

The Matter of Protests

Khan-Cullors, Patrisse, and Asha Bandele. *When They Call You a Terrorist: A Black Lives Matter Memoir*. New York: Wednesday Books, 2020.

THE BLACK CARNAGE OF THE CORONAVIRUS

Racism Can Make You Sick

"Defending Against Unprecedented Attacks on Fair Housing: 2019 Fair Housing Trends Report." National Fair Housing Alliance. 2019. https://nationalfairhousing.org/wp -content/uploads/2019/10/2019-Trends-Report.pdf.

"Africans in America: The Yellow Fever Epidemic." PBS. https://www.pbs.org/wgbh/aia /part3/3p1590.html.

The Shame of Infant Mortality

Williams, David R., and Morgan M. Medlock. "Health Effects of Dramatic Societal Events—Ramifications of the Recent Presidential Election." *New England Journal of Medicine* 376 (June 8, 2017): 2295–99. https://www.nejm.org/doi/full/10.1056 /NEJMms1702111.

Mills, David. "Trump Disorders: How to Cope with a Chaotic Presidency." Heathline, updated August 1, 2019. https://www.healthline.com/health-news/trump-disorders -how-to-cope-with-a-chaotic-presidency.

Torres, Nicole. "Research: Having a Black Doctor Led Black Men to Receive More-Effective Care." *Harvard Business Review*, August 10, 2018. https://hbr.org/2018/08 /research-having-a-black-doctor-led-black-men-to-receive-more-effective-care.

BIBLIOGRAPHY

The Eradication of Public Trust

Shashkevich, Alex. "Stanford Scholar Traces Medical Experimentation on Slaves in 18th-Century Caribbean Colonies." Stanford News. Stanford University, August 10, 2017. https://news.stanford.edu/press-releases/2017/08/10/medical-experimeribbean -colonies/.

Washington, Harriet A. *Medical Apartheid: The Dark History of Medical Experimentation on Black Americans from Colonial Times to the Present.* New York: Doubleday, 2007.

"Fatal Force: Police Shootings Database." *Washington Post*, updated March 28, 2021. https://www.washingtonpost.com/graphics/investigations/police-shootings-database/.

DEALING WITH POLICING IN AMERICA

"They See Us as Thugs"

Lopez, Christy E. "Opinion: Defund the Police? Here's What That Really Means." *Washington Post*, June 7, 2020. https://www.washingtonpost.com/opinions/2020/06 /07/defund-police-heres-what-that-really-means/.

German, Michael. "White Supremacist Links to Law Enforcement Are an Urgent Concern." Brennan Center for Justice, September 1, 2020. https://www.brennancenter .org/our-work/analysis-opinion/white-supremacist-links-law-enforcement-are-urgent -concern.

Pegues, Jeff, Andrew Bast, and Michael Kaplan. "Former Black Special Agents Say FBI's Culture Is 'Not Conducive to Minorities.'" CBS News. CBS Interactive, October 7, 2020. https://www.cbsnews.com/news/fbi-culture-minorities-black -special-agent/.

Steele, Allison, and Sean Collins Walsh. "Camden Disbanded Its Police Department and Built a New One. Can Others Learn from It?" *Philadelphia Inquirer*, updated June 14, 2020. https://www.inquirer.com/news/camden-police-defund -minneapolis-george-floyd-protest-20200609.html.

Hermann, Peter, Carol D. Leonnig, Aaron C. Davis, and David A. Fahrenthold. "How the U.S. Capitol Police Were Overrun in a 'Monumental' Security Failure." *Washington Post*, January 8, 2021. https://www.washingtonpost.com/politics/capitol-police /2021/01/07/fa3114b8-5114-11eb-83e3-322644d82356_story.html.

U.S. Slave Patrols

Martin, Michel. "The History of Policing and Race in the U.S. Are Deeply Intertwined." *All Things Considered*. NPR, June 13, 2020. https://www.npr.org/2020/06/13 /876628302/the-history-of-policing-and-race-in-the-u-s-are-deeply-intertwined.

Tha God, Charlamagne, Angela Yee, and DJ Envy. "Cariol Horne On Standing Up Against Police Misconduct, Her Story Being Silenced, True Justice + More." Broadcast.

Breakfast Club Power 105.1. iHeart Radio, June 18, 2020. https://www.youtube.com/watch?v=IvTgJaGyW2I.

Sweeney, Annie. "Fired Buffalo Police Officer Who Contends She Stopped Another Cop from Choking a Man Finds New Support—in Chicago." *Chicago Tribune*, October 26, 2020. https://www.chicagotribune.com/news/criminal-justice/ct-fired-buffalo-officer-chicago-support-20201026-rifgyniwtffy7nmztj3jdaknkq-story.html.

Sekhon, Nirej. "Blue on Black: An Empirical Assessment of Police Shootings." *American Criminal Law Review* 54, no. 2 (2017): 189–232. https://heinonline.org/HOL/LandingPage?handle=hein.journals/amcrimlr54&div=8&id=&page=.

Elliott, Richard DeShay. "Impact of the Law Enforcement Officers' Bill of Rights on Police Transparency & Accountability." *Southern Political Science Association*, November 19, 2020. https://papers.ssrn.com/sol3/papers.cfm?abstract_id=3690641.

Court Changes and Qualified Immunity

"Charleston Shooting Suspect's Burger King Meal Gets National Attention." *Charlotte Observer*, June 24, 2015, updated May 26, 2020. https://www.charlotteobserver.com/news/local/article25394389.html.

"Criminal Justice Fact Sheet." NAACP. https://www.naacp.org/criminal-justice-fact-sheet/.

"Trends in U.S. Corrections." The Sentencing Project, August 25, 2020. https://www.sentencingproject.org/publications/trends-in-u-s-corrections/.

Ellis, Nicquel Terry. "George Floyd's Family Lawyer Ben Crump Has Often Been the Man Beside the Mourners." *USA Today*, June 3, 2020. https://www.usatoday.com/story/news/2020/06/03/ben-crump-civil-rights-lawyer-also-man-beside-mourners/5274494002/.

"Criminal Justice Facts." The Sentencing Project, September 2, 2020. https://www.sentencingproject.org/criminal-justice-facts/#:~:text=The%20United%20States%20is%20the,explain%20most%20of%20this%20increase.

Nellis, Ashley. "No End in Sight: America's Enduring Reliance on Life Imprisonment." The Sentencing Project, February 17, 2021. https://www.sentencingproject.org/publications/no-end-in-sight-americas-enduring-reliance-on-life-imprisonment/.

"Philadelphia's Jail Population: November 2020." First Judicial District of Pennsylvania Department of Research and Development, November 2020. https://www.phila.gov/media/20201208120806/November-2020-Public-Piktochart-Report.pdf.

Patrick-Stamp, Leslie. "Numbers That Are Not New: African Americans in the Country's First Prison, 1790–1835." *Pennsylvania Magazine of History and Biography* 119, no. 1/2 (January–April 1995): 95–128. https://www.jstor.org/stable/20092927?seq=1.

Patrick, Leslie C. "'New Numbers That Are Not New': Slavery Ends & Prisons Begin: African 'Americans' in the New Nation's First Prisons." Presented Paper, American Corrections Association. August 9, 2005.

LOCKING UP BLACK LIVES

Campisi, Jessica, and Brandon Griggs. "Nearly 100 Bodies Found at a Texas Construction Site Were Probably Black People Forced into Labor—After Slavery Ended." CNN, July 19, 2018. https://www.cnn.com/2018/07/18/us/bodies-found-construction-site-slavery-trnd/index.html.

"Never Going Home Again"

Gamble, Vanessa Northington. "'There Wasn't a Lot of Comforts in Those Days': African Americans, Public Health, and the 1918 Influenza Epidemic." *Public Health Reports* 125, no. 3 (2010): 114–22. https://www.ncbi.nlm.nih.gov/pmc/articles/PMC2862340/.

CHURCH IN THE AGE OF THE BLM MOVEMENT

Harvey, Paul. "Civil Rights Movements and Religion in America." *Oxford Research Encyclopedias*, August 31, 2016. https://doi.org/10.1093/acrefore/9780199340378.013.492.

Calhoun-Brown, Allison. "Upon This Rock: The Black Church, Nonviolence, and the Civil Rights Movement." *PS: Political Science and Politics* 33, no. 2 (June 2020): 168–74. https://doi.org/10.2307/420886.

"Curbing the Coronavirus: Religious Freedom Confers No Right to Spread Sickness." Americans United for Separation of Church and State, May 2020. https://www.au.org/church-state/may-2020-church-state-magazine/editorial/curbing-the-coronavirus-religious-freedom.

Marchese, David. "Rev. William Barber on Greed, Poverty and Evangelical Politics." *New York Times*, December 28, 2020. https://www.nytimes.com/interactive/2020/12/28/magazine/william-barber-interview.html.

BLM and the Black Church

Francis, Leah Gunning. Essay. In *Ferguson & Faith: Sparking Leadership & Awakening Community*, 10–11. St. Louis, Missouri: Chalice Press, 2015.

Jones, Ellen E. "Opal Tometi, Co-Founder of Black Lives Matter: 'I Do This Because We Deserve to Live.'" *Guardian*, September 24, 2020. https://www.theguardian.com/society/2020/sep/24/opal-tometi-co-founder-of-black-lives-matter-i-do-this-because-we-deserve-to-live.

Green, Amy, Samuel Dorison, and Myeshia Price-Feeney. "Implications of COVID-19 for LGBTQ Youth Mental Health and Suicide Prevention." The Trevor Project, April 3, 2020. https://www.thetrevorproject.org/2020/04/03/implications-of-covid-19-for-lgbtq-youth-mental-health-and-suicide-prevention/.

BIBLIOGRAPHY

The Pandemic and the Church

Sze, Shirley, Daniel Pan, Clareece R. Nevill et al. "Ethnicity and Clinical Outcomes in COVID-19: A Systematic Review and Meta-Analysis." *EClinicalMedicine* (*Lancet*) 29, no. 100630 (December 1, 2020). https://doi.org/10.1016/j.eclinm.2020.100630.

Vandenboom, Liza. "George Floyd's Ministry Friends Say He Was Their 'OG,' A 'Man of Peace.'" Religion Unplugged, May 28, 2020. https://religionunplugged.com /news/2020/5/28/george-floyds-ministry-friends-remember-their-og-of-peace?rq =george+floyd.

Chappelle, Dave. "Monologue." *Saturday Night Live*, November 7, 2020.

White Christian Nationalism

Milbank, Dana. "Opinion: Trump's Racist Appeals Powered a White Evangelical Tsunami." *Washington Post*, November 13, 2020. https://www.washingtonpost.com /opinions/2020/11/13/trumps-racist-appeals-powered-white-evangelical-tsunami/.

De La Torre, Miguel A. *Burying White Privilege: Resurrecting a Badass Christianity*, 4. Grand Rapids, Michigan: William B. Eerdmans Publishing Company, 2018.

Tisby, Jemar. *The Color of Compromise: The Truth about the American Church's Complicity in Racism*. Grand Rapids, Michigan: Zondervan, 2019.

Cone, James H. "Black Theology and the Black Church: Where Do We Go From Here?" *CrossCurrents* 27, no. 2 (1977): 147–56. https://www.jstor.org/stable/24458316.

Bailey, Sarah Pulliam. "Seeking Power in Jesus' Name: Trump Sparks a Rise of Patriot Churches." *Washington Post*, October 26, 2020. https://www.washingtonpost.com /religion/2020/10/26/trump-christian-nationalism-patriot-church/.

BLACK POLITICAL LINEAGE: FROM ADAM CLAYTON POWELL TO BARACK OBAMA

Pandey, Swati. "Was It a 'Riot,' a 'Disturbance' or a 'Rebellion'?" *Los Angeles Times*, April 29, 2007. https://www.latimes.com/opinion/la-op-wordwatch29apr29-story.html.

Cottman, Michael H. "COMMENTARY: Obama's Greatest Legacy: Empowering Young Men of Color." Black America Web, June 10, 2014. https://blackamericaweb.com/2014 /06/09/commentary-obamas-greatest-legacy-empowering-young-men-of-color/.

Piccoli, Sean. "Obama: Some Folks Don't Like Me Because I'm Black." *New York Post*, January 19, 2014. https://nypost.com/2014/01/19/obama-some-folks-dont-like-me -because-im-black/.

Remnick, David. "Going the Distance: On and Off the Road with Barack Obama." *New Yorker*, January 19, 2014. https://www.newyorker.com/magazine/2014/01/27 /going-the-distance-david-remnick.

Chisholm, Shirley. *Unbought and Unbossed*. Washington, D.C.: Take Root Media, 40th Edition, 2010.

BLACK WOMEN STAND TALL

Jones, Martha S. *Vanguard: How Black Women Broke Barriers, Won the Vote, and Insisted on Equality for All*. New York: Basic Books, 2020.

THE RISE OF GEORGIA BLACK VOTERS

Clark, Roger. "Dinkins Blazed a Political Trail That Started in Harlem." Spectrum News NY1, November 24, 2020. https://www.ny1.com/nyc/all-boroughs/news/2020/11/24/dinkins-blazed-political-trail-starting-in-harlem.

THE MATTER OF THE WEALTH GAP

Williams, Walter E. "Reparations for Slavery." Creators Syndicate, June 26, 2019. https://www.creators.com/read/walter-williams/06/19/reparations-for-slavery.

Remnick, David. "Ta-Nehisi Coates Revisits the Case for Reparations." *The New Yorker Radio Hour*. NPR, June 10, 2019.

Kijakazi, Kilolo. "Examining the Racial and Gender Wealth Gap in America." Subcommittee on Diversity and Inclusion, Financial Services Committee, United States House of Representatives, September 24, 2019. https://www.urban.org/sites/default/files/publication/101086/kilolo_kijakazi_testimony_on_racial_and_gender_wage_gaps.pdf.

Hwang, Jackelyn, and Lei Ding. "Unequal Displacement: Gentrification, Racial Stratification, and Residential Destinations in Philadelphia." *American Journal of Sociology* 126, no. 2 (September 2020). https://doi.org/10.1086/711015.

"Home Mortgage Disclosure Act (HMDA): FFIEC Issues 2020 Version of *A Guide to HMDA Reporting: Getting It Right!*" FDIC, February 13, 2020. https://www.fdic.gov/news/financial-institution-letters/2020/fil20009.html.

Hairston, Kashief. "The Truth Behind Gentrification in Bed-Stuy." Medium, December 21, 2018. https://medium.com/@kashief.hairston/the-truth-behind-gentrification-in-bed-stuy-6b20cd484e41.

Stasio, Frank. "The Truth Behind the Wilmington Massacre of 1898." *The State of Things*. NPR, January 7, 2020. https://www.wunc.org/post/truth-behind-wilmington-massacre-1898.

ACKNOWLEDGMENTS

Curtis: I'm eternally grateful to God, my mighty African heritage, and my parents, Julia Bunn and the late Edward Bunn Sr., who instilled Black pride and awareness in me, my siblings (Billy, Tami, and Eddie), and cousin Warren J. Eggleston as we were raised in Southeast Washington, D.C. I am steadied by my wife, Felita, and her unwavering support and inspired by the evolution of my son, Curtis Jr., and my daughter, Gwen. I'm proud of niece Tamyah and nephews Gordon and Eddie Jr., and I am uplifted by my alma mater, the great Norfolk State University and my brothers of the luminous Alpha Phi Alpha Fraternity, Inc. (Epsilon Pi chapter and Omicron Phi Lambda).

Significantly, a boisterous thank-you to my brilliant agent, Jennifer Herrera, of the David Black Literary Agency, whose vision and effort are invaluable, and to Grand Central Publishing editor Maddie Caldwell for her leadership and daring to illuminate this project, and to Jacqueline Young for her tireless, important effort.

Also, big thanks to teenager Darnella Frazier, who was aware enough to record on her cell phone the entire murder of George Floyd by Derek Chauvin.

Special thanks to outstanding journalist Karen Robinson-Jacobs.

And thanks to Marcia Davis.

Michael: Thanks to my mother and father, Roberta and Howard Cottman, for reminding me to speak truth to power, to be a champion for those who are disenfranchised, to embrace my proud African American heritage, and, if I'm climbing the ladder, to always reach back and pull someone up to the next step with me.

Thank you to my daughter, Ariane, for always providing words of encouragement.

To Alison LaVigne: thank you for being a creative and intellectual touchstone, a listening ear, embracing our shared mission, and for being a steadfast refuge during proverbial storms.

To my Aunt Pat Favors, Aunt Carol & Rod Jolliffe (& Buster), thanks for all your love and support.

Thank you, Yolanda Woodlee, for graciously offering to help with research on our manuscript under a tight deadline. Your keen journalism skills helped elevate the discussion on these pages and I'm forever grateful.

To my superb literary agent, Jenny Herrera, thank you for your steadfast belief in me and for your encouragement idea by idea, book by book. Your thoughtful guidance from proposal to manuscript is the beacon that helps me navigate the ever-shifting publishing landscape. You always raise the bar. What a blessing.

A special thanks to my publisher, Maddie Caldwell, Grand Central Publishing, and Hachette Book Group. Thank you, Maddie, for publishing *Say Their Names*. When we first approached you with our unconventional idea for five authors you didn't flinch; you rallied around our racial justice narrative with passion and sensitivity, and you gave us a prominent platform to tell this important story. I am greatly appreciative.

And thanks to God for guiding five writers who were separated by miles of highway but connected by an ethereal call for social justice.

Patrice: I am eternally grateful to the talented writers I worked with in creating this book. I am especially thankful to Michael Cottman, who gathered us together and counted me in that number. Thank goodness he introduced us to the dynamic Jennifer Herrera, our passionate agent who guided us with great wisdom through every challenge. I could not do anything without my behind-the-scenes crew: my daughter, Andrea Carter, who encourages me always and who with her life provides a bright light for me to follow. I am thankful to my family for their undying support, especially for my sister and housemate, Carol West, who provides me with food and clean clothes when I'm overwhelmed by a project. And to the members of Allison Creek Presbyterian Church, who with their spirits help me remain sane. Finally, let me acknowledge the brothers and sisters who remain on the other side of the prison wall. I think of you *every* day. My sincere gratitude also to the people who allowed me to interview them for this book and to the infinite number of people fighting for the evolution of humankind and the dismantling of our brutal criminal justice system.

Nick: For those now gone, and on whose shoulders I stand: Albert A. Charles, Emily Cave, Stephen Charles, Andrew Charles, Solomon Charles, Elsie Johnson, Alphus Charles, Eric Chimming, Corina Chimming, Garvin Chimming, David "Bobby" Chimming, Lucita Farroe, Thelma Marshall, Janet Marshall, Ian Marshall, Pearl Ammon, Francis LeeSing, and Carl Byron; and those still here, Monica Charles, Edna Charles, Zita Charles, Cynthia LeeSing, Ruthven Farroe, Mervyn Farroe, Lindell LeeSing, Cheryl Charles, Christine Charles, Coleen Tessema, Patsy Durity, Judy Marshall, Jesse Marshall, Phillip Marshall, Margaret Marshall, Winston Marshall, Gerard Marshall, Dawn Francois, and Anthony Blugh, who continue to sustain me. And for Donna Cohen, Jordi Charles, and Elan Charles. A heartfelt thanks to Jenny Herrera, our intrepid agent, without whom this important work doesn't happen.

Keith: I'm forever grateful to my parents, especially my mother, Alice Harriston, for always emphasizing the importance of education, and to my siblings, who, for as long as I can remember, supported most things I set out to do. My wife, Carol, thank you so much for raising me up and for creating space in our lives that allowed me to work on this project. My sons, Miles and Cole—my inspiration.

And thank you to Tracie Simmons, Bill Ritchie, Dwight Jackson, and Al Hawkins for sharing their time, and to super-agent Jennifer Herrera for helping us to pull this together.

ABOUT THE AUTHORS

Curtis Bunn is an award-winning journalist who has written about race and sports and social and political issues for more than thirty years in Washington, D.C., New York, and Atlanta. Additionally, he is a best-selling author of ten novels that center on Black life in America.

Michael H. Cottman is an author and award-winning journalist. He is the program editor for NBCU Academy, a journalism education and training initiative with the NBCUniversal News Group Diversity, Equity and Inclusion team. He is also the former editorial manager of NBCBLK, a division of NBC News Digital. Cottman is a former reporter for the *Washington Post* and the *Miami Herald*, among other publications. Cottman, who has received numerous awards, was also part of a Pulitzer Prize–winning team for *Newsday*'s coverage of a deadly subway crash in New York in 1992. Cottman has authored, co-authored, and edited eight nonfiction books, and he appeared on *The Oprah Winfrey Show* to discuss his work.

Patrice Gaines is author of the memoir *Laughing in the Dark* (Random House, 1995) and *Moments of Grace* (Random House, 1998). Gaines is a freelance writer, who was a reporter at the *Washington Post* for sixteen years. While at the *Post*, she was a member of a team nominated as a finalist for the Pulitzer Prize. She was awarded a Soros Justice

Media Fellowship to write a series of columns about the impact of incarceration on the Black community. At age twenty-one, Gaines was found guilty of drug charges and forever labeled a "convicted felon." In the decades since, she has spoken and taught in prisons and jails, and also lectured at colleges and conferences on the brutality and failure of America's criminal justice system. Gaines is also a justice advocate and abolitionist.

Nick Charles has reported, written, and edited for various media at domestic and international levels. He has been a reporter/writer and contributor to Long Island *Newsday*, New York *Daily News*, *People*, NPR, the *Washington Post*, and the Undefeated, as well as many other media outlets. He was the editor-in-chief of AOL Black Voices and the vice president of digital content for BET.com. He's currently the managing director of Word In Black, a national collaborative of ten Black-owned media organizations, and an editor and spokesperson for the Save Journalism Project.

Keith Harriston is a writer based in Washington, D.C., who worked for twenty-three years as a senior newsroom manager, department editor, investigative reporter, and beat reporter at the *Washington Post*. As a reporter at the *Post*, Harriston was twice nominated as a finalist by the Pulitzer Prize board. Since leaving the *Post*, Harriston has taught journalism at American University, Howard University, and George Washington University, where he currently is a professorial lecturer in journalism.